NEW HA
GENERAL JOHN STARK

Home of John and Molly Stark, River Road, Manchester, New Hampshire.
Courtesy Manchester, New Hampshire Historical Association.

New Hampshire's General John Stark

Live Free or Die: Death Is Not the Worst of Evils

A fresh look at one of America's relatively unknown defenders of liberty and freedom

BY

Clifton La Bree

Stark served with the famous Rogers' Rangers during the French and Indian War, where he honed the leadership skills that placed him among the most successful military commanders of that conflict and the ensuing Revolutionary War. His extraordinary performance at Bunker Hill, the siege of Boston, the Battles of Trenton, Bennington, Saratoga, and as commander of the Northern Department, has gone relatively unheralded. He was a legendary hero, a true Cincinnatus, who embodies the values that made our country great, and is worthy of our respect and admiration.

Fading Shadows Imprint
New Boston, New Hampshire
2014

Fading Shadows Imprint
126 Wilson Hill Rd.
New Boston, NH 03070

ISBN: 0-9746450-6-0
ISBN13: 978-0-9746450-6-3

Library of Congress Control Number: 2014935353

Third Printing 2014

Published by:

Fading Shadows Imprint
126 Wilson Hill Rd.
New Boston, NH 03070

Book and cover design: Grace Peirce

Frontispiece: General John Stark in full uniform.
Courtesy New Hampshire Historical Society.

Contents

Acknowledgments		vii
Introduction		ix
Chronology		xiv
Chapter One	The Formative Years (1728-1753)	1
Chapter Two	Frontier Warfare (1753-1755)	10
Chapter Three	War on the Hudson (1755-1758)	21
Chapter Four	End of the Conflict (1758-1759)	34
Chapter Five	A Time of Discontent (1759-1775)	42
Chapter Six	The Line Is Drawn (1775)	52
Chapter Seven	Bunker Hill (June 17, 1775)	62
Chapter Eight	British Evacuate Boston ((1775-1776)	78
Chapter Nine	Canada to Trenton (1776)	90
Chapter Ten	Trenton and Princeton (1777)	101
Chapter Eleven	Loss of Fort Ticonderoga (July 1777)	111
Chapter Twelve	Vermont Requests Assistance (July 1777)	119
Chapter Thirteen	Fear on the Frontier (Summer 1777)	132
Chapter Fourteen	Battle of Bennington (August 16, 1777)	142
Chapter Fifteen	The Aftermath (August-September 1777)	154
Chapter Sixteen	Saratoga (September-October 1777)	166
Chapter Seventeen	Post Saratoga (1777-1778)	176
Chapter Eighteen	Rhode Island to the Northern Department (1779-1780)	186
Chapter Nineteen	The Last Post (1781-1783)	197
Chapter Twenty	Fading Shadows (1783-1822)	210
Chapter Twenty-one	In Tribute	221
Appendices	The Bennington Flags	226
	The Bennington Cannons	227
	Children of John and Elizabeth Stark	229
Bibliography		230
Comments on Sources		237
Notes		239
Index		249
About the Author		262

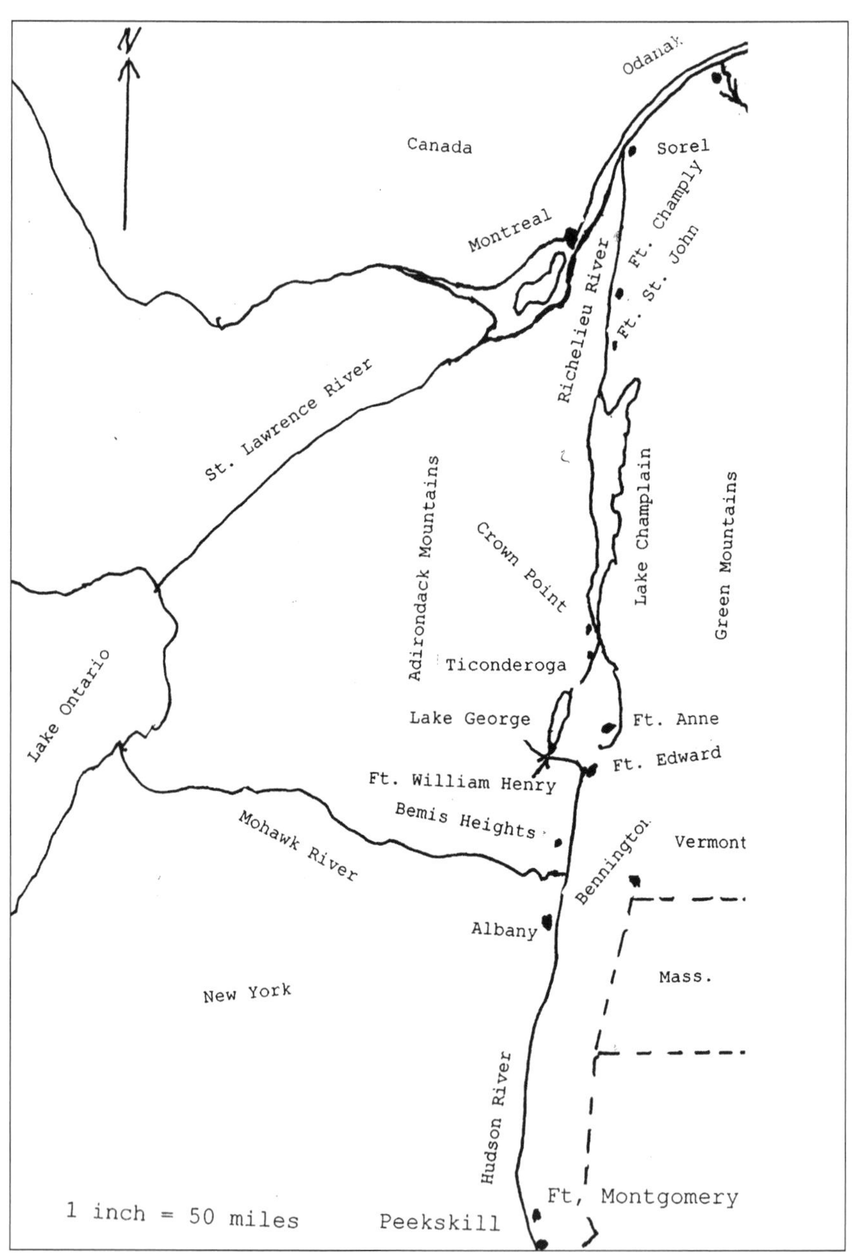

The Northern Department

Acknowledgments

I have written this fresh look at General Stark because I believe that his contributions to our national legacy are underappreciated. I've attempted to tell Stark's story within the time frame it took place so that the readers can appreciate and be grateful for his sacrifices. He is not only a national hero responsible for helping to win our nation's independence on the field of battle: he also uniquely represents New Hampshire's spirit of self-reliance, independence, and love of country, which still defines the people of our state.

It would be impossible to produce this manuscript without the work of those individuals before me who have preserved and documented the information we now have about General John Stark. At the top of the list is his grandson, Caleb Stark, who pulled together all of his grandfather's correspondence in one location for permanent archiving. His *Memoir of General John Stark* is a treasured collection. Another researcher, Howard Parker Moore, wrote the definitive biography, *A Life of General John Stark of New Hampshire*. The book was self-published in 1949, and of his own admission, it was poorly written, and found little popular appeal. The volume suffered from the lack of a good copy editor. Moore obviously worked diligently researching Stark's life, leaving no stone unturned in his pursuit of information. To these authors I am especially indebted.

I have used material that my supportive daughters, Evelyn and Vivian, have obtained from the Internet. My computer illiteracy has been a handicap in this age of technology and I hereby publicly say "thanks."

Over the years I have collected bits and pieces of information about Stark from my visits to Fort William Henry, Fort Ticonderoga, Fort Edward, Fort Anne, Crown Point, Saratoga National Battlefield Park, and the Bennington Battlefield at North Hoosick, New York, while I was stationed in the northern Adirondack region as an employee of the New York State College of Forestry at Syracuse as a young forester on the Pack Demonstration Forest in Warrensburg. I was always fascinated with military history and found much in the area to ignite my curiosity.

Beyond visiting the places where General John Stark served with distinction, I researched this manuscript to corroborate Moore's findings and to review much new material since 1949. The following institutions were especially helpful: the New Hampshire State Library, the Manchester Library (the New Hampshire Room is a researcher's delight!), and the libraries of New Boston, Weare, Bedford, Goffstown, Amherst, Dunbarton, Londonderry, and Portsmouth all in New Hampshire. The John Stark collection and exhibits at the Manchester Historical Association have been most helpful, and it was a pleasure to work in its newly renovated research room. Primary source material such as the papers for George Washington, Henry Clinton, and John Sullivan have been professionally edited and are available to researchers.

I want to say thanks to Brent Armstrong, Dick Moody, and Howard Leonard in assisting me with the section on the New Boston "Molly" Stark cannon.

This manuscript could not have been completed without the unwavering support and encouragement of my family over the period that it has been a part of our lives. My wife, Pauline, heads the list of people to whom I am indebted. She has worked tirelessly to create an atmosphere of tranquility for my endeavors. I appreciate her countless acts of unselfishness, and she must share as a partner in the completion of this work. My oldest daughter, Evelyn, who suggested that I write Stark's story, has been helpful above and beyond, guiding my steps through the process of researching, writing, and publishing. My daughter, Vivian, and son-in-law, Chet, have been most helpful in finding material and providing encouragement. Their computer skills continue to amaze me. They've rescued Dad from innumerable computer "goofs" and made my work so much easier. I hereby give my heartfelt thanks to you all.

Finally, even though several people have contributed to this manuscript, I am solely responsible for any errors that remain. I have tried to be objective in my portrayal of General Stark, but I confess that my respect and admiration for him continued to grow as I progressed through the manuscript, and I do not apologize for the bias.

Introduction

The English settlements expanded inland from the coastal regions on the Atlantic seaboard in the early 1700s. Scotch-Irish immigrants from Northern Ireland soon began to settle in what is now called Londonderry, New Hampshire. They were joined by farmers from neighboring Massachusetts, who increasingly pushed settlements northward into the Merrimack River Valley. By 1740 most of New Hampshire's Indian population had been forced westward and to the north into Canada along the Saint Lawrence River.

Portsmouth became a booming port with many wealthy and influential merchants. Access to unlimited timber resources soon turned the coastal area into a prominent shipbuilding center. Day laborers, sailors, and indentured servants were cultivated for the flourishing enterprises. Slavery even existed, although on a very small scale.

As the inland migration continued to expand, the settlers' ties to Portsmouth decreased and communication links to Boston became stronger. When the British Royal Navy blockaded Boston, New Hampshire sent food and sustenance to the beleaguered Bostonians. When news of the Lexington-Concord exchange was heard, New Hampshire sent some of the best fighting men in the colonies to defend the rights of free men.

New Hampshire was not unique in its allegiance to the Crown as loyal British subjects, but that changed when the Crown ceased to acknowledge their allegiance. New Hampshire was the first state to draft a constitution and to instruct its delegates to the Continental Congress to cast their votes for independence.

The allure of land in the colonies of the New World held the promise of freedom and liberty for the industrious Scotch-Irish settlers, but the land itself and the ability to control the fruits of their labor were the greatest attractions. They came to a new world beset with strife and vicious clashes among the various factions laying claim to the territory. Earlier homesteaders seeking a place in the New World were often met as they stepped ashore by friendly native tribes, fragmented into small bands up and down the eastern seaboard, who had lived in the area for centuries. They traditionally laid claim to the vast primeval forest of the interior.

The native population, the original masters of the land, were displaced and swept aside by the stronger newcomers as if they had never existed. Sadly, they became insignificant players in the monumental events that followed. The introduction of the two vastly different cultures was friendly and beneficial to the new settlers. The Indians had showed them how to raise corn, squash, and other crops suitable to the area, and they shared the bounty of the land and sea with the colonists. Soon, however, the desire of the English-speaking settlers to own the land they worked and to reap the rewards of their labor became the root cause of the bitter confrontations that followed.

British claims to the continent were based on the discovery of Newfoundland by John Cabot, an Englishman, in 1498. English colonies soon thereafter began to take root along the eastern coast.

The French also had been active in the area. They claimed all of the land west of the Ohio River Valley and north of the Saint Lawrence River, based on the explorations of Rene-Robert Cavalier La Salle in 1682, and earlier discoveries by Jacques Marquette and Louis Joliet. The Ohio River Valley marked the eastern boundary of French territory and limited the western expansion of British settlers.

A conflict was inevitable. The French and Indian War (1754-1763) was a viciously fought campaign between two of the most powerful nations in the world. Known in Europe as the Seven Years War, ramifications were felt virtually worldwide. The deadly conflict ended on the Plains of Abraham, on the northern shore of the Saint Lawrence River, near Quebec, when the French surrendered all of their claims on the continent to the English. As hard-fought as the conflict was, it turned out to be only a primer for the larger civil and rebellious war that took place twelve years later, when the fate of a continent hung in the balance.

The French treatment of the Indians had been much more humane and realistic than that of the British. French traders and adventurers came to the continent looking for riches in furs and timber, expecting to return to Europe when they had made their fortunes. They lived with the Indians, shared their culture, spoke their language, and joined forces with them in order to trade goods for furs.

The British, however, came expecting to obtain land. Liberty and freedom of expression were important, but landownership was the main impetus to cross the Atlantic. Without property, liberty and freedom had little meaning. Their claims to the land were, in general, made in good faith. The British negotiated a price and purchased land from native tribes for a fraction of its actual worth and soon established control of their domains, which eliminated future usage of the land by Indians. Ownership, as the British understood the term, was utterly foreign to the native peoples, and they refused to accept the finality of a "sale." The land was like the waters and the air they breathed. It could not be "owned" because it was free to all. This basic misunderstanding was at the heart of all the conflicts that followed. The closest the Indians came to understanding the concept was their traditional hunting and fishing "rights" for certain parcels of forestland set aside for tribal use. Others could use it by request, but the tribes guarded their traditional hunting tracts with as much ferocity as the white men later defended home and hearth.

Frequent raids against isolated settlers in New England by the infamous Abenaki from large communities near the Saint Lawrence River were carried out with aimless cruelty toward the homesteaders. Towns such as Deerfield, Massachusetts (February 29, 1704); Portsmouth, New Hampshire (June 26, 1696); Haverhill, Massachusetts (August 28, 1704); and Durham (July 18, 1694) were victims of murderous attacks. French Jesuit priests frequently accompanied the Abenaki on their raids and urged them to even greater atrocities. The frontier was a dangerous place for many years. The coastal settlements were reasonably free from attacks, but those souls who braved inhospitable conditions in isolated log cabins in the interior were vulnerable to early-morning visits from roaming bands of Abenaki. A few families were lucky and survived. Others were massacred, their bones left to disintegrate in the wilderness, unknowns in the struggle for a new nation.

Archibald and Eleanor Stark's family were Scotch-Irish from Northern Ireland. They landed in Boston Harbor in the autumn of 1720 after an arduous trip across the Atlantic. The ship had been wracked with smallpox and was refused permission to land. Three children died on the trip. The ship then sailed north along the Maine coast, where they disembarked at a small settlement on the Sheepscott River called Wiscasset. The families suffered a terrible winter in the Maine wilderness, and it was not until a year later that they traveled one hundred and fifty miles through wilderness to Nutfield, (Londonderry, New Hampshire) where Eleanor's father, James Nichols, had settled two years earlier.

John Stark was a product of the frontier he grew up in. Survival was the ultimate achievement. Shaped and molded by the wilderness, he developed and became the embodiment of the virtues that defined most frontiersmen, i.e. modesty, self-discipline, independence, frugality, and resourcefulness coupled with a hefty dose of common sense. These virtues remained the cornerstones of his illustrious career. He was one of our great patriots, rising to the challenges of the times and risking everything to turn the dream of independence and freedom from tyranny into the reality that became our United States of America.

The summer of 1776 was a grim period for the American Revolution. After a moral victory at Bunker Hill, the patriots suffered from hunger, smallpox, and lack of supplies, yet they fought courageously even though defeat was a very real possibility. The well-supplied and trained British army was experiencing victory after victory following their humiliating expulsion from Boston.

That summer, a powerful British army commanded by General John Burgoyne began smashing its way south via the Lake Champlain-Hudson River corridor. If he was allowed to link up with other British formations coming from the west and the south, all that the patriots had been fighting for would have been irrevocably lost. A severed New England and New York would allow the British, with the aid of their powerful Royal Navy, to conquer the northern and middle colonies, south of the corridor, one at a time, with a minimum of resistance.

At the height of the national despair, Brigadier General John Stark, who had earned praise from all who participated in the Battle of Bunker Hill, arrived at Bennington with a New Hampshire militia contingent. Independent, cantankerous, and strong willed, Stark had honed his military and survival skills in the vast wilderness known as the New Hampshire Grants as a captain in the fabled Rogers' Rangers. He now reviewed the military situation, and accurately assessed where he could do the most good, disobeying an order from the Continental army to place his command under their control. He steadfastly ignored the demand, leading his formation of irregular fighters against some of the best troops in the world—the British regulars and the Hessian mercenaries. "Undisciplined free men are superior to veteran slaves," said General Stark.

Stark led his New Hampshire soldiers with skill and audacity against a large formation of Burgoyne's soldiers sent to obtain military stores at Bennington. Stark's tenacious attack lasted only a few hours, but he succeeded in crippling Burgoyne's chances for victory by devastating two of his detachments at Bennington. The British campaign to crush the Americans floundered at Saratoga shortly after Stark's brilliant estimation of the situation and daring execution of the enemy's defeat. Saratoga was the most important battle of the Revolution, and Stark's leadership and ingenuity made ultimate victory possible.

After Saratoga, the French were persuaded to come to the aid of the struggling colonials. Troops, supplies, and warships from France helped to ensure a successful ending to the war that gave birth to our nation. General Stark also served General Washington and the country with distinction as commander of the Northern Department for two tours of duty. For all of his independence, however, he was a good team player, and never lost sight of the cause they were all fighting for.

General Stark wrote to General Washington in 1778: "I have no will of my own . . . the good of the common cause is all my ambition . . ." He was a strong symbol and the embodiment of the ideals of the American patriot who risked all for country, and stands proudly with those who made it possible. New Hampshire and the nation have a right, even a duty, to call him a beloved son.

Chronology

1720 Archibald and Eleanor Stark arrive in Boston Harbor and are turned away because some passengers had contracted smallpox. The ship sails north to Wiscasset, on the Maine coast, where the couple found a safe haven over the winter.

1721 The Starks make their way to Nutfield (Londonderry), where Eleanor's father had settled two years earlier.

1728 John is born (August 28), the fifth of seven children.

1736 The family home in Nutfield burns. The Stark family moves to Harrytown, later called Derryfield and then Manchester, where they own six hundred acres of wild land. They build a small house on the east bank of the Merrimack River beside Amoskeag Falls.

1744 Fort Number Four is built on the Connecticut River at Charlestown, New Hampshire.

1747 Saint Francis Indians and French soldiers surround Fort Number Four and lay a siege for three days. They are beaten off by a garrison force of thirty-one men.

1751 John Stark is captured by Indians while hunting and trapping near the Baker River in Rumney, New Hampshire.

1752 Indians receive a ransom amounting to one hundred and three dollars for John's release.

1753 George Washington leads a diplomatic mission to the French forces on the Ohio River.

1754 In July, delegates meet in Albany to discuss Indian affairs. Benjamin Franklin presents his Plan of Union for the colonies.

1754 The French and Indian War formally starts on May 28 when George Washington builds Fort Necessity and then loses it to the French. Stark enlists in Rogers' Rangers as a second lieutenant. Washington returns to Virginia and resigns his commission.

1755 On July 8, General Braddock suffered a crippling defeat by the French as he attempts to attack Fort Duquesne, on the Ohio River. On September 9, colonial General William Johnson wins Battle of Lake George for the British.

1756 May 18, Great Britain declares war on France. Stark serves with Rogers' Rangers in the Lake Champlain Valley.

1757 French lieutenant general Marquis de Montcalm captures and burns Fort William Henry. On August 8, Indians allied with the French massacre British prisoners after they were given permission to leave the fort.

1758 Stark serves under the command of General Abercromby during the mismanaged attempt to capture Fort Ticonderoga (July 8). Stark receives news that his father, Archibald, had died (August 28) at the age of sixty-one, and is furloughed home.

1758 On August 20, John Stark and Elizabeth Page are married in Dunbarton. John returns to duty with the rangers on the frontier shortly after the wedding.

1759 Caleb Stark is born at the Page home, the first of eleven children.

1760 John Stark returns from war duties and lives with his family at the Page residence in Dunbarton.

1761 The Stark family moves to the Stark family house at Amoskeag Falls, leaving Caleb at the Page home in Dunbarton.

1763 French and Indian War ends.

1769 John and Molly Stark build a grand house north of Amoskeag Falls, where they raise their large family.

1771 John Stark is the first Town Grand Juror at Amherst, New Hampshire, the seat of Hillsborough County.

1774 In July, John Stark takes part in a secret session of the illegal Committee of Safety at Exeter. General Thomas Gage arrives in Boston on May 12 to act as royal governor.

1775 Stark also serves at county-level, anti-British meetings in Amherst.

1775 Battles of Lexington and Concord take place on April 18. Stark leaves his sawmill and farm when he hears the news, and rides to Massachusetts to support the colonial blockade of the British in Boston.

1775 On April 23, Stark accepts a colonelcy in the New Hampshire Militia. On May 10, Ethan Allen and Benedict Arnold capture Fort Ticonderoga. The Second Continental Congress convenes in Philadelphia on May 20.

1775 The Battle of Bunker Hill is fought on June 17. Colonel Stark displays courage, discipline, and cool leadership under fire. General George Washington, commander of the newly formed Continental army, arrives in Boston to take charge of the forces conducting the siege.

1776 On March 17, the British evacuate Boston after colonial forces mount cannon transported from Fort Ticonderoga to Dorchester Heights. The Declaration of Independence is published on July 4. The Continental army experiences defeats with heavy losses in and around New York and White Plains.

1776 The Continental Congress moves to Baltimore. Fear permeates the colonial resistance. They are losing the war, and the future looks bleak. On Christmas day, Washington crosses the Delaware River and defeats the Hessians at Trenton. John Stark serves in this campaign under General John Sullivan.

1777 Morale is restored by the victories at Trenton (December 26) and Princeton (January 3). The Continental Congress moves back to Philadelphia. On March 23, John Stark resigns his commission in disgust. Congress has passed over him and promoted several officers with less experience to the rank of brigadier general. One is Enoch Poor, a fellow New Hampshire militia officer who had refused to march his regiment to help at Bunker Hill.

1777 On June 14, Congress adapts the Stars and Stripes as the official American flag. British General Burgoyne captures Fort Ticonderoga on July 6. John Langdon on July 18 announces the formation of a New Hampshire regiment under Stark's control as a brigadier general to assist Vermont.

1777 On August 16, the Battle of Bennington denies supplies to Burgoyne and contributes to his army's October 7 defeat at Saratoga. General Stark commands the force that captures Fort Edward thereby blocking Burgoyne's retreat to the north. On October 14, Brigadier General John Stark is commissioned in the Continental Army. George Washington's forces winter at Valley Forge.

1778 John Paul Jones delivers the message announcing Burgoyne's defeat to Benjamin Franklin in Paris. It is the first voyage of the USS *Ranger*, an armed sloop built at the Langdon Shipyard on Rising Castle Island (Badger Island) in Kittery, Maine. News of the event preceded the arrival by two days. France soon enters the war on the side of the rebels. John Stark assumes command of the Northern Department of the Continental army for the year.

1779 General Sullivan conducts a successful campaign in New York against the Six Nation Indian Confederacy, which had been terrorizing settlements along the northern and western borders of New England, Pennsylvania, and New York. On September 23, Benedict Arnold deserts the patriot's cause. John Stark serves on the court-martial board that finds the British spy Major John Andre guilty and on October 1 condemns him to death.

1780 The southern campaign continues to the end with French assistance.

1781 John Stark is again given command of the Northern Department, until the end of the conflict. On October 19, General Cornwallis surrenders to Continental forces at Yorktown. Stark retires to his farm and sawmill in Derryfield.

1782 Raids continue along the frontiers.

1783 On September 3, a peace treaty is signed in Paris. England officially recognizes the independence of the United States of America.

1783 Stark is promoted to the rank of major general in the Continental army on September 23. The British leave New York City after seven years of occupation. On November 23, Congress disbands the Continental army.

1809 John Stark pens the phrase "Live Free or Die" in a letter to his Vermont comrades dated July 31, declining an invitation to their thirty-second reunion.

1814 Elizabeth "Molly" Page Stark dies on June 29 at the age of seventy-eight.

1818 On April 18, Congress voted John Stark a pension of forty dollars a month.

1822 On April 30, John Stark dies at his home after forty years of continuous farming. He was ninety-four. He is buried in the family plot south of the home, now a part of Stark Park.

I

The Formative Years (1728-1753)

This is the story of John Stark, a simple man of the soil and of the vast forested wilderness that constituted his world as he matured to manhood. All that he became in later years had its origin on the New Hampshire frontier. His virtues of independence and self-reliance were conditioned by the harsh environment that had the capacity to strengthen strong men or to destroy those not up to the challenge.

His parents, Archibald and Eleanor Stark, paid their passage fees and sailed from Port Rush at the northern tip of Ireland in the summer of 1720. The long, perilous journey that had filled their hearts with joy and great expectations now shattered their lives. Their three children died from smallpox during the passage. Three months later, when the ship entered Boston Harbor, they were refused permission to land. Boston officials wanted nothing to do with a ship contaminated with the dreaded smallpox, and ordered them to leave the harbor.

The captain ultimately sailed north up the Maine coast to a small community known as Sheepscott (later called Wiscasset). They landed late in the fall and stayed in the wilderness for the winter. The area was wild and susceptible to Indian raids. The Stark family's losses had been difficult enough, but that winter tested their mettle to the limit.

The consecutive years of poor crops and drought in northern Ireland and Scotland that resulted in starvation and pitiful subsistence living were a powerful incentive to leave their native land. Thousands like the Starks were flocking to the eastern seaboard of the British colonies in the New World.

The decision to emigrate must have been an agonizing one, especially for those with small children. Before they embarked on the overcrowded ship, the passengers knew the journey would be long and dangerous, yet they continued to come in increasing numbers. In general, the old life in Europe, with its traditional prejudices, was displaced by the fervor for what became a homogeneous American culture, defined by independent private ownership of land, the primary means of production. The Starks and their offspring were prominent products of that emerging culture.

One year after landing in Maine, Archibald and Eleanor Stark found their way to Nutfield (now Londonderry), New Hampshire, and moved in with Eleanor's father, James Nichols. He had settled there two years earlier. Nutfield was their original point of destination. Londonderry and the surrounding area were still sporadically harassed by raiding Indian bands, but the frequency was lessening as more and more emigrants established homesteads in the region.

Archibald Stark was a joiner and helped his father-in-law on the farm while they lived together. On June 20, 1722, Eleanor gave birth to a daughter they called Ana. A year later, Archibald purchased a thirty-acre piece of land that adjoined the Nichols property. Archibald was able to read and write, but Eleanor could not, so she had to place her "mark" on the deed. The land was located on both sides of a road leading to the meetinghouse in what is now called East Derry. The tall straight white pine trees that grew in the area were ideal for the construction of cabins and farm buildings. The wood was easy to work and it made sturdy and comfortable homes that stood the test of time.

During the winter of 1725-1726, James Nichols died. Archibald and Eleanor assisted the family in settling their affairs, all the time working hard clearing land and constructing their own home. They raised large patches of flax for linen and candle wicks and enough vegetables to sustain the family through the barren winter months. The Irish seed potatoes they had brought with them grew well in the fertile black soil among the tree stumps they had cleared from the land for construction of their cabin and firewood.

Their fifth child, John, was born August 28, 1728. In addition to Ana, William, Isobel, and Samuel preceded him. Two years later, Archibald was born. The last child, Jean, was born in 1732.

During the winter of 1733-34, Archibald sold off three of the family's thirty acres of land for twenty-eight pounds. He had paid only twenty-four pounds for the entire parcel. Although Archibald worked hard and generally was a good manager of the family's finances, that same year he entered into a new business venture that proved to be unprofitable. His landholdings contained several acres of sandy, well-drained soils heavily populated with pitch pine trees. He attempted to extract turpentine from them, and showed much ingenuity in fabricating the equipment for the destructive distillation of the wood. There was a good demand locally for spirits of turpentine, yet the production was small and required much more physical labor than he had anticipated. Archibald eventually determined that the New England variety of pitch pine could not match the productivity of the southern pines and ceased operations. His turpentine venture lasted about three years, although it failed, it showed his willingness to try new things for the betterment of his family.

The Starks had purchased a pew at the large meetinghouse in Londonderry, where the family attended religious services for as long as they remained in the town. Their tenure came to an end in 1736 when their log cabin burned. Fires were a common occurrence when roofs were covered with dry wooden shingles and chimneys were often clogged with creosote from burning green wood. Once a fire started in the chimney, the accumulation of creosote burned with an intensity and a high temperature that frequently destroyed many homes of the period. We don't know for sure the cause, but a chimney fire seems logical.

As disastrous as the fire was, the family was able to sell the improved land and purchase a six-hundred-acre tract of prime land adjacent to Amoskeag Falls on the Merrimack River in Harrytown. They later sold a twenty-acre and a forty-acre plot to offset the initial cost of the property. The new location placed the Stark family at the center of activities in the lower Merrimack Valley.

Amoskeag Falls was a popular fishing spot. Over the years, "fishing rights" and locations had been purchased and allocated to various families. The fertile fishing grounds produced great quantities of shad, eels, alewives, salmon and sturgeon. A large area near the falls was set aside to dry the filleted fish on wooden racks in the summertime. Every home in the community also had barrels and tubs filled with salt brine and dressed fish. The Stark boys became adept as spearmen and fishermen not only at the falls, but in the nearby streams and ponds as well.

The frontier wilderness began at their doorstep. It ran north to the Saint Lawrence River in Canada and west to the Ohio River Valley. Settlements were growing along the rivers capable of being navigated, but the interior was sparsely populated by a few brave individuals in lonely cabins vulnerable to attack by Indian bands roaming the landscape in search of victims.

The Stark brothers grew to manhood learning to function and survive in the harsh environment. John had a natural aptitude for the isolation and hardships the wilderness represented, especially those long journeys in severe weather. He hunted, fished, and became a marksman of some renown during the formative period of his life. Learning to survive and be self-sufficient regardless of weather or time of year instilled a confidence and a boldness that remained with him for the rest of his life.

He not only adapted to the environment; he also relished his ability to move rapidly for long distances and live off the land for extended periods. His rugged constitution and natural intelligence allowed him to learn and develop woodcraft techniques and skills that would serve him well in the years to come, and, most likely, kept him from being scalped in the numerous engagements he had with his enemies.

A British fort was erected in 1744 on the Connecticut River at Charlestown, New Hampshire, fifty miles west of Harrytown. John Stark was sixteen at the time. The fort represented the most northern and western English-speaking settlement in New England. It was called Fort Number Four because it was located in the fourth chartered town along the river. Number Four, as it affectionately became known, was a welcome addition for the inhabitants of the area. It was a haven from marauding Indians and their French allies. The small British garrison for the fort was commanded by the resourceful and brave Captain Phineas Stevens. We shall meet this stalwart defender of the frontier people as our story of John Stark unfolds.

One other significant event that took place in 1745 while John Stark was practicing and honing his woodland skills was the capture of Fort Louisbourg, the stronghold in Nova Scotia that helped to guard the northern approaches to the Saint Lawrence River. The defeat of the elite French forces holding the fort by an ad hoc New England militia was a source of celebration throughout the colonies.

The French temporarily eased their influence with the Abenaki Indians which resulted in fewer depredations within the Merrimack Valley. Early-morning raids from small bands of Saint Francis Indians were still taking place, however, and settlers maintained a worrisome vigilance. Captain Goffe, who lived a short distance south of the Stark homestead, had patrolled the Merrimack Valley on snowshoes that winter of 1745-46. John's younger brother Archibald accompanied Goffe on several of his patrols. Yet that spring the Indians captured and killed several people. The small hamlet of Derryfield was the northern most settlement in the valley. Beyond lay the wild forested region known as the New Hampshire Grants. The last vengeful act against the settlers here took place in Epsom, when a Mrs. McCoy was taken hostage to the large Indian encampment on the Saint Lawrence River known as Odanak. The Indians killed some of their victims, and many were taken hostage for ransom. They had found the practice to be profitable and they generally took those people who were physically capable of making the arduous journey to and from Canada.

It is interesting that in 1745, when John was seventeen years old, an Abenaki Indian from the Saint Francis encampment temporarily took up residence on a small brook at the southern border of the Stark land. He was called Christo or Christian and was very friendly to the family, especially to the boys, who were fascinated by him. John's view of the native population as an adult was always compassionate. He admired their values and way of life, and respected their ability to survive in such a harsh environment. It is possible that his benevolent attitude can be attributed to his relationship with Christo at such an impressionable age.

All during his teenage years, John Stark spent most of his time hunting and fishing in the wilderness beyond their home on the falls. In March 1752, in the company of his brother William, David Stinson, and Amos Eastman, John left Harrytown for a hunting and trapping expedition about seventy miles to the north on the Baker River. The youths carried provisions, ammunition, traps, and accessories on sledges they dragged behind them on the snow. Upon arriving at the Baker River, they established a camp at what is now called Rumney. There were no inhabitants for miles. The possibility of running into band of Indians was always real and the boys were alert for any signs.

Game was abundant and within a month they had accumulated furs worth five hundred and sixty pounds sterling. On April 28, they met a scout for a band of ten Saint Francis Indians. The previous day they had seen signs of the presence of Indians and had planned to leave the hunting grounds.

John was the youngest in the party and was assigned the task of collecting the furs and traps. He was in the cold water retrieving a beaver trap when he heard a loud hissing sound behind him. He was surrounded by Indians, with their guns pointed at him. There was no place to escape and running would have been foolish so he peacefully surrendered to them.

When John's captors asked him about his companions, he pointed in the direction opposite to where their camp was. He accompanied the Indians for about two miles from his brother and friends in the hope that the boys would take advantage of the time he was giving them and leave the area. They failed to do that, however. Worried at his long absence, they thought John might have gotten lost or disoriented, and began to discharge their weapons into the air. There was no return fire from John. Suspecting that John had been discovered, William and Stinson evacuated the encampment in the canoe while Eastman ran along the shore.

Late on the twenty-ninth, Eastman fell into an ambush and was captured. The Indians ordered William and Stinson to come ashore. John immediately hollered that he and Eastman were captives and warned them to escape to the opposite shore. The canoe veered from midstream as the Indians rose to fire their muskets. Stark was able to knock several weapons closest to him in the air, but those who had a chance to aim killed Stinson. Once the Indians had discharged all of their weapons, John screamed for his brother to escape.

William escaped to the settlements and a party of armed men from Rumford (now Concord) rushed to the scene. They found Stinson's body stripped and scalped. They buried him and returned home. It was a scene that had been playing out on the frontier for years.

John had received a severe beating from his captors for his interference, and they took great delight in confiscating his furs. They headed for Haverhill, on the Connecticut River, an area of fertile soils and bountiful fisheries, where they had procured provisions, and were met by two more Indians from their band. They stayed there overnight and started out for the Upper Coos first thing in the morning. Upon arrival, they sent ahead three Indians with Eastman to the Saint Francis Indian community on the Saint Francis River. The remainder stayed behind with John to hunt and fish around a small stream known as John's River. John Stark was allowed reasonable freedom during the daylight hours. At night he was confined.

After several days of hunting, the party arrived at Saint Francis on the ninth of June. John remained there for five weeks. During that time he studied the language and the Abenaki's mode of warfare, which would serve him well in the years ahead. He was treated adequately, but every captive had to participate in the ceremony known as "running the gauntlet." John and Eastman were no exception.

The warriors lined up in the center of the compound forming two lines. Each was armed with a club or long stick that he used to strike the captive as he ran through the lines. Eastman passed through first and sang the song, "I'll Beat All Your Young Men." The warriors were insulted and beat him so severely that he collapsed from exhaustion and pain at the end of the line.

John started immediately behind his friend with a six-foot pole and a loon skin on one end. He began to sing in a jaunty manner and a loud voice, "I'll Kiss All Your Women." (Nutchipwuttoonapishwameugnonk-kishguog).[1] He was hit several times even as he turned his own pole on his tormentors. They gave him more room and consequently did not hurt him. The elderly, who enjoyed watching the ceremony, were impressed with his bravado and cheered him.

Females of the tribe performed the menial tasks such as hoeing corn, and John Stark was given that job to humble him. He turned the tables on his captives by chopping the corn instead of the weeds. Even his disobedience did not release him from the task, so he boldly threw the hoe in the river declaring, "It [is] the business of squaws, not warriors, to hoe corn."[2]

The tribal leaders removed him from that job and called him Young Chief. The sachem adopted him and he was treated with kindness for his remaining time at the village. "In the latter days of his life, he [John Stark] often related, with much humor, the incidents of his captivity, observing that he had experienced more genuine kindness from the savages of St. Francis, than he ever knew prisoners of war to receive from more civilized nations."[3]

Late in July, a Mr. Wheelright of Boston and Captain Phinehas Stevens, a British army officer, arrived at the Indian village. They were empowered by Massachusetts to redeem colonial subjects from Massachusetts who had been taken hostage. They did not find any, so they paid the ransom price of one hundred and three dollars for Stark and sixty dollars for Eastman.[4] The party then proceeded to Albany, a town John had never visited in his youthful wanderings. From there he made his way home.

Captain Stevens was a much respected and resolute officer. He was the commander of Fort Number Four at Charlestown, New Hampshire, for the duration of the war with the French and Indians. Before his trip to redeem John Stark and Eastman, Stevens, with a garrison force of thirty-one men at Number Four, fought off a vicious three-day siege by the Abenaki and their French allies. They were outnumbered fourteen to one. The French officer in charge requested a parley to demand their surrender or suffer the consequences of a massacre. Stevens replied, "My men are not afraid to die."[5]

The attacks were soon renewed, until the third day, when the French asked for a cessation of arms. They promised to depart the area if the garrison would sell them provisions sufficient to last until they reached Canada. Stevens gave them a curt no, but did offer them five bushels of corn for every captive they would give up. The enemy fired a last salvo and left.

Stevens was given an elegant award by Sir Charles Knowles for his courageous defense. The township was later called Charlestown. Stevens was a frequent participant in the redemption of captives, traveling under a flag of truce to the Canadian Indian village numerous times. He was a prominent player on the New Hampshire Land Grants scene, and many people owe their lives to the dedication and valor of this fine officer. He died in His Majesty's service in Nova Scotia in 1756.

John Stark observed and memorized many things about the area he traveled while he was taken captive. It broadened his already impressive knowledge of the new land. In March 1753, Colonel Lovewell, Captain Page, and Major Talford were ordered by New Hampshire's Governor Sir John Wentworth to explore and check on the feasibility of building a road to the Coos meadow. They hired sixteen men from the Penacook and Amoskeag region. John Stark was hired as a guide because he had recently visited the area. Caleb Page (John Stark's future father-in-law) went along as surveyor. They marked out a road by blazing trees but did no construction. The journey to Piermont on the Connecticut River took seven days. They spent a day and night there and returned to Concord on the thirteenth day from departure.

New Hampshire's interest in the Coos region of the Connecticut River soon reached the French. They protested, using the Abenaki as their surrogates. In January 1753, six Indians arrived at the gates of Fort Number Four with a flag of truce to inform Captain Stevens that they were registering a strong protest against the English interest in the Coos. They claimed that the British had enough land and that if they "...had a mind for war if they would go there, and that they should have a strong war."[6]

In 1754, Governor Wentworth had received a report that the French were erecting a fort on the Upper Coos and authorized Captain Powers and thirty men to travel to the area under a flag of truce and demand that the French leave the area. John Stark was again recruited as a guide to the Little Ox-Bow. They found no evidence of French activity in the vicinity of Haverhill and Newbury. The Indian word *co-has* defines a wide level valley on the Connecticut River that flows through the two towns forming an "ox-bow" of fertile farms.[7]

Once the two scouting projects were completed, John Stark returned north to the Androscoggin River to trap for furs so that he could pay back his ransom money. He traveled and worked alone in an extremely volatile part of the New Hampshire Grants. The fact that he felt comfortable and confident in the hostile environment is a tribute to his courage. In the wilderness a man has the opportunity to test his capabilities. It is both an emotional experience and a physical one. Those individuals who grow from the discovery develop an even greater trust and confidence in their skills, and is a growth experience that lasts a lifetime.

John Stark had obviously attained a level of self-sufficiency that was at least in part responsible for the success and competency he would later display on the battlefield.

2

Frontier Warfare (1753-1755)

The New World was changing rapidly as John Stark crossed the threshold of manhood continuing to develop his skills in the forested wilderness. Perhaps it will be helpful to review some of what was taking place in the world beyond the frontier during that period.

England and France were settling their disputes on the field of battle. Their Seven Years War (called the French and Indian War by the colonists) officially lasted from 1756 to 1763, but it was a small part of a larger struggle that lasted for a hundred years. Their differences were highlighted on the North American continent, specifically within the Ohio River Valley. France claimed all of the land from the Allegheny Mountains west to the Mississippi River and south to Florida. The English refused to accept that claim. The two European superpowers were competing for control of a continent. Each had valid reasons for the position it took, and the prospect for armed conflict was slowly increasing during the early 1750s.

France was governed by an absolute monarch, King Louis XIV. Canada was governed by a Trioka: governor general (a Frenchman); an intendant (Canadian); and the Catholic bishop of Canada. This rigid and unified chain of command helped account for the early successes of the French and their Indian allies.

The British were governed by a constitutional monarchy, with ministers accountable to Parliament. The colonies all had semiautonomous governments administered by governors and council boards with close ties to the English crown. Thirteen different administrations made internal communications almost impossible. Unity of command was nonexistent in the colonies prior to 1757, when the French victories became fewer and the English began to win the war.

The French military was the best in the world, but it had a deficiency in the New World: manpower. At the start of the war, New France had about seventy-five thousand subjects. The population was so light because it was based on the lucrative fur trade, which required few people but large acres of wild land. By contrast, the English had 1,350,000 in the colonies. Some of them were second- and third-generation colonists, anchored in agriculture and shipping, which were labor-intensive. The colonies were capable of supporting reasonable numbers of troops for their protection. The French had to depend on supplies shipped from France and the fish caught off the coast of Newfoundland.

The French had trained European troops to fight "little wars" such as developed in North America. French officers were scattered throughout the tribes of allied Indians, creating a vast forest communication system that worked well. The New France militia was better disciplined than its colonial counterpart. New France, circa 1750, was more a web of trading posts than an empire, depending heavily on the alliances developed with the Hurons and Algonquian-speaking tribes. The French were hunters and trappers who shared many of the Indians' traditional ways of life, and they bonded with the natives better than did their British brethren. However, when they became settlers, they treated the Indians the same as the American colonists, that is, as inferior human beings.

The main attraction for the French was fur. They came to the New World to make their fortune and then would return to France. The English were malcontents, looking for land and an opportunity to expand a new society with an eye on trade. The claim the French placed on the Ohio River Valley was a serious one, and they were determined to back it up with force. They began to accumulate men and supplies to build a series of forts from Fort Lake Erie (Presque Isle) southward into the valley to Fort Le Boeuf (Waterford, Pennsylvania) and down the Ohio River.[1]

When Governor Robert Dinwiddie, of Virginia, heard that the French were fortifying the Ohio, he ordered a small group of men under the command of twenty-one-year-old Major George Washington of the Virginia Militia to travel to the valley and request the French to leave. If the French persisted in their claim on the valley, it would seriously hinder British plans for expansion westward beyond the Allegheny Mountains.

Major Washington left Williamsburg, Virginia, on October 31, 1753, and headed for Willis Creek on the Potomac River, where he hired a seasoned guide, Christopher Gist, and four other woodsmen for the trip. They traveled to the confluence of the Ohio, Allegheny, and Monongahela Rivers in Pennsylvania, where Washington explored the forks and wrote in his journal that a fort built at the site would be capable of controlling the area. They then traveled due north in a blowing snowstorm to an Indian encampment known as Logstown (now Cambridge Springs, Pennsylvania). Winter was fast setting in and the journey by horse and foot one hundred miles to Fort Le Boeuf was difficult. The fort was heavily defended with cannon and about one hundred French troops.

The British diplomatic mission was received cordially and offered refreshments including fine French wine. When Washington presented the letter from Governor Dinwiddie, the French commander told him that he was a new replacement officer and was unable to comply with his request. He would have to transmit the letter to Marquis Duquesne for a response. The mission stayed at the fort as guests of the commander until a reply was received. The French firmly stated that the Ohio country belonged to France by right of discovery and exploration and they intended to stay!

The mission left the fort December 16, 1753 clothed in heavy buckskins and with a generous supply of food and wine from their friendly hosts. The return journey was arduous, and perilous, but a month later, Washington arrived at Williamsburg, Virginia, to make his report.[2]

Events were rapidly propelling the French and the British into a war that neither wanted. Delegates from the thirteen colonies assembled at Albany in July 1754 to discuss mutually important subjects. Benjamin Franklin presented his Plan of Union for the colonies. It was the first step in uniting for a common cause. Another important achievement was securing the Indians in New York, known as the Six Nations, as allies of the British. This would have important consequences for John Stark for the next six years. They were lavishly feasted. Each of the colonies contributed to the cost of the conference. New Hampshire's bill for liquor, food, and gifts amounted to eighty-three pounds. The Nations were governed by consensus of the Great Council which spoke with one voice, one mind and one heart. [3]

Robert Rogers was born in 1727 in Londonderry. He grew into manhood on the New Hampshire frontier under much the same circumstances as John Stark. Robert's family moved to Starktown later called Dunbarton shortly after he was born. He developed an athletic physique and was known on the frontier for his bold and fearless disposition, and feats of strength won him much local esteem. All who knew him described him as having a very large nose! Alert and quick of mind, yet always calm and confident, he had few peers for presence of mind in combat.

In 1755, Governor Wentworth authorized the formation of three companies of militia appointing Robert Rogers, John Goffe, and John Moore as captains. John Stark joined the company and was made a lieutenant. Also in the company were Lieutenant Noah Johnson, Abraham Perry as the ensign, and Hugh Stirling as clerk. Stirling was married to John Stark's sister Isabel. The company was to be used for scouting, collecting of intelligence, and anything else that required its unique talents in the forest. Shortly after formation, the elderly Johnson was exchanged for Lieutenant Richard Rogers, Robert's brother.

The volunteers were some of the hardiest and most resolute men in the area. Most served for the duration of the conflict, which ended in 1760. Regardless of terrain or season, the rangers performed superhuman feats of physical endurance. The French and Indians alike feared them and were in awe of their accomplishments. They roamed the wilderness in search of information and intelligence about the enemy, living off the land summer and winter, frequently penetrating settlements hundreds of miles away. They became the scourge of their foes making silent day and night raids against formations many times stronger than their own ranks. It was not uncommon for them to hit an Indian encampment by surprise, taking a heavy toll on its inhabitants, and then silently retreat to the dark shadows of the wilderness. Most of the time, they were all that existed on the borderland to protect the vulnerable, isolated settlers from capture or death. Even a hint that Rogers' Rangers were in the vicinity was deterrent enough to make the wily Abenaki and their French handlers make a detour rather than take a chance on meeting the green-clad rangers.

Robert Rogers gave an astounding performance during the French and Indian War, but even then there were questions and rumors about his character. Parkman writes that his character "leaves much to be desired. He had been charged with forgery, or complicity in it, seems to have had no scruples in matters of business, and after the war was accused of treasonable dealings with the French and Spaniards in the West."[4]

Rogers's defects in character did not detract from his accomplishments on the frontier, where his gift of leadership contributed to the successful conclusion of the war against France. His rangers, at the least, were the equal of the best British troops in the field and were "the most formidable body of men ever employed in the early wars of America... To their savage and French foes, they were invincible."[5]

During a hunting trip to the Asquamchumauke River, near Mount Moosilauke, in about 1753, Robert Rogers, John Stark, and Samuel Orr, of Goffstown, were spending a rainy day in their camp when they were visited by three friendly Indians. The Indians departed just before dusk and Robert left camp a few minutes later. He returned in the middle of the night with three fresh scalps. Stark objected to the murder of the Indians during a time of peace. Rogers replied that war would take place within a year anyway.[6]

The story above illustrates a distinct difference between Stark and Rogers. It is remotely possible that Stark did not know about Rogers' illicit activities, even though it was the talk of the sparse rural community. John's father, Archibald, was definitely aware of Rogers's transgressions. Regardless of the closeness of the two intrepid bordermen, Stark was never tainted by his friend's tendencies, his inherent decency and stability of character fortified him against temptations, if they ever presented themselves.

He continued to grow in stature and wisdom during the French and Indian War. Rogers, on the other hand, seemed to deteriorate under the attraction of personal gain. It is a sad commentary on a man who served so valiantly the struggle for an empire. In the end, he became a Tory and fought against his former brethren, sharing that ignoble position with John's brother William.

Following George Washington's report to Governor Dinwiddie about the French in the Ohio River Valley, Washington was commissioned a lieutenant colonel and was the second in command of the Virginia militia regiment authorized by the governor. Colonel Joshua Frye was the commander. In the winter of 1754 a small group of workers were assembled and sent to the location where Washington had recommended a fort, at the juncture of the Ohio and Allegheny Rivers. The men began construction immediately upon their arrival. The structure was to be named Fort George. Two months later, a large force of French marines forced the surrender of the work crew, who were allowed to leave with their supplies intact.

The French forces then proceeded to continue the construction of a formidable fortress which they called Fort Duquesne. Washington heard of the capitulation and moved a portion of his regiment to a place he called Great Meadows, about sixty miles from the Ohio, to await reinforcements from his superior, Colonel Frye. Frye had two additional companies in his train and was close to linking up with Washington when he fell off his horse and was killed, leaving Washington in full command of the regiment.

Washington's reinforcements had not caught up with him when his Indian scouts reported to him of a French formation in the area. He observed the French contingent while they were eating breakfast, and attacked them. It was a brisk firefight that lasted only fifteen minutes. Half-King, one of his Indian chiefs, killed the French officer, Ensign Joseph Coulon de Villiers, brother of a popular French officer, then serving on the Ohio. Several French soldiers were killed in the fight and twenty-one surrendered. This ill-conceived attack was the opening salvo in the French and Indian War.

Returning quickly to Great Meadows, Washington ordered the erection of a wooden stockade, which he called Fort Necessity. He knew that some of the French soldiers had escaped and would warn the main camp of their action. The French responded immediately with seven hundred soldiers and three hundred and fifty Indian allies, attacking the frail stockade on the morning of July 3. A sniping siege raged for several hours, then the French offered Washington surrender terms that would permit them to return home with the arms and supplies they could carry on their persons, because the two countries were not officially at war. Washington accepted the offer and retreated hastily. On July 4, 1755, the French flag was raised over Fort Necessity. Years later, Washington would recall the irony of the date. He returned to Williamsburg and resigned his commission for the failed campaign. The Virginia House of Burgesses gladly agreed.

War had not been officially declared, but it was certainly being planned by both sides. In January 1755, the British sent two powerful regiments with General Edward Braddock to take command of British forces. Braddock had formulated a strategic plan for the destruction of the French in North America and discussed it with a convention of colonial governors in Alexandria, Virginia.

The plan was a simple one but it would require a large number of militia from the colonies. It proposed to attack four French strongholds all at the same time. They were Fort Niagara, on Lake Ontario; Fort Beausejour, in Nova Scotia; Fort Duquesne on the Ohio; and Crown Point (Fort Frederick) and other objectives in the Lake Champlain-Hudson River Valley.

The New England regiment under Colonel Blanchard had rendezvoused at Stevenstown (now Salisbury) while Rogers's company was sent to the Coos meadow, where they commenced construction of a small fort at the junction of the Connecticut and Ammonoosuc Rivers. They were then ordered to proceed to Fort Number Four, thence on to Lake Champlain. They crossed the Vermont wilderness and reached Albany on August 12, 1755.

The New Hampshire companies were assigned to the area north of Albany on the Hudson River flats and were incorporated into Major General William Johnson's army, with men from Massachusetts, Connecticut, and Rhode Island. General Johnson was an energetic and inexperienced commander who had immense influence over the New York Indian Confederacy contingent under his command. Intelligent and affable, he was well liked by the native populations and held the position of Indian agent in New York.

The news of General Braddock's devastating defeat on the Ohio caused alarm across the colonies. The Merrimack River valley communities observed the twenty-third as a day of fast.[7] Great expectations had accompanied Braddock's approach to the Ohio River Valley. He was a competent commander with excellent troops and was well supplied. Parliament believed that all that would be needed to resolve the conflict in the colonies were two British regiments, which it authorized. Now the regiments were neutralized, Braddock was dead, and the New York and Pennsylvania frontiers were defenseless against the rampaging Indians and their French allies. Fear gripped the borderland. The colonial governments moved with maddening indecisiveness. Money to support militias was scarce and there was very little coordination among the colonial powers, despite Benjamin Franklin's call for unity at the Albany conference.

Governor William Shirley, of Massachusetts, became responsible for Fort Oswego, on Lake Ontario, and maintained a large garrison at the facility. Braddock's defeat left the western frontier west of the Alleghenies wide open for Indian depredation. The main fear was of a general uprising of the Indians against the British. The selection of General Johnson helped to alleviate that fear.[8]

When General Johnson's army left Fort Lyman, named for a Dutch trader in the Albany area and later called Fort Edward, the fort was garrisoned by five hundred New Hampshire men from Colonel Blanchard's New England regiment. Johnson changed the name Lac St. Sacrament to Lake George, in honor of the British king. At the southern end of the lake, his army began the construction of a flotilla of rafts, whaleboats, and radeaux, sturdy rafts that were essentially floating forts. Johnson planned to use these to travel to Lake Champlain and attack Fort Frederick at Crown Point. He also started to build a fort.

Fort Frederick was commanded by a French officer, Baron Ludwig Dieskau. As soon as he learned of the British buildup at Lake George, he led a force of French, Canadian, and Indian troops south to trap them. He laid an ambush on a trail leading to Lake George against a force commanded by Colonel Phineas Lyman, General Johnson's second in command and an able soldier. When he was attacked, Lyman instantly ordered his troops to retreat to the incomplete fortifications at the edge of the lake. Dieskau followed on Lyman's heels. After several attempts to dislodge Lyman from the fortifications, Dieskau's forces were ordered to retreat to Fort Frederick. Dieskau, however, was captured while trying to disengage his troops.[9]

Colonel Blanchard, at Fort Edward, received news of the battle at Lake George and sent Captain Nathaniel Folsom of the New Hampshire regiment with eighty men and forty from a New York regiment. Captain McGinnis was in charge. He was killed early in the engagement and Captain Folsom took over, leading his men against the retreating French with audacity and courage. At that point, General Johnson refused to follow up on his victory, which became known as the Battle of Lake George.

While the above engagement was taking place, Robert Rogers and John Stark were scouting the Hudson River. When they returned to Fort Edward, they learned of the battle and were ordered to continue scouting operations in the area throughout the winter, beginning on September 3, 1755. It was customary at that time for military formations to go into winter quarters leaving a minimum number of troops to garrison isolated facilities.

That fall Colonel Blanchard wrote to Governor Wentworth informing him that the New Hampshire regiment was obliged to return home, and requested that Robert Rogers and a few of his men remain on duty to continue their valuable scouting work. Stark returned to New Hampshire at that time. Rogers remained behind with his brother, Richard, and conducted numerous scouting operations in and around Fort Frederick and Lake Champlain.

Stark was twenty-seven years old and had received valuable experience in handling large numbers of men during scouting operations. He waited out the winter at home and was most likely aware of events then taking place beyond the Hudson Valley-Lake Champlain corridor. British forces had seized Fort Beausejours in Nova Scotia. It was part of the grand scheme to reduce Canada's dependency on the French. Governor Shirley was instrumental in insisting that the population of the province take an oath of allegiance to the British crown. Many refused, and the overwhelming task of evacuating six thousand residents of Acadia took place in November and December. Many of the Acadians, scattered throughout Canada and New England, went to Louisiana. At the end of the Seven Years War, a large number returned to their homes. The helpless Acadians suffered severe hardships. A century later, the poet Henry Wadsworth Longfellow, immortalized the cruel event in his poem *Evangeline.*

In March 1756, Governor Shirley, who had replaced General Braddock as commander in chief of British and colonial forces, summoned Robert Rogers to Boston for a conference, where he was warmly received. Shirley gave him a commission to recruit an independent company of sixty rangers. Shirley instructed Rogers "to destroy the French and their allies by sacking, burning and destroying."[10]

Rogers wrote that most of the men were enlisted from the Merrimack region and from the New Hampshire regiment. He again enlisted John Stark as a lieutenant to be his second in command. The company was assembled, and a group under the command of Lieutenant Richard Rogers departed for Albany, which was to be their rendezvous and staging area. Rogers and Stark traveled by way of Fort Number Four, where they received new orders to proceed to Crown Point. On the second day of their march through the mountainous terrain, Stark became ill and left the formation with an escort of six men headed for Fort Edward. The course to the fort was extremely hazardous and the small detachment remained vigilant to any sign of danger. Stark had noted a formation of four hundred Indians as he got closer to the Hudson River. He was quick to recover from his illness once he arrived at Fort Edward.

In the meantime, Rogers and his men were at Lake Champlain south of Crown Point, where they observed more than five hundred French troops. They evaded the French and on May 11 reached Fort William Henry, where Rogers learned that Governor Shirley had been replaced by Lieutenant General James Abercromby, who authorized Rogers' request for a larger ranger company. Abercromby recognized the value of irregular combat units in the wilderness. The command of the new company was given to Robert's brother Richard. The ensign for the new command was

Caleb Page, of Starkstown. He was the brother of Elizabeth Page who became John Stark's wife and achieved enduring fame as Molly Stark. John Stark was named Richard's second in command. The new company was ready to function within twenty-eight days and left on a patrol up the Mohawk River Valley.

English and colonial authorities were building an army capable of capturing Fort Frederick. Stark remained at Fort Edward, where General Johnson assigned a company of Stockbridge Indians to the ranger company. Stark sprinkled a few of his men within the ranks of the Indian detachment and sent them to scout the area west and north of Fort Ticonderoga. They returned a few days later with four French scalps taken near the fort.

Stark's reinforced company embarked in whaleboats with Robert's company for a rendezvous twenty miles north of Crown Point on the west bank of Lake Champlain. They encountered a schooner but were unable to capture the vessel. The following day, they returned to within eight miles of Crown Point and landed on the eastern shore. On the twenty-ninth, they entered a village east of the fort and took prisoner a man, his wife, and his fourteen-year old daughter, returning them to Fort William Henry on the twenty-second.

The ranger companies gathered valuable intelligence information, but a lot of their effort, time, and energy was spent escorting supply columns to and from the area, acting as flanking guards. The young General Abercromby was often critical of the rangers' discipline, or lack thereof. He accompanied them as an observer on a scouting mission and described the men as follows:

"They even rebelled against their own officers. All I could do or say to the officers they could not prevent firing on our march. They slept one night near Ticonderoga and the next morning a few of them were seen about to capture a prisoner. Captain Stark who was with me set up the Indian holler, upon that the whole party jumped up and yelled as if Hell had broke loose and all afiring at a few men running away. I did everything in my power to make them hold their tongue and behave as they ought to do. I even knocked several of them down and damned their officers for a set of scoundrels. A month later the rangers encamped on an island off Fort Edward and began a riot in an effort to rescue two of their number who had been imprisoned by their officers . . . Captain Shepherd confronted them with a firelock in his hands. After that they began to desert . . . The rangers refused to take orders or to do any duty but that of scouting."[11]

The summer of 1756 slipped away quickly and both sides began preparing their winter quarters. The French had captured Fort Oswego on Lake Ontario in August. This gave them secure communications from the Saint Lawrence to the Mississippi River.

Robert Rogers wrote: "Both armies now retired to winter quarters. The rangers were stationed at Forts William Henry and Edward, and were augmented by two new companies [British] from Nova Scotia under Captains Hobbs and Spikeman. These two companies were posted at Fort William Henry, and the two at Fort Edward. Captain Richard Rogers was sent to New England for recruits. He waited upon the Boston government to obtain pay for the rangers' services in the winter of 1755; but could obtain none, although Lord Loudoun generously supported the claim."[12]

3

War on the Hudson (1755–1758)

John Stark and a small band of rangers whiled away the bleak winter months listening to the wind howl across the barren north woods, where the wolves lifted their heads into the night to call to their mates from distant hills. The unnerving monotony of winter cooped up in hastily built shelters tried the patience of many of the hardy rangers. They hoped for the occasional glimpse of Indians so that they could be used for target practice, and the occasional lone Indian accommodated them.

In the middle of January 1757, Robert Rogers came from Fort Edward to Fort William Henry and spent two days there making snowshoes so that the men could conduct patrols over the deep snow. They marched north on Lake George as far as the Narrows and camped overnight. At that point, a few of the men lacked the physical stamina required for snowshoeing in the cold climate. They turned back to Fort William Henry, leaving the company with seventy-four able-bodied men.

On the nineteenth, they reached the western shore of Lake George four miles south of Rogers's Rock and proceeded inland on an azimuth west of north about eight miles, then set up camp for the night. The next morning they took a course east of north for the day, passing Fort Carillon unnoticed and continuing for another five miles. By then it was raining and the heavy snow clung to their snowshoes, making travel difficult. That night they slept in holes dug into the snow with soft spruce and fir boughs piled as bedding to protect them from the slush that covered the ground. The drizzle continued through the night as the company rotated its guard detachments. Standing watch in the bleak cold night, wrapped in heavy furs to protect against the cutting winds that swept the lake, was a lonely and often frightening vigil that drove some men mad. It was a frigid and gloomy environment in which the rangers had to exercise prudence in taking care of themselves. The threat of pneumonia or a bad cold could spell the difference between life and death.

The next morning the men continued their patrol in the rain to the western shore of Lake Champlain, where they immediately spotted a sledge being drawn by horses over the ice between Crown Point and Carillon. Rogers ordered Stark to rush to the left toward the shore so that he could head off the sledge while Rogers reentered the forest to block its retreat.

Stark had left on his mission when, seconds later, Rogers noticed several more loaded sledges (he claimed eight or ten), and sent a messenger to alert Stark. It was too late; Stark had already shown himself on the ice. Suddenly the sledges, alerted to their plight, turned around and raced toward Carillon. The rangers captured three of the sledges along with seven men and six horses and began to interrogate the prisoners. The patrolling rangers were amazed to learn that Carillon had more than three hundred and fifty regular French soldiers, two hundred Canadian militia, and about forty-five Indians with more expected to arrive that evening.

The information made the rangers realize that they were in great peril. The escaped sledge operators would give away their presence and location, and with the troops available at the fort, an overwhelming force could successfully cut off their retreat. They were soaking wet and exhausted, and alarmed that they had fallen into a trap.

Rogers evaluated their predicament and ordered the company back along the trail toward their most recent camp to warm themselves and to dry their weapons. They then started off in single file with a sense of urgency that reflected their true status. Rogers and Lieutenant Kennedy were in the vanguard while Lieutenant Stark positioned himself at the tail end of the column. They moved steadily and as swiftly as aching bones permitted until two in the afternoon, when they filed through a heavily forested valley a few hundred feet wide. The front of the column descended the first hill and was mounting the opposite hill when the forest erupted in gunfire from the bushes above their line of travel. The volleys echoed across the frozen land, killing instantly Lieutenants Kennedy and Spikeman.

French soldiers and Indians leaped from their hiding places killing several rangers and taking several more prisoners. The outnumbered rangers returned fire as best they could. Rogers was wounded in the head in the first volley. Stark was at the top of the knoll when they were hit and quickly organized a counter fire that checked the enemy long enough for many of the rangers to fall back across the hollow and up the incline where Stark had established a defense. They then began to take cover behind trees and fire at targets of opportunity, stubbornly holding their ground.

The assailants twice tried to outflank them at their rear and were repulsed by a group Stark held in mobile reserve for just such a move. The fight lasted several hours, with the French trying to convince Rogers to surrender by offering him and his men kindness and good treatment. They even told him how much they admired his courage. Sporadic firing and conversation continued the stalemate until darkness.

Both Stark and Rogers realized that to stay put was a death sentence, so they cautiously withdrew under the cover of darkness with forty-eight able bodied men and six wounded. They reached the northern portion of Lake George with no further contact with the enemy. The next morning, Stark and two men left the group and rushed ahead to obtain a sledge for the wounded and weakened men. The balance of the group made their way to the narrows and encamped to wait for the relief column. Stark was exhausted by the sprint for assistance, and sent fresh men and a sledge to the narrows. His trek was a tribute to his physical fitness and determination.

Shortly thereafter, on January 23, 1757, the column of weakened rangers filed through the welcome gates of Fort William Henry with their prisoners. They had survived an ambush that could have wiped out the ranger company. Rogers must bear the blame for the order to backtrack on their original trail. It violated one of his own tactical rules of operation: never use the same route to and from a destination!

Later, General James Abercromby sent a letter of commendation and thanks for the men's gallant effort from his Albany headquarters. As a result of the rangers' performance, several British officers were eager to adopt many of the ranger's rules of engagement for their own light-infantry regiments.[1]

Stark related many years later that this ambush was the only time when he consciously killed another human being. He had been a successful hunter all of his life and was well known as one of the best marksman of his time. Caleb Stark wrote:

"While the rangers were defending their positions on the crest of the hill, he [Stark] observed that several balls struck near him from a certain direction . . . he discovered an Indian stretched at full length upon a rock, behind a large tree. His gun was soon ready and he saw an Indian rising for another shot at him. His fusee was instantly leveled, discharged, and the savage rolled from the rock into the snow pierced by a bullet through the head."[2]

With the death of Captain Spikeman, Stark was promoted to Captain as the rangers were reorganized after the January debacle.

※

The first siege of Fort William Henry at the southern end of Lake George took place in March 1757 while Stark was commander of the ranger detachment at the fort. William Henry was located fifteen miles from Fort Edward on the Hudson River, north of Albany. The nearest French fort was Fort Carillon, forty miles north of William Henry, at the southern tip of Lake Champlain. Prior to the siege, smallpox had weakened the garrison, even though the men were still functioning well. Caleb Stark gives a figure of one hundred and twenty-eight invalids from disease and old wounds leaving a force of three hundred forty-six effective soldiers.[3]

Robert Rogers had contracted the disease while he was at Albany and was confined for a month and a half. Stark, always ready to assist, took over Rogers's duties, attending to many details pertaining to the provisioning and equipping of the ranger force. His ability to accept and carry out responsibilities would serve him and the country well. He was comfortable with command, which reflected his self-confidence.

On the evening of March 16, while Stark was making his rounds at Fort William Henry, he became aware that the Scotch-Irish members of the garrison intended to celebrate their patron, saint Patrick. He had always disliked the excessive carousing and rowdy Irish drinking habits and took steps to curb some of their excesses by ordering the sutler to refrain from anything other than normal rations to the rangers unless Stark personally ordered the change. Then he notified his aides that he was not to be disturbed after he retired to his quarters.

The Irishmen and Scotsmen began their celebration with exuberance and the rangers were eager to enjoy the same privileges. The officer of the day was having a difficult time assigning sober soldiers to the sentry posts. Giving up in disgust, he substituted rangers in place of those men who were unfit for duty. Stark's rangers were the only members of the garrison available.

Later that evening, a sentinel looked out across Lake George and noticed a light on the water. Closer scrutiny indicated that a large force was descending on the fort, and he sounded the alarm with Captain Stark. Stark then alerted the fort commander and ordered all of his ranger contingent to the barricades. It was a wise decision.

An army of twenty-five hundred French soldiers and a number of Indians commanded by General Marquis Vaudeville were slowly approaching the fort under the cover of partial darkness. They stopped about five hundred feet from the stockade and sent forward a number of courageous men with scaling ladders to be placed at the foot of the stockade. They were elated that they had achieved surprise. Stark had ordered his men to hold their fire until he gave the command, and just as the vanguard of soldiers reached the top of the ladders, he gave the order to fire in a loud clear voice that echoed through the still of the darkness.

The rangers' musket fire was followed by grapeshot fire from several cannons, which took a terrible toll on the assailants. The French fell back, confused and intimidated by their reception. They had assumed that the Scotch-Irish population of the fort would be drunk or well on their way to that state. Stark urged even heavier fire at the retreating enemy. After the first salvo, those who had been celebrating began to take their positions at the barricades, increasing the rattle of muskets and cannon grapeshot.

Shortly after daylight, a flag of truce carried by a French officer appeared at the main gate. He was blindfolded and brought into the fort. He carried a summons for the fort's garrison to surrender, claiming that the British occupied territory belonging to the king of France. The summons offered them their lives and personal weapons and the officers whatever baggage they were capable of carrying. Because there was a large contingent of Indians beyond the stockade, the summons suggested that they provide some gifts to keep them orderly. If terms were not accepted, they would attack with an overwhelming force and no quarter would be given.

The unanimous decision to refuse the surrender offer was passed on to the French courier. Memories of Braddock's costly defeat on the Monongahela River in Virginia were fresh, and the men were determined to hold out for as long as possible and be buried in the ruins of Fort William Henry rather than surrender. The French officer received the verdict and was escorted to the gate. He was given twenty minutes to reach the French lines.

The fort was then assaulted several times. Each time the fire from the barricaded walls stopped the attack. The defenders were as determined as the attackers and the situation settled into a wary waiting game. The French burned several boats and outbuildings. The siege lasted for five days, at which time the French disengaged themselves and retreated to Fort Carillon, carrying away most of their dead and wounded. The French tried to conceal their losses by cutting holes in the ice on the lake giving their dead comrades a cold-water burial.

Caleb Stark claims that many of the French soldiers were scalped by the Indians before being inserted in their watery graves. Those French soldiers taken prisoner after the engagement told their captives that they had orders to put to death every man, woman, and child once the fort was captured.

Very few of the garrison were wounded and there were no fatalities. Stark was struck by a spent ball, which left a small bruise on his body. It was the only time in his active military career that he sustained an injury from an enemy's weapon. He received praise from many quarters for his spirited defense of the fort. One show of appreciation came from a group of Nantucket whalers who gave him a cane made from a whalebone with an ivory handle. (The cane is still in the Stark family.)

In 1757, Prime Minister William Pitt, recognized that the colonies were the key to future prosperity and began to allocate more funds, materials, and manpower to the execution of the war effort. One of the strategic actions he recommended was the capture of Fort Louisbourg, Nova Scotia. A garrison of four thousand men was left at Fort Edward as the British began to scale down operations in preparation for the assault on Nova Scotia.

Stark was selected to be one of the participants, but he contracted smallpox while at a staging area in New York, and remained there until he recovered; the rangers sailed north without him. In October 1757, he returned to Fort Edward as soon as he was strong enough to assume command. Normally the armies of all the nations involved went into winter quarters and garrisons of vital installations were whittled to the bone. Supplying them under winter conditions was difficult. Stark stayed at Fort Edward for the winter.

Early in the summer of 1757, while Stark was recuperating from smallpox, the most famous battle of the French and Indian War took place. This time, Fort William Henry fell to the French and their uncontrollable Indian allies. Montcalm had been using Fort Carillon as a staging area and when he was informed of the British pullout within the Hudson River–Lake Champlain corridor between the Adirondack Mountains to the west and the Green Mountains to the east, he determined that the time was right to capture Fort William Henry. Altogether he had assembled a force of eight thousand Canadian and French soldiers and a force of six thousand Indians from all over the eastern seaboard. He even had a few Iowans.[4]

Conditions looked promising to Montcalm. He had amassed together an impressive and well-supplied force. At the same time, the British had weakened their garrisons. Perhaps it would be possible, Montcalm hoped, to go all the way to Albany. That would give him control of the northern half of the corridor. He entered the summer with a powerful army under his command and high expectations for success.

The French army moved south from Carillon by boat and over land to Fort William Henry. The commander there, Major General Daniel Webb, viewed the intelligence about the French intentions and force makeup with alarm. When the French appeared on the water before the fort, he cowardly fled William Henry for the relative safety of Fort Edward, leaving the brave and resourceful Major George Munro in charge of two thousand three hundred seventy-two men with only eleven hundred fit for duty. Disease and wounds had plagued both sides in the contest.

Montcalm ordered a tight siege on the fort while the occupants put up a spirited defense for four days. General Webb, fourteen miles away at Fort Edward, had a garrison of fourteen hundred men and another eighteen hundred available in camps nearby the fort. That gave him a potential total of three thousand two hundred men in which to come to the aid of his brothers fighting for their lives at William Henry. Webb was fully aware of the desperate situation. Separated by only twelve miles, he could hear the thunder of the cannons and still failed to come to his comrades' rescue.

Munro fought on with a determined defense and sent several urgent appeals for assistance to Webb, to no avail. Webb answered that he would capitulate! His cowardly behavior made possible an easy victory for the French. After four days of constant combat, Munro had lost three hundred killed and wounded and smallpox was continuing to run rampant through his garrison. Munro had no honorable choice but to surrender the badly damaged fortress, and was ordered to march out with the able-bodied men and to leave behind the wounded and sick.

As soon as they evacuated the ruins, the Indians rushed to the interior in search of food and rum. They found the vulnerable injured and sick and proceeded to butcher all of them. Their savagery sickened even Montcalm, who tried unsuccessfully to control them. Crazed by the blood inside the ruins, the Indians turned outside to the surrendered group whom Montcalm had promised safe passage to Fort Edward. Even his British enemies praised the French officer's efforts to stop the massacre that was about to occur.

The British column remained together that night and at first light continued to Fort Edward. Members of the New Hampshire regiment were among those at the rear of the column. Eighty of them were killed instantly or dragged off and slaughtered.[5]

The stalwart defense of Fort William Henry and the ensuing massacre of the defeated inhabitants have been beautifully and passionately described by James Fenimore Cooper in his classic novel *The Last of the Mohicans.* The episode displays the full spectrum of human virtues and vices, when courage and chivalry opposed cowardice and bestiality.

Stark returned to Fort Edward in October 1757 after a full recovery from smallpox. It was a highly contagious disease that was generally fatal to children and to individuals with a weak constitution. When it strikes, it has a crippling effect on the patient. A high fever, headaches, and vomiting are common symptoms. Stark and Rogers were lucky to survive the scourge. They shared that experience with George Washington who contracted the disease while as a young man in Barbados.

General Augustus Vincent Lord George Howe, whom many of his peers considered to be one of England's finest and most competent soldiers, was in command at Albany. He was a good administrator and put in a great deal of effort supervising the execution of his orders, especially among his rangers. Stark traveled often between Albany and Fort Edward during this period and became an ardent admirer of Lord Howe. One wonders what he had thought of Webb's performance in regard to the defeat of Fort William Henry!

On March 10, 1758, Rogers was ordered to make a reconnaissance around Fort Carillon and to bring in a prisoner if possible. The mission required more men than Rogers assigned to the task, and they were badly mauled in several intense engagements. They had camped at the narrows of Lake George and proceeded to ambush an Indian scouting party, scalping all who were killed. The rangers' ambush triggered a response from a larger contingent at Fort Carillon who entered the field with the intention of destroying the bothersome ranger force.

When Rogers encountered the main body of this task force he was woefully outnumbered and in danger of being overrun. The Indians allied with the French came upon their scalped comrades and were roused to a high fever for revenge. They succeeded in pushing the rangers to the west side of Bald Mountain, which became known as Rogers' Rock.

Tired and worried, the rangers had little time to secure good defensive positions before they were attacked on three sides. At that time, Rogers gave the order to scatter. It was every man for himself. Confusion reigned on the hilltop. Lieutenant Philips accepted the offer to surrender and receive fair treatment. He was deceived, for most of his men were tied to trees and systematically hacked to pieces. Philips later escaped to tell the harrowing story to Rogers.

A cluster of rangers with Rogers made their way over the frozen lake. He had lost one hundred twenty-eight men, which caused much grief in many New Hampshire homes. He sent word to Fort Edward for assistance and recorded the following in his journal for March 15, 1758:

"In the morning we proceeded up the lake and at Hoop Island, six miles north of William and Henry met Captain John Stark coming to our relief bringing with him provisions, blankets and sleighs. We encamped on the island, passed the night with good fires and on the evening of the next day arrived at Fort Edward."[6]

After the rangers' worst defeat, Rogers traveled to New York, with Howe's consent, to confer with General Abercromby about his plans for an enlarged ranger presence. He was promoted to major and given authority to form a battalion. In the meantime, Stark remained in charge of the rangers in and around Fort Edward and Albany. Robert Rogers relied on Stark's serious and steadfast attention to all details of his command. On April 18, 1758, Stark promoted his brother Archibald to the rank of lieutenant.

Conferences between Abercromby and Howe generated a desperate need for more information about the enemy's defenses and strength. Four separate parties were sent to the Fort Carillon area to obtain prisoners. Stark was ordered to scout the west side of Lake George and Lake Champlain up to Fort Carillon. He returned on May 8 with six prisoners and a detailed account of his patrol.

The regal Lord Howe and the sturdy frontiersman Stark got along well. They enjoyed mutual respect. Howe, a grandson of King George I, was thirty-four years old and had left England for the express purpose of capturing the French forts on Lake Champlain in order to open the gateway to Canada. He was Prime Minister Pitt's choice for the command, but it was given to Major General James Abercromby, the senior British officer in North America.

General Abercromby, with Howe as second in command, had assembled sixteen thousand men at the burned site of Fort William Henry, poised to strike and capture Fort Carillon. Originally the fort was to be called Fort Vaudreil in honor of the governor-general of Canada. Carillon, a chime of bells, was agreed upon for the sound of three sets of rapids and waterfalls that joined lake Champlain and Lake George.[7]

When William Pitt became England's prime minister a year earlier, he began supplying more men and equipment to defeat the French in North America and prepared a war plan to implement that policy. He proposed a three-pronged attack. First, the powerful Fort Louisbourg at Nova Scotia, defending the approaches to the Saint Lawrence River, was assaulted with twelve hundred men and the assistance of a powerful British fleet of gunships. Second, General Forbes was to secure Fort Duquesne, on the Ohio River. The largest and third prong of attack was to be conducted by Abercromby and Howe at Fort Carillon as the initial assault in the strategy to secure Canada, the reverse of what Montcalm had envisioned.

The army set sail on July 5, 1758, in whaleboats and rafts from the southern end of Lake George. The rangers and Colonel Gage's light-infantry regiment were in the vanguard of the flotilla. In late afternoon, they stopped at Sabbath Point, twenty-five miles up the lake, to wait for their artillery and supplies to catch up with them.

The next day, the rangers approached the bridge on the La Chute River with Rogers in the lead position and Stark bringing up the rear. Rogers ran into a band of French troops and Indians who disputed his passage. After a short exchange of fire, the French retreated, leaving the bridge open.

In the rear of the rangers, the main body of British and provincial troops formed four columns and plunged forward into the dark forest. Lord Howe was leading the way. A Connecticut colonel Israel Putnam, was at his side with the advance elements of troops. They encountered a French force of about three hundred and fifty troops near the La Chute River. Montcalm had sent them out to locate the main position of the British force. The French troops were surprised to find the British where they were, between them and the fort, and a certain amount of confusion accompanied the brisk firefight that ensued.

Upon hearing shots to their rear, the rangers doubled back to assist the leading elements of the British army. The rangers caught the French in a crossfire. Most of the French scouting force was either killed or captured. This skirmish at the river unnerved many of the British regulars, despite a lot of training from Lord Howe and Colonel Gates in forest tactics. Without the timely assistance of the rangers, the initial contact with the enemy at the river might have ended the campaign before it really got started.

Lord Howe was killed by a bullet through his chest during that first contact with the enemy, and that night a somber mood settled over Abercromby's army. Howe was the one person whom all ranks admired and genuinely liked. "Lord Howe was probably the most respected officer in British North America," Pitt later wrote, "a character of ancient times, a complete model of military virtue."[8]

The next morning, Abercromby ordered the troops back to the landing site to reorganize. He planned to take a circuitous route to the northwest and approach the fort from the west along a rocky plateau that was higher in elevation than the surrounding terrain. It was a logical tactic to approach the heights from the west. In doing so, the men had to reconstruct the bridge over the La Chute River that the French had burned.

Montcalm did not commit himself until he was in possession of firm intelligence as to where and when the main British attack was coming. When he had reports of them approaching via the portage road between Lake George and Lake Champlain, he instantly ordered his troops to construct breastworks and abatis to impede their advance. His troops cut down a huge forest so that the trees pointed away from the French defensive lines. The entanglement of large oak, maple, hemlock, and white pine canopies created an impressive fortification measure. The weary French troops slept well the night of July 7. Their method of breaking up the unit cohesion of the British formations with the abatis was a stroke of genius, and it worked better than they had imagined.

The attack by the British started at about noon. The area looked as if it had been hit by a hurricane. The attack is aptly described by a Stephen Smith:

"As the British and American troops advanced up the Heights of Carillon they would have to pass through the abatis: trees felled so that their tops faced the direction of the attack, with limbs interfaced and sharpened. This obstacle extended up to 25 paces in depth—it not only slowed the attack, but it would break-up formations, forcing the men to advance individually instead of in ranks. Once past the abatis, the troops would face an open field of fire up to 50 paces wide. Surviving that obstacle, they still would have to climb the eight- or nine-foot breastworks before they could cross bayonets with the French."[9]

The advance was a disaster, yet the British troops tried valiantly to pick their way through the entanglement in a hail of bullets. The slaughter was complete and unit cohesion was lost a few minutes after they entered the abatis. An hour after the initial assault, not one British or provincial soldier had made his way to the breastworks. Reports of the disaster came to Abercromby's headquarter a mile to the rear, yet, time after time he callously ordered the assaults to continue against the impregnable field of fire and brush. His army was needlessly destroyed. The troops endured seven hours of hell before the much-awaited order to withdraw arrived. Their valorous effort was of no avail. The rangers and Gage's well-trained light-infantry covered the withdrawal of the main body.

There was much jubilation in the French ranks when they saw the British and provincials retreat. In contrast, the mood of the retreating troops bordered on mutiny. Abercromby became the most hated man in the British army. The men sullenly climbed into their whaleboats and rafts and rowed south on Lake George to the ruins of Fort William Henry. The valiant 42nd Highlands Regiment (the Black Watch), in which his nephew, Captain James Abercrombie, served; the Royal American Regiment (60th) and other regiments ceased to exist. The army of sixteen thousand men had lost two thousand dead and wounded. The French defense force of thirty-five hundred men lost three hundred seventy-five killed and wounded.

Abercromby's decision to attack the French fortification was based on the report of a young, inexperienced engineer, Colonel Clerk. He had viewed the situation from Rattlesnake Mountain (Mount Defiance) with

John Stark and a company of rangers. Clerk believed the enemy works to be of little importance. Stark, on the other hand, adamantly disagreed and stated forcefully that they were formidable defenses. Abercromby dismissed the opinion of an experienced campaigner like Stark and chose to rely on Clerk's point of view, and attacked without his artillery in support. The arrogant decision doomed his army to failure. Caleb stark wrote:

"The regret of Captain Stark for the fate of the gallant Lord Howe, who was thus fell at the age of thirty-three, lasted his lifetime. He often remarked, however, during the Revolution, that he became more reconciled to his fate, since his talents, had he lived, might have been employed against the United States. He [Stark] considered him the ablest commander under whom he ever served."[10]

On June 22, 1758, Archibald Stark, John's father, died while attending to his will. Notice of his death reached John sometime during the first or second week in July. He was immediately granted a leave of absence and furloughed home.

4

End of the Conflict (1758-1759)

While General Abercromby was witnessing the methodical destruction of his army at Fort Carillon, another piece of Prime Minister William Pitt's strategy for eliminating French influence from the North American continent was taking place miles away in Nova Scotia. Pitt recalled General Jeffrey Amherst from Germany to command the land troops against Fort Louisbourg on Cape Breton Island, arriving at Halifax on May 28 to take charge of an army of three divisions. The troops boarded ships for Cape Breton shortly after his arrival.

Tall and thin, Major General James Wolfe did not look like a soldier. His pallid complexion and red hair tied in a knot at the back of his head belied the fiery passion and intensity of purpose that guided his every step. He went into battle carrying only a walking stick. His troops had captured the southeastern side of the harbor at Lighthouse Point by June 12. For another forty-five days the bombardment continued, until the French capitulated on the 26 of July. The British took six thousand French prisoners and celebrated their victory two and a half weeks after the tragic failure at Fort Carillon. Now they could sail up the Saint Lawrence and destroy all of the French settlements along the shores and bays. The battle for Louisbourg and the upper Saint Lawrence also saw the destruction of the French fleet by the more powerful Royal Navy.

General Jeffrey Amherst was informed of Abercromby's defeat, and he personally led troops to his post at Albany and then returned to his winter quarters at Halifax, where he learned that he had been named commander in chief of all of His Majesty's troops in North America. Realizing that he would need even more manpower for the number of tasks ahead, he began advertising and soliciting for more funds. He also postponed a decision to capture Fort Carillon.

John Stark had taken a leave to settle his father's estate. Archibald Stark's financial affairs left much to be desired, but John and his brother William had worked hard to settle matters to the satisfaction of the family. William had married Mary Stinson, from a prominent family in Starkstown, four years earlier. On this same furlough, John married Elizabeth Page, on August 20. She was the daughter of Captain Caleb Page, one of the original proprietors of the town. John had known the family for several years and Elizabeth had captured his heart. John returned to duty at Fort Edward late in February 1759.

During that winter of 1758-1759, the rangers were almost constantly on the move, scouting the area around Crown Point, Fort Carillon, and the western shore of Lake Champlain. John Stark was not mentioned in accounts of these long and difficult expeditions, but it is safe to say that he participated in some of them after he returned to duty. By that time, Amherst's appointment as commander in chief was beginning to be felt. Men, equipment, and supplies were rapidly accumulating to replace those lost by Abercromby.

London had ordered Amherst to invade Canada via Fort Carillon and Crown Point, then on to Montreal. Wolfe was to command the main force against Quebec. The two coordinating movements created a giant pincer that was mutually supportive, especially as they drew closer to each other.

Amherst arrived at Albany on May 3, 1759, to review his army of eight thousand men. The troops came from New England, New York, and Virginia. By June 1st he was eager to get under way. He was already a month behind schedule, rainy weather and a muddy spring had postponed the anticipated assault on the first objective—Carillon.

Robert Rogers wrote in his journal: "I was directed to send Captain Stark with three companies to join Gen. Gage. I remained with the other three."[1] Stark and Gage had known each other before they came together under Amherst. Gage's light-infantry had been trained in the same tactics used by the rangers, and were some of the best troops in the British army. The two officers had also served side by side during the unsuccessful assault on Carillon. Little did the two officers know that, in seventeen years, they would oppose each other in a desperate struggle for Breed's Hill, in Charlestown, Massachusetts.

In Amherst's journal entry for June 13, 1759, he wrote: "Captain Stark with his company of rangers will join the detachment from the

4-mile post." The next day a few members of each battalion were fishing in Lake George to supplement their food supply. The fishing party had drifted too far north and was pursued by three enemy boats. Rogers had seen what was taking place: "I sent Captain Stark out with a party to secure their retreat and try to catch the enemy."[2] The party returned without incident.

Two companies of grenadiers, rangers, and Indians covered the fishing boats off Diamond Point. Organized fishing parties were part of the General Orders for June 27, when Amherst wrote:

"Capt. Stark will have a red flag in his bateau and every bateau must be near enough to call to each other and to follow Captain Stark immediately as he knows where the covering party is located and will row in that direction at the proper time. The fishermen will take their arms, which Captain Loring will deliver and great care must be taken that they are not too much crowded. Captain Stark will receive his orders when the whole is to return to major Campbell."[3]

Amherst sent two splinter groups to the west from Lake Champlain, one to secure Fort Niagara on Lake Ontario and the other to relieve Fort Pitt, in Pennsylvania. He had also built impromptu fortifications between the old ruins of Fort William Henry and Albany at three to four mile intervals. While he was at the head of Lake George, he began to build a fort where the British had made their stand in an entrenched camp during the unsuccessful first siege of Fort William Henry. General Amherst completed one bastion of the fortress, known as Fort George, before leaving to lead the assault on Fort Carillon. He chose to lead the central advance up the Champlain corridor to Montreal and ultimately to link up with Wolfe's force on the Saint Lawrence River at Quebec City.

The southern tip of Lake George had been the mustering place for the French and British alike for the past five summers. It was at this staging area that he opted to collect his men and supplies and train them. Half of the men were British troops and half were from the various provinces. They drilled daily and practiced marksmanship and small-unit tactics. Amherst's aim was to condition the troops to forest fighting as much as possible in the time available before he moved on to assault Fort Carillon.

Amherst proved to be a demanding leader. Every company fell in for daily parade. Those who were on sick call were ordered to march to the lake and wash their faces and hands. Courts-martial were frequent, with many floggings publicly administered to culprits before their regiment. A few were shot for cowardice and treasonable acts. Discipline improved immediately.

One chore the troops carried out without shirkers or complainers was the practice of cutting tips of branches from spruce trees native to the area, for the brewing of spruce beer. The north woods brew was reputed to have been successful against scurvy, a dread disease causing loss of teeth and spongy skin that bleeds easily from lack of vitamin C. Every garrison in the wilderness had a large supply of West Indian molasses available to manufacture the brew. The men were allowed to drink as much as they wanted at a halfpenny a quart.[4]

By the third week in July, Lake George was once again filled with British and provincial troops. The pageantry of their colorful uniforms and banners filled the water as they wove among the small islands of the lake. By nightfall, the advance contingent of rangers was near the outlet. The men remained overnight in their boats on the water. They landed in the morning and fought off a small French patrol, and marched up the familiar portage route to the sawmill and waterfall south of Fort Carillon. To the surprise of all who participated, the advance was meeting only token resistance as they approached the heights and entrenchments where General Abercromby had hurled his army, in vain, at the strong French defenders.

The French Commander Bourlamaque chose not to contest the newly constructed earth fortifications even though he had as many men as Montcalm had when confronting Abercromby. While the fort's cannons pounded away at the attacking formations, the British quickly took refuge from the barrage in the shelter of the entrenchments, which served them well. Then Amherst brought up his artillery, the "queen of battle," and began his assault on the fortress. It was not long before he realized that Bourlamaque had retired to the north up Lake Champlain, leaving behind a token force of only four hundred French troops to slow down the British assault. He had been ordered to abandon Fort Carillon and retreat to Isle aux Noix, in the center of the Richelieu River, north of Lake Champlain.

On the evening of the twenty-sixth at about ten o'clock, three French deserters entered the British camp to report that the magazine was rigged to blow up. An anxious army looked toward the fort wondering what was happening. At eleven o'clock an explosion ripped through the fortress, sending a fiery display of exploding munitions into the air mixed with remnants of the fort itself. The British entered the fort shortly after the first detonation to discover that the damage was limited to the destruction of only one bastion. Thus, the proud stronghold, a symbol of French empirical expectations for the New World, was now in the hands of their opponents. One cannot help but wonder what the ambitious Amherst would have done if he had been in Abercromby's place a year earlier. Without question, he would have pounded the treacherous abatis into splinters with his superior artillery train before sending his troops into the assault, as Stark had suggested.

Amherst advanced as far as Fort Frederic at Crown Point after his ranger scouts told him that the position had been abandoned and destroyed. He immediately occupied the fort and deliberated his future moves to link up with Wolfe at Quebec. As usual, Amherst insisted that his army in the field keep active, so he put them to work building a new fort at Crown Point that would "give plenty, peace and quiet to his Majesty's subjects for ages to come."[5]

Amherst also ordered two roads to be blazed and opened, one between Crown Point and Fort Carillon (now called Fort Ticonderoga by the new British occupants), and another from Crown Point to Fort Number Four on the Connecticut River at Charlestown, New Hampshire, a popular rendezvous for New Hampshire and Massachusetts troops. Stark was selected to do the road across the Green Mountains in Vermont mainly because his ranger company was filled with frontiersmen experienced in forest operations and they were familiar with the area. Amherst assigned two hundred men to Stark for the arduous task. On September 9, 1759, General Amherst entered the following in his journal while at Crown Point: "Captain Stark with 200 Rangers was employed in cutting a road from Crown Point through the wilderness to No. 4."[6]

The roadway started at Chimney Point on the eastern shore across from Crown Point through Bridport, Shoreham, Sudbury and Pittsford. The terminus at the Connecticut River began two miles north of Fort Number Four and ran adjacent to the Black River as far as Ludlow. The roadway or forest track ended up little used except by supply trains between the two forts. Later, during the Revolution, it remained rough and in need of much repair.[7]

In the meantime, General Amherst was directing hundreds of his troops as they transformed the rubble at Crown Point into a new fortress next to the old. Stark's task of cutting a road kept him from being a part of the ranger raid against the Saint Francis Indian village at Odanak,

Canada, on the south side of the Saint Lawrence River. Amherst had sent two messengers, Captain Kennedy and Captain Hamilton, to the large village complex under a white flag of truce with a message of peace for the Abenaki.

The two couriers were seized and taken to Montreal as prisoners. The Abenaki were the scourge of the frontier, killing men, women, and children with equal savagery. They professed to be Christians but that did nothing to dampen their creative ways to butcher and torture helpless settlers. Earlier, Jesuit priests had encouraged the depredations in their zeal to eliminate any and all English influence on the continent. Their dominance on the border between organized settlements and the vast wilderness was supreme for decades.

Outrage over the rejection of his peace proposal and the detention of his couriers gave Amherst the justification he needed for his harsh order. On September 13, 1759, Major Robert Rogers and the rangers selected for the risky mission were instructed by Amherst as follows: "Remember, the barbarities that have been committed by the enemy's Indian scoundrels. Take your revenge, but don't forget that, those dastardly villains have promiscuously murdered women and children of all ages, it is my order that no women or children be killed or hurt."[8]

Rogers' version of the operation lists one hundred and forty men on the expedition with him. They left Crown Point in whaleboats and ten days later arrived at Missisquoi Bay, at the northern tip of Lake Champlain, where they hid their boats and proceeded inland toward the Saint Francis River. Two days into the march, Rogers was warned by his Indian trackers that a large French force had discovered the boats and were hard on their trail. Rogers was determined to reach the village before the alarm could be raised, so he drove his rangers at a fast pace, arriving at the outskirts of the village encampment twenty-two days later.

They attacked the village an hour before sundown, when sleeping inhabitants would not suspect their presence. By seven in the morning the raid was over. More than two hundred Indians were killed and twenty women and children were taken prisoner. Five English captives were rescued. The village was set afire and its canoes destroyed. The town had been ravaged as Amherst requested. The rangers had suffered one Indian killed and six men wounded.

The rangers left the village intent on reaching Fort Number Four at Charlestown. Several hundred Indians and French soldiers, filled with rage, were pursuing them intent on revenge. The retreating rangers followed the Saint Francis River southward to the eastern shore of Lake Memphremagog, where their supply of confiscated corn ran out and hunger became another burden to bear. At this point, the rangers broke up into small groups, the better to find food and escape their followers. Dense spruce swamps hampered their progress through the wilderness, requiring extraordinary physical effort. They marched for eight days with little or no sustenance.

The group with Robert Rogers proceeded to the Coos Intervale on the Connecticut River. Earlier he had sent a message to Amherst that food stocks be provided for his men at the junction of the Connecticut and Amonoosuc Rivers. The food was not there. The men were starving and unable physically to continue, so Rogers fashioned a raft and left alone for Number Four. He promised that he would send food as soon as possible. On the verge of collapse, Rogers arrived at the fort five days later. From there he sent canoes of food upriver to his dying men. The harsh wilderness and starvation took a terrible toll on the rangers. The pursuing enemies contributed to their ordeal; they took a few prisoners, whom they tortured and on whom they vented their fury.

For years after the episode, the bones of dead rangers were discovered along the retreating trail. The raid was immortalized by Kenneth Roberts's novel *Northwest Passage* and in the movie *Rogers' Rangers,* starring Spencer Tracy.

While Rogers was absent, John Stark remained Amherst's senior ranger officer. Stark had fought the Indians for ten years and was well aware of the degree of savagery the Abenaki were capable of. However, he did not blame the Indians as much as he did the French, who had successfully bribed, cajoled, and pushed the Abenaki into believing that they were carrying out a holy, even noble war against those who violated their lands. The French Jesuit priests taught the Abenaki that Jesus was killed by the English. Their "brainwashing" techniques included liberal amounts of alcohol.

While Robert Rogers was carrying out the Saint Francis raid and struggling for survival in the wilderness, an important achievement took place—Quebec had been captured. Wolfe and his opponent, Montcalm, were killed during the battle. With news of Quebec, Amherst canceled his plans to invade Montreal that winter and continued to build Crown Point. His journal entry of November 22, 1759, records: "It is time I should get the troops away but I must see the Forts first in a defensive state of cover for their garrisons, which two days more will accomplish. Captain Stark could prevail only on 157 Rangers to engage for the winter and next summer if wanted."[9]

The capitulation in Canada brought military operations in the colonies to a halt, other than maintenance of basic security at forts and other installations. Stark left Crown Point with a promise from Amherst that he would be able to re-enter the service with his rank of captain. There is no evidence that Stark remained in British service after 1759.[10]

The modest and competent Stark, like most of his colonial contemporaries, harbored a growing resentment against many of the British officers he associated with. The newly created lieutenants and captains who had purchased their commissions held many of the attitudes unique to their social status. Stark must have been offended by some of the dandified officers who purchased their commissions with money they had not earned. Many of them were uninterested in learning about their trade. Their antipathy to hard work and an unwillingness to get their hands dirty must have generated a great deal of animosity, or at the least amusement, in the hearts of the sturdy colonials who were entrusted, even ordered, to perform arduous and unpleasant tasks.

Stark probably saw a decline in good fellowship after the death of Lord Howe. Between battles, the average British officer remained distant and refused to fraternize with the colonials, who were poorly equipped, and frequently illiterate, and cut an unrespectable figure. Stark understood his provincials because he was one of them. Within the provincial ranks, there was a growing feeling that their sacrifice and contribution to a successful conclusion of the war was disregarded, if not ignored, by many of the British. That fact more than anything else generated disdain for posturing and pompous British officers who always acted as if and believed that they were superior to the homespun warriors in ragged clothes. Stark detested their elitist airs for as long as he lived.

5

A Time of Discontent (1759–1775)

The winter of 1759-1760 brought an end to the war after the capitulation of Canada, and the colonial troops began to return to their homes and farms. The French and Indian War had been a training exercise; many of the veterans would be tested again on the field of battle within fifteen years. The British now ruled most of North America.

John Stark was thirty-two years old when he left Crown Point and made his way through the wilderness to his wife, Elizabeth, who was living at her father's home in Starkstown, New Hampshire. Their first child, Caleb Stark, was born on December 3, 1759.

The couple stayed at the Page homestead for the balance of the winter and then moved into John's mother's home at Amoskeag Falls. Caring for the family and maintaining the home was a lot of work for John's mother, so "Molly," the nickname John affectionately gave to Elizabeth early in their marriage, tried to lessen the burden of his widowed mother. When they moved to Derryfield, the couple left little Caleb with his grandfather, Caleb Page, in Starkstown. Molly's father had become very attached to young Caleb, his namesake, since his wife had passed away. Caleb grew into manhood as a part of the Page family, yet he was also close to his mother and father and would serve with his father in the war looming on the horizon. Molly soon became pregnant again and gave birth to their second child, Archibald, on May 28, 1761.[1]

While John Stark was settling into family life, the British completed the capture of Niagara and Montreal, and peace talks were taking place with the native Indian tribes to the north and west of New England and New York. The 1763 Treaty of Paris, signed by the French and the British, formally marked the end of the war. The British influence in North America now included all of Canada and the western lands south as far as

Florida, which was eventually traded with the Spanish for Cuba. England also became master of the seas, and the white ensign was flown in every corner of the world.

The cessation of hostilities had strengthened the ties of the very independent colonies to the homeland. Bloodlines, rules of law, and language bound the progeny to the parent, but there were murmurs of discontent that could be discerned by those who took the time and effort to examine the relationship closely. Symptoms of revolt arose from taxation by Parliament because the colonists considered themselves to be free men. The passionately independent colonies were finding a new source of strength as they united into a larger and more influential body, which soon developed into the United States of America. Yet each colony jealously maintained its individual autonomy, even when success in war had shown that collective cooperation was more effective than individual enterprise. Francis Parkman offers the following advice to the colonies:

"The string of discordant communities along the Atlantic coast has grown to a mighty people, joined in a union which the earthquake of civil war served only to compact and consolidate. Those who in the weakness of their dissensions needed help from England against the savage on the borders have become a nation that may defy every foe but the most dangerous of all foes, herself, destined to a majestic future if she will shun the excess and perversion of the principles that made her great, prate less about the enemies of the past and strive more against the enemies of the present, resist the mob and demagogue as she resisted Parliament and King, rally her powers from the race for gold and the delirium of prosperity to make firm the foundations on which that prosperity rests, and turn some fair proportion of her vast mental forces to other objects than material progress and the game of party politics."[2]

An uprising known as Pontiac's Conspiracy, on the western frontier around the Great Lakes and the Ohio River Valley during the spring and summer of 1763, had been squelched. The death of Pontiac brought peace to the troubled region. Stark's old commander, Robert Rogers and his rangers, had played an active part in putting down the bloody affair. As a result of his efficient handling of the uprising, he was given the responsibility of administering the various posts in the region. This peaceful interlude gave the colonists, such as John Stark and his growing family, an opportunity to stamp their imprint on the land they were working.

The inhabitants of Derryfield held a town meeting on October 6, 1760 at which they offered John Stark one hundred acres of land if he would build a sawmill and saw "for halves" (Stark would keep for himself half of the lumber he processed). He agreed to the proposal and diligently went to work producing a dam built out of wood to collect water for a pond. The man-made structure became known as Stark's Pond and was located next to the falls on the river.

John's brother William had already built a home on the high ridge near the street (Elm) where Town Meetings were held for several years. William had been a Captain in the rangers and became a leading citizen of the community. His participation in civic affairs was in contrast to that of John, who preferred to work his land and leave politics to others.

The decade between 1765 and 1775 was one of foment and agitation. Opposition to the oppressive acts passed by Parliament was generated primarily by the leading citizens in the areas of heaviest population such as Portsmouth, Boston, and New York and coastal Virginia.

The manufacture of durable goods by the colonists had been strictly forbidden and the edict vigorously enforced by the Crown for many years. According to Parliament, the main reason for the existence of the colonies was to produce raw materials such as cotton, wool, sugar, grains, and lumber for England to manufacture into consumer products, which were then sold to the colonists. Controlling the restrictive monopoly was accomplished by questionable regulatory acts as passed by Parliament.

The Sugar Act was designed to help offset the debt created during the French and Indian War by doubling the duties on foreign goods sent to England, then to the colonies. Foreign imports of rum and wines were strictly forbidden. It should be noted that a brisk and profitable source of commerce for coastal communities was the building and operation of fast, shallow draft privateers that plied the heavily traveled trade routes. The success of the privateers was such that later, General Washington would order several of them into action soon after he became the Commander in Chief of the Continental army. They paid handsome dividends by supplying food, military stores, and liquor to supplement the meager quantities of supplies.

The Currency Act of 1764 prohibited the colonial usage of legal tender. In March 1765 the Stamp Act imposed the first direct tax on the American colonies. It was intended to defray the high cost of maintaining the British military in the New World. The act levied a tax on all printed material, including newspapers, deeds, bills, legal transactions, licenses, etc. and drew a strong reaction from the colonists. It was instrumental in the formation of a resistance organization dedicated to oppose "taxation without representation," as voiced by James Otis at a town meeting in Boston, in May 1764.

Sons of Liberty were established in almost every community to oppose the Stamp Act. It was an underground organization of loosely affiliated patriot groups. It began in New York City and spread rapidly to include all groups opposed to the British dominance of their lives. Some groups used violence to protest, but generally the Sons of Liberty opposed outbursts of violence, preferring to adhere to agitation and intimidation to gain support for their resistance to the Stamp Act.

Once the Stamp Act was re-appealed in 1766, the Sons of Liberty remained an organization loyal to the king. Regardless of how much opposition there was to Parliament's indifferent attitude, most colonists still considered themselves as loyal English subjects. Initially, the colonists asked only for the opportunity to be masters of their own lives, free of interference from the Crown. Their allegiance to England deteriorated commensurate with Parliament's attempts to enslave them. England lost her prize colonies because of her indifference to their demands to stand alone as a free peoples.[3]

Unlawful demonstrations were not uncommon in New Hampshire. On October 29, 1771, unknown Portsmouth residents stole a cargo of molasses from a merchant ship, anchored in their harbor, in defiance of a new import duty. Portsmouth was a favorite port for the privateers. As a matter of fact, John Langdon, one of its leading citizens, had built and commanded several privateers that operated openly up and down the Atlantic coast and the Caribbean Sea.

That same winter, the Queen's surveyor general tried to enforce the law calling for the seizure of all logs suitable for the king's navy. The largest and best white pine trees growing in New Hampshire's forests had been marked with the broad arrow designating them the king's property. They were used primarily for masts on ships. The trees were carried, one at a time, on large wagon wheels drawn by oxen from the forest to Portsmouth. The roadway from Weare to Portsmouth Harbor was known as Mast Road. Today, only a portion of the route is so designated.

The surveyor general's deputies were beaten up and run out of the town of Weare by irate woodsmen who reserved the right to cut their own trees for their own use. The surveyor general was a neighbor of John Stark.

During this period of unrest and uncertainty, John Stark purchased and sold land, lumber, and produce grown on the rich Merrimack River floodplain. He remained quiet and tended to his farming and sawmilling enterprises. Occasionally, he went to court to settle differences as a plaintiff or as a defendant. Most of the cases were insignificant and simply highlighted the fact that Stark brought a passionate energy to all aspects of his life. As far as we can determine, he was a fair, competitive businessman who worked hard to achieve success. Caleb Stark called his father "friendly to the industrious and enterprising, severe to the idle and unworthy."[4]

While John Stark quietly tended to his affairs, his old companion and commander Robert Rogers completed the Detroit campaign and returned to New Hampshire in February 1761 to claim his back pay and expenses for the war. Their old farm on Mountalona Road in Dunbarton near the Bow town line was still occupied by his mother. On June 30, he married Elizabeth Brown, the youngest daughter of Rev. Arthur Brown, rector of St. John's Church in Portsmouth.

Six days after his wedding, General Amherst ordered him to North Carolina to fight Indians. The following November he again returned to Portsmouth, where he ran up serious debts and was the subject of several lawsuits. He was drinking heavily. The Reverend Brown became more and more disappointed in his son-in-law and forced him to cede title to five hundred acres of land located between Bow and Rumsford (now Concord) on the Merrimack River to pay a debt of one thousand pounds. He and his brother James speculated on twenty thousand acres of land near Lake Champlain and five thousand acres near Readboro, Vermont.

Robert Rogers rarely saw his wife. He was not suited for domestic life and sailed for England, where he wrote his now famous Journals. King George III appointed him governor of Fort Michilimackinac, between Lake Huron and Lake Michigan. Rogers left England and brought his wife to this harsh outpost. This appointment earned Rogers the animosity of William Johnson, of New York, for his duplicity and questionable activities. On December 6, 1767, Rogers was arrested for treason, but the trial collapsed for lack of evidence. His dream of finding a northwest passage to the Orient was part of a calculation on his part to set up an independent republic with him in charge. It withered on the vine for lack of commitment.

By 1775, Rogers had become a shadowy figure showing little evidence of discipline or moral conviction. One day he was a Tory and the next he was a patriot. It is unlikely that John Stark had anything to do with his old companion during this period between the two wars. Rogers's own writings support such an assumption.

One day while John and Molly Stark were living with his mother, a man was crushed to death when his wagon swerved around the house and he was caught between the wagon and the corner of the house close to the roadway. After the accident, John placed a large rock at the corner of the house to prevent it from happening again. (The Daughters of the American Revolution had placed a plaque on the rock.)

With a rapidly expanding family, and a large farming operation, John and Molly decided the time had come for them to build a home on a site half a mile north of the falls near the center of their property. They began construction in 1768, when John was forty years old. The mansion was a typical Colonial-style structure with large chimneys located so that a fireplace could be built in each of the rooms, upstairs and down.

John was an admirer of fine wood and refrained from painting, varnishing, or papering over the wide white pine panels, wainscoting and corner cupboards that filled the house. Elaborate wooden mantels were built over the fireplaces in each room. Years after Molly and John had died, the house became part of a reform school, and was burned by the inmates in 1865.

When the Committee of Safety met at Exeter on July 1, 1774, to discuss current state affairs, John was present. He was not comfortable in the circle of politicians and influence peddlers, but his passion and commitment to the cause of liberty strengthened his normal reticence. Lawyers and politicians were not his favorite people, for he was more pragmatic and straightforward in his thinking. However, he recognized the value of civic groups such as the Committee of Safety and voluntarily joined their gatherings. The fiery spirit of resistance was now flowing through the colonies, and it is probably safe to assume that Stark was swept along by that same spirit.

Parliament imposed an import tax on tea, giving the East India Company a virtual monopoly on all tea shipped and sold to agents throughout the colonies. This sparked greater fervor for independence. A mass meeting was held in Philadelphia to oppose the tea tax and the monopoly of the East India Company, and to force the resignation of British tea agents. In

November 1773, a group in Boston was unable to secure the tea agents' resignation. Later, three ships loaded with tea sailed into Boston Harbor. The royal governor of Massachusetts ordered the harbor officials to hold the ships until the tax on the tea was paid. On December 16, 1773, colonial activists dressed as Mohawk Indians boarded the ships and dumped the tea into the water.

John Adams wrote in his diary: "This [Boston Tea Party] is the most significant movement of all. There is a dignity, a majesty, a sublimity, in this last effort of the patriots that I greatly admire. This destruction of the tea is so bold, so daring, so firm, intrepid and inflexible, and it must have important consequences, and so lasting that I cannot but consider it as an epocha in history."[5]

Patriots of Portsmouth, New Hampshire were the first to commit an act of war against the British. The town had always been an important shipping and mercantile seaport as well as a prolific shipbuilding center. Stately mansions still lining some of her city streets are testimony to the industrious nature of her inhabitants. On December 13, 1774, Paul Revere rode into town to warn the inhabitants that General Gates, military commander of Boston, was planning to send troops to Fort William and Mary to confiscate the gunpowder and military supplies in storage there. (That fort is known today as Fort Constitution, located beside the Coast Guard station on the Piscataqua River.) Revere told Portsmouth's most prominent citizen, John Langdon, that the British were making a major effort in all of the colonies to deny rebellious citizens access to powder and arms.

Langdon recognized that time was of the essence. He called out the Sons of Liberty in the greater Portsmouth area, which included Rye and New Castle, the town where Fort William and Mary was located. The next day four hundred men arrived at the gates of the fort, where they easily overpowered the guard detachment. They then removed ninety-eight barrels of gunpowder and stored them in secure places for future use. Gunpowder was extremely scarce in the colonies, because the Crown had prevented them from producing it. Throughout the conflict on the horizon, the presence or absence of sufficient gunpowder was a major factor in all of the military decisions, and it remained scarce until the French entered the war after the defeat of the British at Saratoga in 1777.

Governor John Wentworth had proved to be an able administrator and worked tirelessly for the province. He became a sad victim of the war looming in the shadows. He tried to uphold British authority with grace and understanding, and to maintain the confidence of the people of New Hampshire. It was an impossible task. When he became aware of the raid on Fort William and Mary, he was unable to locate a person to warn the small garrison at the fort.

On the evening of the raid on Fort William and Mary, another party of men was led by John Sullivan, a prominent lawyer from Durham, to carry off the balance of the stockpile of supplies, which included sixteen small cannons with ammunition and powder. This overt act by New Hampshire patriots was the first instance of armed rebellion against the British. Tensions in the area ran even higher than usual. Governor John Wentworth and his family felt threatened by the bold deed and requested assistance from Boston.

Help came a week later in the form of the armed sloop *Canceaux* and the forty-gun frigate *Scarborough.* The latter gunboat also carried one hundred British royal marines, which prevented any further raids on the fort, creating a state of tension among the populace.[6]

A British officer described the situation three weeks later in his diary: "Govr. Wentworth issued a proclamation couched in the most spirited terms, accusing those people who forcibly entered the Castle of William and Mary at Portsmouth and taken from thence barrels of powder, cannon balls and small arms, of treason and rebellion; and exhorting all His majesty's loyal subjects in that Province to exert themselves in the detection of those high offenders, and to use every means of bringing them to a punishment equal to the crime."[7]

The governor and his family moved into the fort for protection in the spring of 1775. By summer, they abandoned the fort and sailed for Boston. The royal governor's final official proclamation was to abolish the New Hampshire Assembly. With his hurried departure, royal authority ceased to exist in New Hampshire.

John Langdon and John Sullivan were prominent New Hampshire personalities who had significant influence on John Stark's adult life during the Revolutionary War. Sullivan was perhaps the most controversial and best-known public figure from the state. Born in 1740, he became

Durham's first lawyer and was a good friend of Governor Wentworth, who commissioned him a major in the New Hampshire militia. He had wealth, power, and respect and was an able leader. Early in 1775, Sullivan and Langdon were both elected to the First Continental Congress, which convened at Philadelphia. At that congress, Sullivan was appointed a brigadier general. His military career was long and controversial. He had a tendency to talk too much.

Sullivan's grandson described him: "About five feet six inches or seven, erect, well formed, hair and complexion dark, cheeks red, hospitable, fond of display. Prodigy of money, honest, generous. His mother was small, beautiful, vain and had a violent temper."[8]

Stark would serve under Sullivan's leadership faithfully and competently without any serious complications. Their temperaments and demeanors were opposite, yet they ended the war with mutual respect and friendliness, despite the fact that they traveled in different social circles. Sullivan enjoyed the company of individuals of influence and positions, the very private Stark shunned higher society. Sullivan freely expressed his opinion on every subject and never seemed to learn the value of holding his tongue, Stark kept his thoughts to himself. Perhaps the Fraternal Order of Freemasons, to which both men belonged, contributed to their amicable relationship.

John Langdon was born in Portsmouth on June 16, 1741, and attended Portsmouth Public Grammar School. After that, he was a self-educated man with little interest in scholastics. When he was twenty-two years old he was a sea captain of sloops and brigantines sailing the Atlantic trade routes. He fell victim to the restrictions and limitations of the Stamp Act of 1765 and the American Revenue Act of 1764, losing a cargo of sugar and rum and the ship carrying them as well. Langdon was a true patriot who placed his life and fortune on the line to advance the independent ideals in which he so strongly believed. He was an active member of the Committee of Correspondence, which helped to maintain communication among the colonies. Langdon was a member of the Naval Committee authorizing the construction of thirteen frigates and securing a contract to build one ship at his shipyard on Rising Castle Island (now Badger

Island) across the Piscataqua River from Portsmouth. The first ship was christened, *Raleigh*.

John Stark worked diligently at improving his business enterprises during the period of discontent, but he found time to be active in community affairs. He was chosen to be a representative of Derryfield at a Hillsborough County congress in Amherst, attending several anti-British meetings—one on January 16, 1775, again in March, and one on April 5.

The Amherst meeting was attended by thirty delegates from throughout the county, including Stark of Derryfield, Paul Dudley Sargent of Amherst, Captain Blood of Temple, Captain Lovewell of Dunstable (Nashua), Jonathon Martin of Wilton, Dr. Jonathon Gove of New Boston, and Daniel Campbell of Amherst. The committee of delegates adopted a resolution to form militia companies for training and discipline to counteract riots or licentious acts against individuals and/or property. There was a large segment of the population that still opposed any form of independence from the Crown. Stark, Sargent, and Campbell acted as a subcommittee of three to write a formal declaration of opposition to the oppressive acts of the Crown and an expression of solidarity and support to the people of Massachusetts, particularly Boston, who were being held hostage by the British troops. They intended to insert the document in the *Essex Gazette* and one of the Boston papers, and had planned to meet again on May 4, 1775, but the eruption of violence and the loss of life at Concord and Lexington (the shots heard around the world) changed everything. After April 19, 1775, a way of life in the American colonies was forever changed.[9]

6

The Line is Drawn (1775)

The coercive acts passed by Parliament closed the port of Boston to commerce until the province paid the East India Company for the destroyed tea dumped into Boston Harbor. Since the famous Boston Tea Party, the city had been the major recipient of repressive measures by the British. It soon became apparent that her plight would be repeated throughout the colonies. The line had been drawn by the Boston patriots. George Washington wrote: "[T]he cause of Boston . . . now is ever and will be considered as the cause of America."[1]

General Gage was ordered to enforce the acts and to suppress the open rebellion. He had three thousand British troops in Boston and more were on their way from England. His "get tough" orders were intended to crush the rebellion before it spread out of control. The recent passage of the Fishery Act, which forbade New Englanders to trade with England, Ireland, or the West Indies and banned fishermen from the productive fisheries of Newfoundland, set in motion an irreversible chain of events.

First, General Gage ordered the leaders of the Massachusetts Provincial Congress—Samuel Adams, John Hancock, and Dr. Joseph Warren—to be arrested and detained. The British general had received information from his intelligence network that Adams and Hancock were on their way to attend the Second Continental Congress in Philadelphia. His most successful spy circulated freely within the inner circles of the Committee of Safety, betraying his friends and companions because he needed money to maintain a secret love affair. The informant told Gage that Adams and Hancock were passing through Lexington and planned to stop overnight at an acquaintance's house on the Lexington square. Gage's informant also told him that there was a large depot of gunpowder and other military stores in Concord. Pleased at the prospect of seizing the arms cache and capturing Adams and Hancock all in one swift operation, Gage ordered it to proceed with all haste and in utmost secrecy.

Gage's secret plan soon became known to the patriots' ubiquitous informer in Boston, Paul Revere, who had a network of informants throughout the colony and was passionately loyal to the movement toward independence. On the night of April 18, he had evidence that the British troops were on the march and began his famous ride through the countryside to Lexington, warning the inhabitants along the way that "the regulars are coming." Revere rowed across the Charles River to Cambridge and set out from there on horseback while his companion, William Dawes, left at the same time across the Charlestown Neck toward Lexington, sounding the alarm as he went. Revere was captured between Lexington and Concord. He was able to escape, but without his horse. He had successfully warned Adams and Hancock of the advancing threat and accompanied them to safety in the waning hours of the night.

The alarm had been sounded. Militia members who had trained to be ready on a moment's notice, hence the name Minute Men, assembled for the defense of their homes and families. Hundreds of determined farmers, shopkeepers, and tradesmen of all descriptions came together to protest the acts of the British regulars.

The first clash of arms came that day at the Lexington triangle. A small group of militia under the command of Captain Parker confronted the British advance group commanded by Major Pitcairn. The British formed a battle line. Captain Parker ordered his men to stand their ground and not to fire unless fired on: "If they want a war, let it begin here!"[2]

Major Pitcairn had nothing but contempt for the rebels assembled before him and ordered the militia to lay down their arms and disperse. Parker, in turn, asked his men to disperse, as he was hopelessly outnumbered. Suddenly, shots rang out and both sides started shooting at each other. Ten militia were wounded and eight were killed, including Captain Parker, who had stood his ground until he was repeatedly bayoneted. Only one British soldier had been wounded. The Battle of Lexington ended as the militia scattered for cover, and the British continued to Concord, where they searched for the cache of powder. They came up empty-handed.

While Pitcairn and his men were in Concord, militia companies from surrounding towns began to congregate along the British route of retreat until they numbered over four hundred men. Stationed on a ridge overlooking the North Bridge, the men under Colonel Barrett watched the British regulars burning old gun carriages. Barrett led his men down the hill, concerned that the smoke they saw might be the British trying to burn the town. The regulars were waiting for them at the bridge. The British fired first, hitting several of the militiamen. A scream pierced the air from the militia officer: "[F]ire, for God's sake, fire!"[3]

The militia withdrew toward the ridge, carrying their dead and wounded, while the British quickly returned via the same road toward Boston. They would soon experience the wrath of hundreds of angry patriots who followed their progress from both sides of the roadway. Every stone wall and every tree seemed to shelter a sniper who took aim at the helpless redcoats in their rush to the safety of Boston.

The heaviest and most costly fighting occurred at Menotomy (now Arlington) as the British retreating columns wove their way south. At the beginning of the day, militia units were independent groups of armed men, but as the day progressed, with more and more men assembling from surrounding communities, they became a more structured and disciplined force under a Roxbury farmer, General William Heath, who formed circles of skirmishers attacking the retreating columns at every vantage point. They were taking a heavy toll against the redcoats who dropped by the wayside. British discipline vanished as they received withering fire from both sides of the road all the way to Charlestown. A relief column from Boston gave the tired and frightened redcoats some protection, but sporadic sniper fire continued to kill and harass the retreating redcoats all the way to Charlestown.

When the bloody retreat ended, the British casualties were sixty-five killed and two hundred and seven wounded. The patriots suffered fifty killed and forty-four wounded.[4]

The siege of Boston began just as soon as the British column reached the city. Large numbers of militia placed a ring of armed men around the city, effectively eliminating any projection of force by the British troops beyond the confines of gunships anchored in Boston Harbor.

When word of the exchange of fire at Lexington came to New Hampshire, several of the first responders for the call to help sought out John Stark. His previous service in the French and Indian War positioned him at or near the top of the list for a commission. He was at his sawmill in Derryfield when he first got the news. Potter, in his *History of Manchester*, wrote:

"Stark was at work in his sawmill at the head of Amoskeag Falls when he heard the news and without a moments delay he shut down his mill, repaired to his house, took his gun and ammunition, mounted his horse in his shirt sleeves as he came from the mill and rode on to meet the enemy. As he journeyed on he left word for volunteers to meet at Medford and without delay made the best of his way to Lexington. On his entire route his force continually increased so that the following morning when he arrived at Lexington he had at his command a large force of backwoodsmen."[5]

Stark traveled from Lexington to Cambridge, where he met with the Massachusetts Committee of Safety on April 21. He was granted a colonel's commission in the Massachusetts militia with authority to enlist recruits. Captain James Reed from, Cheshire County, and Captain Dudley Sargent, from Hillsborough County, were also commissioned as colonels. The latter two men had enlisted four companies each while Stark had enlisted fourteen. Stark would act under Massachusetts authority until New Hampshire acted to confirm the commissions. Caleb Stark wrote:

"The late venerable Jonathon Eastman, senior, informed the writer that the election [of Stark] took place at the hall of a tavern, in Medford, afterward called the New-Hampshire Hall; that it was a hand vote, and he held up his hand for his friend John Stark."[6]

New Hampshire regulations called for nine companies for a regiment, with seventy men per company. Stark's regiment was the largest in the siege around Boston and considered by many to have been handled with extraordinary efficiency. The Massachusetts Bay Authority found barracks for the New Hampshire companies under Stark and Sargent. Stark and a small staff were quartered until early July in an impressive mansion in Medford called the Isaac Royall's Mansion. He was later asked to give up his quarters to General Charles Lee.

As soon as the regiment settled into an acceptable routine of discipline, Stark left for home to arrange personal affairs and to settle any discrepancies his New Hampshire benefactors were concerned with. It was planting season and labor was hard to find. The logs Stark had stockpiled at his sawmill skidway would rot as the war progressed, there was no experienced help to do the sawing. Young Caleb was a part of his regiment at Medford, and the next son, Archibald, twelve years old, worked long hours under his mother's direction. Eleanor was eight, Sarah was six, Elizabeth was four and Marty was two. The family must have worked hard just to plant, cultivate, and harvest the food necessary for subsistence living with the absence of their father.

On May 8, 1775, John Stark wrote a letter to his superiors in Exeter:

"Gentlmen—About the 29th of April last a Committee sent from Provincial Congress of the Province of New Hampshire to the Provincial Congress of the Province of Massachusetts Bay, having discretionary instructions from said Congress advised to raise a Regiment from the Province of New Hampshire as soon as possible under the Constitution or Establishment of Massachusetts bay; but to be deemed as part of the quota of men of the Province of New Hampshire and the New Hampshire Congress would establish measures. In consequence of which a number of officers from the Province of New Hampshire conven'd and made choice of their field officers for said Regm't., who have raised the same, 584 of whom are now at Medford, exclusive of drummers and fifers, and the remainder are hourly expected; and as a great number of those already here (who expected when they enlisted to draw arms from the Provincial stocks are destitute of the same and cannot be furnished as no arms are to be procured here at the present) must inevitably return from thence they came unless they are supply'd from some quarter speedily; I humbly pray that you would maturely consider our defenceless condition and adopt some measure or measures whereby they may be equipped. In confidence of your immediate compliance with the above request, I am in the Country's common cause, your most obedient and devoted humble servant.

John Stark

N.B. The gentleman who presents this to the convention, can give you particular information as to our present situation."[7]

The New Hampshire delegates received the letter on Friday the nineteenth. The Massachusetts Bay Colony had proposed a union so that each colony would contribute money and men commensurate with its population. At the above meeting they proposed another two thousand men to serve until December. The vote on Stark's request was prompt:

"That the Selectmen of the respective Towns where the persons Inlisted under Col. Stark, who are destitute of fire arms belong, be desired to procure the same and forward them to the Persons so destitute, and if such towns can not furnish them, Coll. Stark or any of the officer's under him are desired to purchase the same and upon a just acc't thereof being rendered to this Convention it shall be allowed and paid—and Coll. Stark is desired as soon as circumstances will permit to transmit to this Convention what shall be done in consequence of this vote, and every soldier supplied as afres'd is required to give a Receipt for such fire-arms that he will at his dismission from service return the same or have the value thereof deducted out of wages."[8]

The volunteers in Stark's regiment may not have been drilled in parade ground formality, but with his experience in the French and Indian War, he knew that without discipline, a group of armed men was nothing but a mob. He made sure that at a minimum, the manual of arms and the basic movements of an infantryman within a military formation were taught, to instill pride and cohesion of the unit and adherence to orders. An independent-minded Yankee farmer did not yield to authority without some form of resistance. Stark probably experienced the same thing with the fiercely individualistic rangers, and was able to apply just the right amount of firmness. He was an officer who preferred to lead from the front instead of the rear and from example rather than words. His reputation as a veteran of many campaigns gave stature to his authority, which was frequently lacking from newly assigned officers.

Late in May, the Massachusetts Bay Committee of Safety was determined to remove the livestock on Noodle Island and Hog Island, situated in Boston Harbor. General Artemus Ward, the commander of all armed forces in Massachusetts, regardless of origin, ordered Colonel Stark to remove the livestock. He used a combined force from New Hampshire and Massachusetts numbering about three hundred men. At ebb tide, the water between Noodle Island and the mainland was shallow enough for men and cattle to wade across the two landmasses.

Late in the day while Stark and some of his men were herding four hundred sheep through the knee-deep water, they were attacked by British regulars. Both sides fired but neither inflicted much damage. As soon as Stark's men returned fire, the British left. It was late in the day and most of Stark's men were still on Hog Island, so they waited until dark before herding the rest of the sheep across the shallow water to the mainland of

Chelsea, where he sent for reinforcements. General Ward dispatched a Colonel Nixon with a company to the scene to assist Stark's men with the livestock.

While the siege around Boston was being tightened, the Second Continental Congress authorized defensive force against the British. The skirmish at Lexington fell into that category. As soon as the siege of Boston was intact, several officers realized that they lacked firepower to attack the fortifications the British had erected in Boston. Benedict Arnold knew that cannons were available at Fort Ticonderoga. The Massachusetts Committee of Safety authorized him to raise a small force in western Massachusetts and to capture the fort. Arnold easily raised and organized an expeditionary task force capable of doing the job, and headed for Lake Champlain.

The lightly defended British stronghold was also the destination of another independent force, under the command of the charismatic Ethan Allen with a group of his Green Mountain Boys of Vermont. They had the same objective as Arnold's group. The two forces met at Lake Champlain where strong language was exchanged between the two strong-willed leaders arguing over who was in charge. After a lengthy and loud discussion, they agreed on a joint command. On May 9 they crossed the lake with eighty-three men. They took the fort by surprise, capturing it without a shot being fired. Colonel Benedict Arnold's May 11, 177 report to the Massachusetts Committee of Safety on the capture of Fort Ticonderoga, reads:

"Gentlemen:—I wrote you yesterday that arriving in the vicinity of this place, I found one hundred and fifty men collected at the insistence of some gentleman from Connecticut (designed on the same errand on which I came), headed by Colonel Ethan Allen, and that I joined them, not thinking proper to wait the arrival of the troops I had engaged on the road, but to attempt the fort by surprise; that we have taken the fort at four o'clock yesterday morning without opposition and made prisoners one Captain, one lieutenant and forty-odd privates and subalterns, and that we found the fort in a most ruinous condition and not worth repairing; that a party of fifty men were gone to Crown Point, and that I intended to follow with as many men to seize the sloop. Etc., and that I intend to keep possession here until I had farther advice from you.

"On or before our taking possession here I had agreed with Colonel Allen to issue farther orders jointly . . . Colonel Allen, finding that he had the ascendancy over his people, positively insisted I should have no command, as I have forbid the soldiers plundering and destroying private property. The power is now taken out of my hands...

"There is here at present near one hundred men, who are in the greatest confusion and anarchy . . . There is not the least regularity among the troops, but everything is governed by whim and caprice-the soldiers threatening to leave the garrison on the least affront . . .

"I have therefore thought proper to send an express advising you of the state of affairs, not doubting you will take the matter into your serious consideration and order a number of troops to join those I have coming on here . . . Colonel Allen is a proper man to head his own wild people, but entirely unacquainted with military service . . . I think it my duty to remain here against all opposition until I have farther orders."[9]

After securing Ticonderoga, Arnold boldly seized Crown Point and commandeered the only British warship on Lake Champlain, an armed sloop. He sailed it north to Saint Johns, just north of the border, where he opened fire on the outpost and captured it. It was a stroke of luck. Now, the Americans lightly controlled the most strategic corridor into Canada, the famous Lake Champlain-Hudson River corridor the French so vigorously defended in the last war.

The ragtag army of citizen-soldiers holding General Gage hostage in Boston were despised, but dismissed as little short of a nuisance. On June 12, 1775, Gage wrote to Lord North in London describing their condition:

"The situation these wretches have taken in forming the blockade of this town is judicious and strong, being well intrenched where the situation requires it and with cannon. Their numbers are great, exclusive of every inhabitant armed coming in to join that part of their army that may be attacked; upon the alarm being given, they come far and near, and the longer the action lasts, the greater their numbers grow. Their mode of engaging is (like all other inhabitants of a strong country) by getting behind fences and every sort of covering, firing from thence; then retire and load under cover and return to charge; or take another situation from which they fire. The country for 30 miles is amazingly well situated for manner of fighting, being covered with woods and stone walls inclosures, exceedingly uneven and much cutt with ravines . . .

"In our present state all warlike preparations are wanting. No survey of the adjacent country, no proper boats for landing troops, nor a sufficient number of horses for the artillery nor for the regimental baggage. No forage, either hay or corn of any consequence-no wagons or harnesses for horses, except some prepared by Colonel Cleveland for the artillery.

"No fascines or pickets. The military chest at the lowest ebb, about three or four thousand only remaining, which goes fast for the subsistence of the troops.

"The rebellious colonys will supply nothing. Some of these articles will, I hope, be furnished from Quebec, but unless Government enters heartily into the wants here by immediately sending all the supplys wanting, particularly for the winter, the army will do them little service. Flat bottom boats are much wanted. Our intelligence is so scanty that what we get from the inland country for the most part is sent to the general by Rebels. Very few or no spies; we are therefore intirely ignorant of what they are about in the neighborhood."[10]

Colonel John Stark wrote to the New Hampshire Committee of Safety late in May listing the men he had signed up in the service of the province of New Hampshire with the expectation of being paid. He took the side of his men in stressing the need for pay and listed armorers tools, a chest of medicine, and the services of a sutler to provide personal goods to the troops.

At a meeting of the New Hampshire Provincial Congress on the last day in May, it was voted to divide the field forces of New Hampshire into three regiments as recommended by the Committee of Safety. At the same meeting the delegates requested that Stark appear before them in order to be commissioned. Stark was to be commissioned a colonel, Wyman a lieutenant colonel and McClary a major of the First New Hampshire Regiment. The famous First enjoyed the distinction of having the longest service in the war of any active regiment in the country.

Stark traveled to New Hampshire as requested and presented himself in Exeter before the Speaker, and was informed that General Folsom was to be the commander of the First New Hampshire Regiment with Stark in command of the Second. Stark bluntly informed the assembly that he had already been assured command of the First New Hampshire Regiment:

"It is a great honor to address such an august body and powerful body that can make a baby born yesterday older than a baby born last month." If the Committee was not able to recognize that fact, he would bring about another Committee of Safety that would do it for them. With that statement, he left the room."[11]

Stark's disdain for the ruling elite, and the fact that he had just accepted a Massachusetts commission, generated powerful enemies among the legislators. His stubbornness and blunt language did little to curry favor with the power brokers of the day. Nathaniel Folsom, a man with no military experience, was promoted to brigadier general over Stark. He had just reason to be upset, for his experience as a combat leader had been supplanted by political expediency.

Ultimately he was given the command of the First New Hampshire Regiment, with twelve companies. Colonel James Reed was commander of the Second New Hampshire Regiment, with ten companies and Colonel Enoch Poor was given command of the Third New Hampshire Regiment, also with ten companies. Poor's regiment stayed in New Hampshire during the Battle of Bunker Hill.

Stark always referred to the "Exeter crowd" with derision and only lightly veiled contempt, and he must have been glad to return to his troops. Immediately after his return to Medford, Stark gave Captain Henry Dearborn, one of his company commanders and a soldier who served with great honor during the Revolution, a written order to perform guard duty. It is one of the earliest recorded orders:

"Medford, June 8th, 1775. Capt. Henry Dearborn; You are required to go with one sergeant and twenty men to relieve Guards at Winter hill and Temple tomorrow morning at nine o'clock, there to take their place and orders but to first parade before the New Hampshire Chamber." John Stark."[12]

7

Bunker Hill (June 17, 1775)

The British Royal Navy's attempt to isolate and blockade the city of Boston and its rebellious citizens actually unified the city and helped strengthen the resolve of many who had lingering doubts about the soundness of going to war. All of New England recognized that Bostonians were in need of support, and they sent food and other supplies overland to relieve their neighbors' suffering. The blockade actually hurt the British more than it did the people of Massachusetts. When the ring of patriots around Boston became complete, they blocked off all food and fuel from entering the city. The British were existing on salted meat and slim rations.

London had ordered General Thomas Gage to issue a proclamation offering everyone, except John Hancock and Samuel Adams, forgiveness if they would simply lay down their arms. Otherwise they were threatened with death as traitors. The moment of truth had arrived. Those who were faint of heart must have wondered if they were on the right side of the issues, but the vast majority of the men laying siege to Boston simply snarled or laughed at the threat.

Once blood had been shed, the chances for a fair settlement of differences seemed nonexistent. Still, very few Americans wanted a complete break from the motherland. Dr. Joseph Warren, a beloved Boston physician, head of the Massachusetts Committee of Safety and president of the Provisional Congress, was a favorite spokesman for moderation. Dr. Warren made a passionate plea to the British in the form of a speech entitled *On the Dangers of Standing Armies in Time of Peace.* It was a true characterization of prevailing sentiments, and was given before a mixed congregation of Tories and Whigs:

"An independence of Great Britain is not our aim. No: our wish is, that Britain and the colonies may, like the oak and ivy, grow and increase in strength together, but whilst the infatuated plan of making one part of the empire slaves to the other is persisted in, the interest and safety of Britain as well as the colonies require that the wise measures recommended by the Continental Congress be steadily pursued, whereby the unnatural contest between a parent and child beloved may probably be brought to such an issue as that the peace and happiness of both may be established upon a lasting basis. But if these pacific measures are ineffectual, and it appears that the only way to safety is through fields of blood, I know you will not turn your faces from our foes, but will undauntedly press forward until tyranny is trodden under foot, and you have fixed your adored goddess, Liberty, fast by a Brunswick's side, on the American throne."[1]

Gage was confident that he could squelch the rebellion with the additional troops that had already arrived in Boston, and refused to see or have any contact with Dr. Warren. Three of England's best generals accompanied the soldiers: William Howe, Henry Clinton, and John Burgoyne.

Howe was an able and courageous professional soldier and the younger brother of Lord George Howe, admired and respected by many including John Stark, when he was killed at the battle for Ticonderoga in 1758. Clinton, former governor of New York, was a colorless professional soldier and somewhat of a martinet. Burgoyne was a gentleman, a playwright and a former member of Parliament. They came with the intention of cleaning up an untidy mess that should never have gotten out of control. The generals had low military expectations from the rebels opposing them. The universal feeling was that one real show of British military force was all that was necessary to quell the rebellion. They would soon regret their miscalculation.

Boston is located on a peninsula pointing northward toward Charlestown, which is on the southern shore of another peninsula connected to the mainland by a narrow isthmus called Charlestown Neck. A band of water in Boston Harbor separates the two communities. Charlestown was nestled on the flatlands, with Bunker Hill the highest elevation of the peninsula. Breed's Hill, located at the center of the peninsula, was closest to the town of Charlestown. Both the British and the colonials knew that the commanding heights north of Charlestown and the Dorchester Heights south of Boston were strategically important positions. With cannons on either prominence, they could pound the city and much of the harbor into submission.

General Artemas Ward was commander of all colonial forces in Massachusetts. He had served as a colonel in the French and Indian War and was an able tactician. Ward was suffering from a debilitating disease of the kidneys called "the stones," and was unable to exercise firm control of the situation around Boston. He had decided to act before the augmented British forces in Boston made the first move to occupy the valuable high ground at Bunker Hill, while at the same time maintaining a ready reserve to protect the impressive heights at Dorchester in case the British made an unexpected move in that direction.

Caleb Stark was sixteen years old when his father went off to Boston to participate in the siege around that city. He had watched his father leave the farm and his family eager to show his devotion to the righteousness of the patriots' cause. Caleb first sought approval from his grandfather, Caleb Page, and was told that he was too young to experience the carnage of warfare. The adolescent gave in to his grandfather's wishes and for weeks bided his time and let the subject drop. On June 3, he collected food, clothing, and a musket with lead and powder, and quietly left the house where he lived with his grandfather in Starkstown. Young Caleb was on his way to the New Hampshire encampment at Medford.

En route on the Boston Post Road to the rebels' lines, Caleb met a stranger on horseback dressed in the fatigue uniform of a British officer. He was a tall, fine-looking man who inquired Caleb's destination. Caleb replied that he was going to be with his father at the camp in Medford.

"You are, then, the son of my old comrade. Your father and I were fellow-soldiers for more than five years. I am traveling in the same direction, and we will keep company."[2]

The impressive-looking stranger turned out to be the famous commander of Rogers' Rangers, Robert Rogers, who insisted on paying for meals and tolls along the way. That evening Rogers left Caleb, requesting that he carry a message soliciting an interview with Colonel Stark at the Medford Tavern.

When Caleb showed up at his father's camp, Colonel Stark was not pleased to see his son and inquired what he had come for at such a difficult time, admonishing him that he should have stayed at home. Caleb bravely

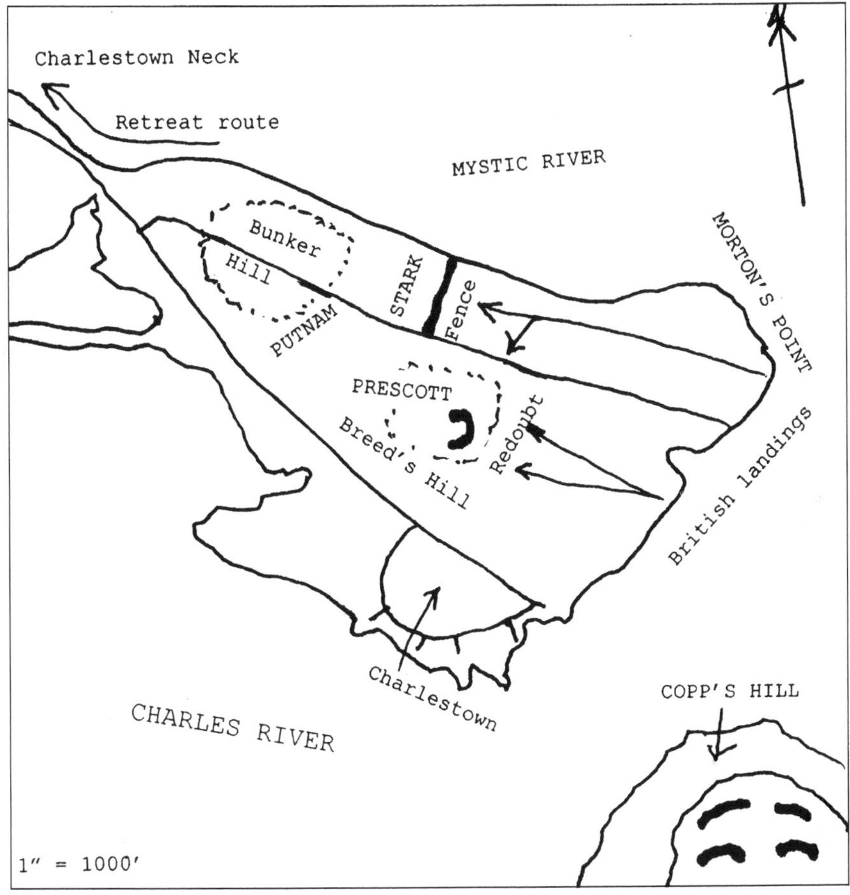

Battle of Bunker Hill, June 17, 1775

defended his actions, replying that he had come to fight and that, as his father knew, he could handle a musket very well for his age. Though his father must have seen his presence as one more worry, he had to have been proud of his firstborn son's courage and resolve.

"Very well..." his father had replied, turning to Captain Reid, [a company commander] continued: "Take him to your quarters; tomorrow may be a busy day. After that we will see what can be done with him."[3]

Busy day indeed! It was on the eve of the battle at Bunker Hill. Caleb served in Captain Reid's company during the battle.

The colonial militias facing the British were from Connecticut, Rhode Island, New Hampshire, and the fabled Massachusetts Minutemen, troops prepared on a minutes notice to rush to the defense of their cause. The militias were concentrated in a semicircle around Boston from Roxbury to Medford. General Ward's second in command, General Thomas, was in command at Roxbury, covering the Dorchester Neck and Boston Neck with about eight thousand men. Ward controlled the center with six thousand men, and the area closest to Boston was commanded by Brigadier General Putnam, with one thousand Connecticut troops. Colonel Stark was positioned on the Mystic River at Medford to guard against any amphibious assault up the river. The other New Hampshire regiment under Colonel James Reed, was stationed at Charlestown Neck. Stark's regiment of about eight hundred men was the largest in the area.

There were approximately ten thousand colonial troops around Boston. The British had slightly fewer men, but experts claim that between twenty-five hundred and four thousand were actually engaged in the battle.

Espionage was rampant on both sides, and relatively accurate. Gage had the services of Dr. Benjamin Church, who informed him of every move the colonials made, including the patriots' best spy, Paul Revere. Revere had an efficient network that produced a constant flow of information about the British. The Massachusetts Committee of Safety called for the occupation of Bunker Hill when it became known, from Revere's intelligence, that the British were planning to assault the peninsula. In a letter from Cambridge, dated June 15, 1775, Chairman Benjamin White wrote:

"*Whereas,* it appears of importance to the safety of this colony that possession of the hill called Bunker's hill, in Charlestown, be securely kept and defended; and also, some one hill or hills on Dorchester neck be likewise secured; therefore, *resolved,* unanimously, that it be recommended to the council of war that the above mentioned Bunker's hill be maintained by sufficient forces being posted there; and as the particular situation of Dorchester neck is unknown to this committee, they advise that the council of war take and pursue such steps, respecting the same, as to them shall appear to be for the security of this colony."[4]

In compliance with the above order, Colonel William Prescott led about fifteen hundred men across Charlestown Neck to Breed's Hill with his engineering officer, Captain Richard Gridley. Gridley, a veteran of Wolfe's defeat of the French on the Plains of Abraham in Quebec, had proved his skills when he lifted two cannons to the top of the Plains. He suggested that it would be easier to position their defenses at Breed's Hill instead of at Bunker Hill. Artillery, skillfully used, could even duel with the more powerful warships in Boston Harbor, which controlled all the waterways around the city. Gridley had two fieldpieces available for Breed's Hill, and the men feverishly began to dig the trenches for defense and placement of the cannons.

General Israel Putnam stubbornly began to build defenses around Bunker Hill at the same time. It was farther away, but it had the advantage of being less vulnerable to bombardment from the ships in the harbor. Gridley and Prescott believed it to be too far away for the light cannons they now had. Building the two defenses weakened the colonial force and doubled its workload.

General Artemas Ward quickly recognized the deficiency in manpower and ordered John Stark and his New Hampshire Regiment of one thousand men forward to augment the defenses of Breed's Hill. Estimates vary on the exact number of troops, but it is safe to assume that Stark, with remnants of Reed's regiment, commanded at least one thousand men in the battle. Without a doubt, the First New Hampshire Regiment possessed the best troops in the colonial army at that time. Desertions from the militias were commonplace throughout the war. It is a fact that Stark never experienced a desertion from his regiment while he was in command, a tribute to his leadership skills.

The First New Hampshire Regiment was renowned for its marksmanship. It was a skill that Stark demanded. Most of the New Hampshire volunteers were frontiersmen or pioneers living beyond city or town centers, so good marksmanship was a part of their every day lives. They had little means to pay for powder and bullets, which further encouraged shooting skills. Stark gave his regiment orders that were clear and precise. His men, in turn, executed them rapidly and as instructed. The First New Hampshire Regiment was proud of its reputation as the most professional of all the militia units, and many claim that its finest commander was John Stark.

Ward's order to call upon Stark, who was four miles away in Medford, was what Thomas J. Fleming, the noted historian, called, "[T]he best order Artemas Ward would give all day."[5]

Stark immediately detached two hundred men to aid Prescott in the preparation of the platforms for the two four-pounder cannons with a Colonel Wyman as their commander. These men fought at the redoubt under Massachusetts control.[6]

Stark's men were described by an observer as follows:

"To a man they wore small-clothes, coming down and fastening just below the knee, and long stockings with cowhide shoes ornamented by large buckles . . . The coats and waistcoats were loose and of huge dimensions, with colors as various as the barks of oak, sumach and other trees of our hills and swamps could make them, and their shirts were all made of flax and, like every other part of the dress, were homespun. On their heads was worn a large round-top and wide-brimmed hat. Their arms were as various as their costume. Here an old soldier carried an old Queen's Arm, with which he had done service at the conquest of Canada twenty years previous while by his side walked a stripling boy with a Spanish fusee . . . which his grandfather may have taken at the Havana, while not a few had old French pieces that dated back to the reduction of Louisbourg. Instead of the cartridge box, a large powder horn was slung under the arm, occasionally a bayonet might be seen bristling in the ranks. Some of the swords of the officers had been made by Province blacksmiths, perhaps from some farming utensil; they looked serviceable, but heavy and uncouth."[7]

Finally, all of Stark's regiment left Medford for Breed's Hill following two dimly lit lanterns. They carried their weapons, a day's food ration, and some water. Lack of water the next day caused much suffering among the ranks in the hot humid weather. A very young Captain Henry Dearborn, one of Stark's company commanders, was about to embark on his first campaign. He had raised and trained a company of men from his native Nottingham and headed for Cambridge after hearing the news of Lexington-Concord. Dearborn was walking beside Stark as they started across the small isthmus at Charlestown Neck. Captain Dearborn described the situation:

"At Charlestown Neck we found two regiments halted in consequence of a heavy enfilading fire thrown across it of round, bar and chain shot from Lively Frigate and floating batteries anchored in Charles river and a floating battery laying in the River Mystic. Major McClary went forward and observed to the commanders if they did not intend to move on he wished them to open and let our regiment pass; the latter immediately done. My company being in front I marched by the side of Col.

Stark, who, moving with a very deliberate pace I suggested the propriety of quickening the march of the regiment that it might sooner be relieved of the galling cross-fire of the enemy. With a look, peculiar to himself, he fixed his eyes on me and observed, with great composure, "Dearborn, one fresh man in action is worth ten fatigued ones' and continued to advance in the same cool collected manner."[8]

After the battle, Stark proudly explained to Exeter authorities that when he had received the express rider with his orders to move the whole regiment, his was the first regiment to report on the line although he received his orders an hour later than the other troops and had two more miles to travel. General Dearborn described Stark's regiment to a reporter:

"Col. Stark's was quartered in Medford distant about four miles from the point of anticipated attack. It then consisted of thirteen companies and was probably the largest regiment in the army. About ten o'clock in the morning he received orders to march. The regiment being destitute of ammunition it was formed in front of a house occupied as an arsenal where each man received a gill cup of powder, fifteen balls and two flints. The several captains were then ordered to march their companies to their respective quarters and make up their powder and ball into cartridges with the greatest possible dispatch. As there were scarcely two muskets in a company of equal caliber it was necessary to reduce the size of the balls for many of them and as but a small proportion of the men had cartridge boxes the remainder made use of powder horns and ball pouches."[9]

Stark met with Reed's regiment under Lieutenant Colonel Gilman at the Charlestown Neck. Reed was absent because he was ill, so Stark took over the regiment, forming one line with himself in the lead. He always led from the front, it would have been completely out of character for him to issue orders from a more secure location at the rear. One of his finest gifts was his ability to quickly survey a situation and come up with a workable plan. That kind of leadership can only be administered from where the action is. He met General Israel Putnam, from Connecticut, after crossing the Neck. They had campaigned around Lake George and Lake Champlain during the French and Indian War and knew each other well. The choice of where to go was left up to Stark, with the certainty that he would perform well under fire.

Major McClary, Stark's second in command, observed the field with Stark and recognized the weakness of Prescott's position. Stark concluded: "I took my post on the left wing [at the fence] and could have kept it if it was not for the right wing which gave way and the left of the Regulars almost surrounded me before I retreated."[10]

General Howe landed with his light-infantry Royal Welsh Fusiliers on a sandy point between Morton's Point and the redoubt, expecting to be opposed the minute he landed. No shots came however. He sent one hundred and fifty picked troops along the shore of the Mystic River to act as skirmishers in a shallow hollow about two hundred yards from Morton's Hill. Then he ordered his light-infantry to the brow of the hill, thus securing the beachhead. It was always an impressive sight to see the colorful pageantry of red-coated soldiers marching in formation with bayonets leveled at their enemy, and it must have given some pause to the inexperienced militia members who were viewing the performance for the first time. General Howe planned to attack in columns of four with the Welsh Fusiliers in the vanguard.

Prescott never intended to oppose the amphibious landings, but he did order Captain Knowlton and his Connecticut troops to do just that. When the young and energetic Knowlton left the redoubt, he was aghast at what he and his small detachment of one hundred and fifty men were asked to do. His problem was solved when General Putnam rode up and told him to man the fence between the Mystic and the redoubt. The fence line was slightly to the rear of the redoubt and closer to Bunker Hill. Putnam screamed that they were in danger of being outflanked. The fence was more than two hundred yards long, too long for the small company. Putnam promised that he would get reinforcements, and spurred his mount away.

Stark also saw the weak link in Prescott's defenses. The rail fence at the beach left a hole through which Howe could easily outflank the redoubt. He later said, "It was a way so clear that the enemy could not miss it."[11]

Captain Knowlton and Stark got along well and coordinated their forces without difficulty. Stark then ordered two hundred of his best marksmen to break down parts of the wood rail and build a breastworks to the water's edge. After, he had them lie down behind the crude barrier in three ranks, and then took personal command of the position.

Stark gave them a short address of encouragement and ended with three cheers for the success of their endeavor. With that the men began reinforcing the line with grass, mud, and stones—anything to give it a more permanent look to deceive the British. The work did not add much to the safety of the men manning the barricade, but it gave the illusion of strength. C.E. Potter wrote in his 1856 *History of Manchester*:

"After arriving upon the ground Stark's men threw up a sort of breast work of stone across the beach to the water, and continued the rail fence down the hill to the stone wall or breast work. This wall served a most excellent purpose as the sharpshooters from behind it could take the most deadly aim at the advancing enemy. Here was posted Capt. John Moore and his company from Amoskeag [Stark obviously knew and trusted his neighbors with the most important section of the line]. And it is a well established fact that the British troops in front of this wall were almost completely annihilated . . . After completion of this wall [the one across the beach] and the British were advancing, Col. Stark stepped in front of the line, thrust a stick into the ground about 80 yards distant and remarked to his command 'there, don't a man fire till the red-coats come up to that stick, if he does, I'll knock him down.' The killed and wounded were all betwixt the stick and the line, showing with what coolness Stark's troops obeyed his orders."[12]

❧

General Henry Clinton and the rest of the British command were amazed at the speed with which the colonists had built a workable redoubt. Their regular troops could never have built such a structure in one night's time. The two four- pounders Prescott had on Breed's Hill could not compete with the battery of twenty-four-pounders located on Copp's Hill across the harbor. General Howe planned to attack the redoubt with a flanking movement to the north, which placed the main thrust of the attack directly at Stark's position.

General Gage was watching the scene of the battle from the observation cupola of the Province House in Boston. One of his staff inquired whether the rebels would stand and fight. Gage, remembering the resourceful rangers whom he used as a model for his light infantry, and the respect he held for John Stark, replied: "[T]hat if John Stark was with them, they would fight; for he was a brave fellow and had served under him, in 1758-9, at Lake George."[13]

Gage was referring to the abysmal attack by General Abercromby upon Fort Carillon in which he and Stark both served under Lord Howe, the brother of General William Howe who was in command of the troops then attacking Bunker Hill.

At about three o'clock in the afternoon, the British troops had successfully established a beachhead and were ready to advance against the colonials' strongholds. General Howe elected to lead his light-infantry, his favorite troops, against Stark's line of defense while his second in command, Brigadier General Robert Pigot, led the charge against the breastworks and redoubt held by the wiry and indomitable Colonel Prescott and an ad hoc force from Massachusetts, New Hampshire, Connecticut, and Rhode Island.

The second the redcoats, marching at double time with bayonets leveled, passed the stake, Stark yelled the order for his first line of troops to fire. Silent musket muzzles of every description pointing from behind their line, suddenly belched fire and death, ripping through the frontal British ranks like a scythe mowing grain. The Welsh Fusiliers were considered the finest regiment in the British army. It mustered about seven hundred men before it marched against Stark's line. The following morning there were only eighty-three men!

The advance hesitated. The ground was littered with dead and wounded soldiers wearing red uniforms, and the mournful cries from the wounded men pierced the smoke-laden air. Then the second company started forward, less confident in its mission but still resolute. Stark had trained his troops to form lines of three men deep. When the first line fired, it made way for the second line to take its place to fire while the second began to reload its weapons. It was the same with the third line and then it started all over again. It created a withering volume of concentrated fire that stopped the British advance. As long as powder, bullets, and flints remained plentiful, a steady volume of fire could be maintained indefinitely. It took courage and a hand from lady luck to withstand such a barrage.

The concept of "continuous fire" was one of Colonel Robert Rogers' rules of ranging service. Excerpts from rule number VII states: "If the enemy push upon you, let your front fire and fall down, and then let your rear advance thro' them and do the like, by which time those who before were in front will be ready to discharge again, and repeat the same alternately, as occasion shall require; by this means you will keep up such a constant fire, that the enemy will not be able to easily break your order, or gain your ground."[14]

While the attack was under way, some sniping took place against the British troops from Charlestown. To counter that, an order was given to fire hot shots of cannon with boiling-hot pitch into the village proper. Within a short time, the whole town was in flames, contributing to the nightmarish appearance of the battle scene.

The British lines continued to reform and advance against colonial breastworks. Prescott's men at the redoubt and breastworks gave an honorable account of themselves. When Stark gave the third order for his lines to fire, the British formation crumpled and retreated, leaving the battlefield littered with dead and wounded. The advance had been stopped. Stark looked out upon the field and was amazed at the carnage. Where whole companies had stood, only a few bewildered soldiers were left standing. It was one of the most costly frontal assaults in military history. Eighty percent casualties of forward echelons was unheard of.[15]

Stark and Knowlton braced themselves for another assault, but the British now ignored them to concentrate on the redoubt and breastworks on Breed's Hill. A large number of British officers had been killed, among them Major Pitcain, of the marines, who was a very able and popular officer. Dr. Joseph Warren, of the Continental Congress, had joined Prescott's line of defense as a private soldier. He was one of the very last men to be killed. The kind doctor was beloved by friends and foes alike and was sorely missed by those responsible for planning future operations.

By now the colonials had run out of powder, and they followed the only prudent and logical tactic available to them: they retreated in haste, but without panic. At this critical point in the Battle of Bunker Hill, Stark displayed uncommon valor and sound judgment, for he had foreseen such a movement and began a slow fighting withdrawal so that he could cover the retreat of his fellow colonials on Breed's Hill. The only route available to them was over Bunker Hill to Charlestown Neck, so Stark held his regiment between the retreating columns and the attacking British formations until everyone had evacuated Breed's Hill. The British pressed hard against Stark's blocking regiment. He took most of his casualties during this contested withdrawal period. His heroic stand during the retreat saved countless lives.

Caleb Stark described the end of the battle:

> "While the British were storming the redoubt, these troops could hardly be prevented from leaving their lines and attacking the enemy's rear. Their commander had witnessed such scenes before. He foresaw the fate of the redoubt; knew that his men had few bayonets, and but one or two rounds of ammunition remaining. He therefore considered any attempt to succor the right of the line would be an act of madness . . . When the redoubt was carried, and retreat became unavoidable, Colonel Stark drew off his troops in such order as not to be pursued. The men were willing to quit their position, having repulsed the enemy so often as to consider themselves completely victorious."[16]

Stark's New Hampshire regiment was the last to leave the battlefield, and the men did so in good order. Some of the New Hampshire men were able to drag a cannon from the battlefield. They made their way through Charlestown Neck north to Ploughed Hill and Winter Hill in Medford along the Mystic River, where they dug entrenchments in case the British followed up on their victory. The enemy now occupied Breed's Hill and Bunker Hill, but what a hollow victory it was! They stood in shock at what had just taken place.

British casualties were eleven hundred and fifty killed and wounded out of a total of twenty-five hundred men committed to the battle. The colonials' casualties were about four hundred out of fifteen hundred to sixteen hundred men committed to the battle.

British losses stunned the entire British contingent. That a group of undisciplined rabble could fight so tenaciously seemed unbelievable. Thoughts of what future conflicts might hold left them in a state of confusion. They never recovered from the shock so ably administered by the rebel militias. Almost eleven hand-picked companies of the best trained soldiers in the world were decimated in front of Stark's regiment.

The horror that descended upon the British camp shattered any preconceived notions they may have harbored pertaining to the determination and resolve of the rebels to fight. The fact is that only the lack of gunpowder saved the British formations from total destruction. General Howe wrote a letter to King George III a few days after the battle. A few excerpts from the letter follow:

"Camp upon the Heights of Charlestown, June 22, and 24.

" . . . the troops were no longer ashore than it was instantly perceived the enemy were very strongly posted, the redoubt upon their right being large and full of men with cannon. To the right of the redoubt they had in the houses of Charlestown, about 200 yards distant from the redoubt, the intermediate space not occupied, being exposed to the cannon of the Boston side battery.

"From the left of the redoubt, they had a line cannon-proof, about 80 yards in length; and from thence to their left, close upon the Mystic river, they had a breastwork made with strong railing taken from the fences and stuffed with hay, which did not stop musket balls, but looked more formidable to the British. This breast work about 300 yards in extent-they made the whole in the night of the 16th.

" . . . the Light Companies upon the right were ordered to keep along the beach to attack the left point of the enemy's breast work, which being carried, they were to attack them in flank. The Grenadiers being directed to attack the enemy's left in front, supported by the 5th and 52nd, their orders were executed by the Grenadiers and the two battalions with a laudable perseverance, but not with the greatest share of discipline, for as soon as the order with which they set forward to attack with bayonets was checked by a difficulty they met with in getting over some very high fences of strong railing, under heavy fire, well kept by the Rebels, they began firing, and by crowding fell into disorder, and in this state the 2nd line mixt with them. The Light Infantry at the same time being repulsed, there was a *moment that I never felt before,* but by gallantry of the officers it was all recovered and the attack carried."[17]

At the height of the battle, Stark was notified by a courier that his son Caleb had been killed. Stark immediately replied: "If he is it is no time to talk of private affairs while the enemy are advancing on our front. Back to your post."[18] The report turned out to be erroneous. Caleb had been "blooded" to combat in one of the most costly battles of the war. He would go on to become a staff officer and was present when the cornerstone of the Bunker Hill Monument was laid in 1825.

Colonel John Stark had a right to be proud of his New Hampshire regiment at Bunker Hill. It is fitting that we give him the final word on the battle in his report to his superiors:

"Colonel Stark to Hon. Matthew Thornton, President of the New Hampshire Provincial Congress.

Medford, June 19, 1775

Sir,—I embrace this opportunity, by Colonel Holland, to give you some particulars of an engagement in battle, which was fought on the 17th inst., between the British troops and the Americans.

"On the 16th, at evening, a detachment of the Massachusetts line marched, by the general's order (General Ward) to make intrenchment upon a hill in Charlestown, called Charlestown hill, near Boston, where they intrenched all night, without interruption, but were attacked on the morning of the 17th, very warmly by the ships of war in Charlestown river, and the batteries in Boston [Cobb's Hill]. Upon this I was ordered by the general to send a detachment of two hundred men, with proper officers, to their assistance; which order I promptly obeyed, and appointed Lt. Col. Wyman to command the same. At two o'clock an express arrived with orders for my whole regiment to proceed to Charlestown, to oppose the British who were landing on Charlestown Point; accordingly we proceeded, and the battle soon came on, in which a number of officers and men of my regiment were killed and wounded. The officers killed were Major McClury, by a cannon ball; Captain Baldwin and Lieutenant Scott, by small arms.

"The whole number, including officers, killed and missing, 15; Wounded, 45

"Total, killed, wounded and missing, 60

"By Colonel Reed's desire, I transmit the account of those who suffered belonging to that portion of his regiment who were engaged:

Killed, 3; wounded, 29; missing, 1.

Total in both regiments, 93.

"But we remain in good spirits, being well satisfied that where we have lost one, the enemy have lost three. I should consider it a favor if the committee of safety should recommend to the several towns and parishes of New-Hampshire the necessity of detaining and sending back all the soldiers belonging to the New-Hampshire line, stationed at Medford, whom they may find at a distance from the army, without furlough from the commanding officer.

I am, Sir, with great respect,
Yours and the country's
To serve in the good cause.
John Stark."[19]

The historian, Rev. Increase N. Tarbox, in his biography of General Israel Putnam, wrote, "We have the full conviction that the time will come when the whole nation will give honors of the battle of Bunker Hill to the common soldiers of New Hampshire who more than any other men, fought it."[20]

An interesting footnote to the Bunker Hill battle is that gunpowder from the stocks removed from Fort William and Mary arrived too late to have any influence on the outcome, but it helped to resupply depleted stocks. How different the battle might have been if the powder had arrived prior to the battle.[21]

The American defenses for Bunker Hill were as complete as time and resources had permitted. Considering that Stark, Putnam, Prescott, and Gridley all worked relatively independent of each other, without the benefit of staff officers, they had shown more professionalism than the British imagined possible. After the battle, Stark is reported to have said:

> " . . . That there was no commander of all the American troops on this hard fought day, and . . . most of the officers who conducted the men there, all being moved by one common impulse, and to one common end, fought the common enemy much as they deemed best, each acting pretty much on his own hook."[22]

8

British Evacuate Boston (1775-1776)

The British had always intended to occupy the Dorchester Heights and had made provisions to carry out the operation on June 18, 1775. The sudden presence of Americans on Breed's Hill in Charlestown disrupted that schedule. Their losses on the seventeenth so weakened the British forces that the Dorchester operation was postponed.

We last saw Robert Rogers as he accompanied young Caleb Stark on the way to Medford, when he asked Caleb to carry a message to his father requesting a meeting. Colonel Stark had been Rogers's second in command of the ranger service. The two men had shared many harrowing experiences. Long marches in inclement weather and smoky campfires during lonely nights in the middle of the wilderness are never forgotten by those men who had experienced them.

We do not know for sure, but it's likely that Stark cordially met his old companion, even though he must have been distressed by Rogers's conduct since their discharge from the ranger service. It is believed that Robert Rogers's visit in 1775 to America was to review both sides of the dispute taking place, so that he could most likely chose the winning side for personal gain. Stark had assured Rogers that no offers of rank or wealth could induce him to abandon the cause of his oppressed country. He said: "I have taken up arms in her defense, and, God willing, I will never lay them down until she has become a free and independent nation."[1]

George Washington had expelled Rogers on the grounds of being a British spy. He later visited Congress and eventually joined the British, obtaining the rank of colonel. He had bounced from one side to the other, and ultimately devoted his energy to developing loyalist ranger groups in the New York area, which failed to distinguish themselves.

Rogers traveled to England in 1780 and lived the rest of his life in obscurity, a sad ending for a man whose brilliance and physical courage shined so brightly in his youth. That flame flickered because of his flawed character. It is believed that he died in Algeria or the East Indies.

❧

The siege of Boston continued after Bunker Hill. The British seemed more reluctant than ever to venture far from their fortified placements within the city. In the aftermath of the battle, Stark was busy taking care of his regiments, seeing that the dead were properly buried and the wounded were given the best care available. He quickly sent word to his family that he and young Caleb were doing well.

Wages for the men were badly in arrears and Stark was pulled into an incident that ruffled the feathers of a lot of politicians. Men were in distress from lack of funds and the paymasters had been ordered to pay the three New Hampshire regiments, Stark's First, Reed's Second, and Poor's Third, if the rolls proved to be satisfactory. It was close to the end of the year and the paymaster figured to pay only up to August 4. The men were outraged and a group of them with a fife and drum forcibly marched the paymaster to Stark's headquarters. Stark demanded the men be paid. The paymaster claimed that some of his money was missing, and the matter was passed on to Exeter who launched an inquiry.

The matter was ultimately passed on to General Sullivan who was inclined to settle the affair in an amicable manner as quickly as possible. Stark took all of the blame, disciplining nobody. His "Confession" or apology is vintage John Stark copy and reads as follows:

"Whereas on the 30th day of December last some persons belonging to my regiment without order or warrant from me for so doing proceeded under arms from their barracks on Winter Hill to the lodging of Samuel Hobart, Esq. at Medford and there assaulted and took him prisoner and brought him to my encampment at Winter Hill and I being at that time much perplexed with business and not knowing the many aggravated circumstances attending said assault & not considering at that time the dangerous tendency of such an insult offered to him while in the execution of his office as paymaster of the troops from the Colony of New Hampshire neglected to confine and punish those offenders but being before wearied by their complaints for want of pay and much perplexed with other business hastily and inconsiderately threw out some warm an illiberal reflections [Stark had called him a coward] upon some members of the Congress in that Colony for which I am sincerely sorry and heartily ask their forgiveness and beg leave to assure them that those reflections proceeded only from heat & passion & not from any settled design to slander or defame them."[2]

Several important events preceded the battle for Bunker Hill. When the Connecticut colonial assembly learned of the Lexington-Concord exchange, they authorized Ethan Allen and his renowned Green Mountain Boys to seize the fortress of Ticonderoga, the former Fort Carillon built by the French on the southern tip of Lake Champlain. Allen enthusiastically gathered his flock and headed for the lake. Unbeknownst to him, Massachusetts had authorized Benedict Arnold to carry out the same mission. The men met on the shore of Lake Champlain and heatedly discussed who was going to be in charge of the operation. Neither of the strong-willed commanders would give in, so they shared command.

Fort Ticonderoga was garrisoned by forty British soldiers unfit for field duty. The assault was accomplished with eighty-three men, all that could be ferried across the lake in the boats available in the early morning-darkness. A sentry from the fort fired on them, sounding the alarm, as the Americans scaled the wall crying "no quarter."

Once inside the fort, the stairs leading to officer quarters at the end of the parade ground were climbed in a rush by Allen and Arnold. An officer clutching his britches was at the top of the landing. Allen shouted, "Come out of there, you damned old rat."

The officer demanded, "By what authority?"

Allen hollered, "In the name of the Great Jehovah and the Continental Congress," and demanded "the fort and all the effects of George the Third." The captain handed over his sword.

The strategic fortress holding the gateway north to Canada and south to New York was now in American hands. The richest prize of all consisted of the valuable stockpiles of military stores, especially cannons and mortars. Two days after the capture of Fort Ticonderoga' Seth Warner, Ethan Allen's second in command, occupied Crown Point, slightly north of Ticonderoga at a strategic overview of the lake. It was taken without firing a shot. Buoyed by their success, Arnold saw an opportunity to push northward and took command of a schooner that had been captured from a Tory at Skenesborough by the Green Mountain Boys. He was the only man present who could sail a ship.

Arnold sailed north on Lake Champlain and entered the Richelieu River to Fort St. John, where he engaged a fourteen-man garrison and briefly occupied the site. The arrival of a large British formation hastened Arnold's retreat southward in the schooner with all the supplies he could remove in the time he had available. All in all, it was a profitable venture carried out with dash and enterprise.[3]

The day after the fall of Fort Ticonderoga, the Second Continental Congress met in Philadelphia and assumed responsibility for coordinating the rebellion then taking place. On June 15 the Congress mandated that: "a General be appointed to command all the Continental forces raised or to be raised, for the defense of American liberty."[4]

The Congress chose George Washington, a Virginian who had served in the Virginia militia during the French and Indian Wars. His favorable vote of approval solicited the following statement:

> "Mr. President . . . I . . . declare with the utmost sincerity, I do not think myself equal to the command I am honored with. As to pay, Sir, I beg leave to assure the Congress that as to no pecuniary consideration could have tempted to have accepted this arduous employment at the expense of my domestic ease and happiness, I do not wish to make any profit from it."[5]

Shortly, George Washington was on his way to Boston to take command of the military formations surrounding the city, He stopped in New York, where he was informed about the Bunker Hill battle, a misnomer that exists today. Congress had also selected Artemas Ward (Massachusetts), Israel Putnam (Connecticut), Philip Schuyler (New York), Charles Lee (a former Polish officer), and Horatio Gates (Virginia) as Washington's assistants.

Washington arrived in Boston on July 2, 1775. He had always hated British officers, from the time he first served with them in the Ohio Valley during the French and Indian War. In that respect, he and John Stark were in agreement. The haughty and condescending manner of the British infuriated most colonials, but the feature of the British army that allowed incompetent officers to purchase their commissions was perhaps the most detested tradition, and Washington was determined not to let that happen in the new army he was about to command. We do not know for sure, but given Stark's no-nonsense set of values, he probably concurred.

General Gage had about twelve thousand men in Boston: Washington counted about sixteen thousand. The siege circle was eight to nine miles in length. Washington's first glimpse of the militias he would incorporate into the Continental army was a shocking disappointment. He found them exceedingly "dirty and nasty people." Washington believed that soldiers who had enlisted should be held to their commitment, and asked Congress for the right to hang deserters. The answer was slow in coming. As conditions improved, Washington found that the men wanted to decide which officers they would serve under and insisted that they come from the same colony. Regional loyalty was, at that time, greater than national aspirations. Shortages of supplies was the most severe problem facing the new army, and it would plague the army for the duration of the conflict. Each soldier had, on the average, nine bullets to contain the British in Boston.[6]

Early in September, a mysterious ciphered letter came into Washington's hands at his Cambridge headquarters on the Charles River. Three members of his staff deciphered the message. It was addressed to a Major Cane, one of General Gage's staff, and was from a Dr. Benjamin Church. Washington was crushed by the betrayal of the man he had recently appointed general director of hospitals in the Continental army. Church had been a long-standing member of the Massachusetts Provincial Congress and a close colleague of Samuel Adams and John Hancock.

Paul Revere, the ultimate patriot, had always been suspicious of Church's loyalty to the patriot cause. On April 20 after Lexington and Concord, Church had told Revere that he was at the clash of arms at Lexington commons, encouraging the American militia to resist the British and was splashed with the blood of a patriot. After that exchange, Revere had changed his mind until he later learned that Church was charged as a traitor. In 1780 he was found guilty and sent to Martinique. The sloop sank in a storm taking the traitor to his death.[7]

❧

The shoulder-held weapons of Stark's First New Hampshire Regiment were perhaps typical of, if not slightly more serviceable than those in the militia units around Boston. The diversity of firearms was a tribute to the ingenuity and can-do spirit that motivated the colonists. After April 18, 1775, thousands of farmers and tradesmen from New England flocked to Boston, armed with a large variety of weapons. The colonists were aligning themselves against the finest military in the world with a vast manufacturing capability to support its armies in the field. In contrast, The colonists lacked a manufacturing base to produce arms or support a war. At first glance, it looked like an impossible job ahead of the ragtag army that had risen from the soil to oppose tyranny. Their lack of manufacturing facilities and know-how was overcome by the pioneering spirit which motivated them.

The aggressive colonel Henry Knox was responsible for locating the nation's first armory in Springfield, Massachusetts, in 1776. It was relatively safe from combat operations and enjoyed an ideal location on the Connecticut River. The first musket produced at the Springfield Armory was called U.S. Model 1795. It was based on the popular French Charleville of 1763 vintage. The armory turned out two hundred and forty-five guns with forty workers—a small beginning for what would become a world-class producer of fine military arms:

> "The rebels possessed an explosive vitality and ability to innovate. How they deified the impossible and drew from this 'new world' energy to successfully equip their spawning armies is one of the untold stories of our incredible path to freedom."[8]

The militia units from different communities generally included the able-bodied males from sixteen to sixty years of age. They were armed with an assortment of muskets, trade guns, fowling pieces, and rifles of various diameters. The desperate shortage of serviceable firearms in Massachusetts, even within Stark's regiment, when Washington arrived on the scene was typical and widespread within the colonial militias. At first usable weapons were assembled from supplies of broken and discarded weapons. The availability of two to three thousand gunsmiths in the colonies formed the nucleus of a flourishing firearms industry.

Committees of Safety issued contracts for weapons based on the popular and sturdy British Land Pattern Army musket—the famous Brown Bess. Weapons shortage was alleviated somewhat by importing arms from the European countries, especially France. It is estimated that three hundred thousand long arms were used by the American troops during the revolutionary War. Local gunsmiths using mixed components, produced over eighty thousand.[9]

Meanwhile, Stark and his men continued to improve their entrenchments and quarters at Winter Hill. A period of relative inactivity followed the Battle of Bunker Hill. Replacements were accepted in the regiments to replace those who had returned home. Enlistments had generally been for the remainder of the calendar year, and as December approached, many men were anxious to go back to their farms and families to get ready for winter. Both armies went into "winter quarters," where they could be reasonably protected from the bitter cold. It was also a time when plans for the coming spring were formulated.

❧

While the British army was licking its wounds in Boston, the Royal Navy was active all along the eastern seaboard. Fast sloops and privateers that had been plying the waters for years were a thorn in the side of the navy officials, who in their slow, heavily armed frigates could never catch them. The home ports of such vessels were harassed and a few were destroyed. The inhabitants of the communities on the shore had no means of defending themselves. Places like Bristol, Rhode Island, and Falmouth, Maine were viciously attacked.

On October 16, 1775, the captain of the British man-of-war *Conceau,* had sent ashore a warning message to the people of Falmouth:

"After so many premeditated attacks on the legal prerogatives of the best of Sovereigns . . . and in place of a dutiful and grateful return to your King and parent state, you have been guilty of the most unpardonable rebellion, supported by the ambition of a set of designing men, whose insidious deeds have cruelly imposed on the credulity of their fellow-creatures . . . my having it in orders to execute a just punishment on the Town of Falmouth. On the name of which authority, I previously warned you to remove without delay the human species out of the said Town, for which purpose I give you two hours . . . should your imprudence lead you to show the least resistance, you will in that case free me of that humanity so strongly pointed out in my orders, as well as in my inclination."[10]

On January 15, 1776, the Selectmen of Falmouth reported what took place after they refused the request:

"It was about 9 o'clock on Wednesday, being the 18th of October, that the firing began from all the ...vessels, with all possible briskness, discharging on every part of town which lay on a regular descent toward the harbour an horrible shower of balls, from three to nine pounds weight, bombs, carcasses, live shells, grape-shot and musket-balls. The firing lasted without many minutes cessation, until six o'clock P.M., during which time several parties came ashore and set buildings on fire by hand. Parties of our people, and others from neighboring towns, ran down to oppose them, and it is thought killed several. . .through the goodness of God no life was lost on our side and only one man wounded... Had no opposition been made, we do not believe they would have left one building standing; and more opposition would have been made had not the people's attention had been taken up in securing their effects.

" . . . three quarters of the buildings . . . are consumed, consisting of 130 dwellinghouses of two or three families apiece, beside barns, and almost every store and warehouse in town. St. Paul's Church, a large new building, with a bell; a very elegant and costly court-house, not quite finished; a fine engine almost new; the old town house and the publik library, were all consumed . . . All the compact part of town is gone; and among the hundred dwellings that are standing, there are but few good buildings, and those damaged with balls passing through them or bombs bursting."[11]

General George Washington wrote on October 24, 1775, to the Second Continental Congress in Philadelphia from his camp in Cambridge:

"Sir: My conjecture of the destination of the late squadron from Boston in my last has been unhappily verified by an outrage exceeding in barbarity and cruelty every hostile act practiced among civilized nations. I have enclosed an account given me by Mr. Jones, a gentleman of the Town of Falmouth, of the destruction of that . . . village . . . THE ORDERS SHOWN BY THE Captain for this horrid procedure by which it appears the same desolation is meditated upon all the Towns on the coast, made it my duty to communicate it as quickly and extensively as possible. As Portsmouth was the next place to which he proposed to go, General Sullivan was permitted to go up and give them assistance and advice to ward off the blow. I flatter myself the like event will not happen there, as they have fortification of some strength, and a vessel has arrived at a place called Sheepscut, with one thousand five hundred pounds of powder."[12]

General Washington and his staff were busy studying the tactics available to select those with the best chance of defeating the British within Boston. It was difficult to maintain a siege without sufficient siege guns. Therefore, Washington dispatched Henry Knox, a studious young bookseller to Fort Ticonderoga to transport its cannons to Boston. Weapons and all manner of military store were scarce or unavailable in Boston. Washington could not deliver the fatal blow to the British until he had the weapons capable of doing the job.

Knox's heroic epic deserves a more detailed description than we can present here, but let it be noted that the superhuman efforts of a gentle giant of a man may have been the pivotal act that ensured the success of the rebellion. His party was equipped with eighty-two sleds, one hundred sixty oxen and over one hundred and twenty-five horses, and hauled forty-three cannon and sixteen mortars weighing over one hundred twenty thousand pounds from the southern tip of Lake Champlain down Lake George to Albany, across the Hudson River, through the deep snows and rugged peaks of the Berkshire Mountains, to Boston. It took seventy-five days of excruciating labor and effort. Colonel Henry Knox had earned the respect and admiration of his peers. He rolled into Cambridge on January 24, 1776.[13]

Now the cannons could be placed at Dorchester Heights, but the ground was frozen and the heavy artillery needed to be emplaced in such a way that the British were unaware of the positioning. Working parties hauled wagonloads of barrels filled with rocks, soil, fascines, and pressed-hay bundles to build battery positions. They even wrapped the heavy wagon wheels with cloth to muffle their sound. On March 2, General Washington ordered Colonel Knox to begin a diversionary bombardment while the gun emplacements were built and secured in the frozen ground at Dorchester Heights. The bombardment was capable of covering all of Boston proper and the harbor anchorage area. The scope and rapidity of it unhinged the British high command.

General Howe had the option of attacking and face the likelihood of Washington counterattacking and capturing most of British army, or he could evacuate the city. They decided to evacuate. Historian Leckie wrote:

"On March 17, 1776-St. Patrick's Day, forever more in Boston to be joined to Patriot's Day-the last of Howe's soldiers and about one thousand dejected Tories sailed from Boston Harbor for Nantasket Harbor. Ten days later this woebegone fleet of perhaps 170 vessels set sail for Halifax."[14]

During this period, John Stark's brother William Stark appeared to be sympathetic to the patriots' cause. He had served with distinction in Rogers' Rangers as a captain during the French and Indian War. He was even offered a commission under General Sullivan, but after a series of questionable financial transactions came to light, he left for New York, where he received a colonelcy in the British army. His son was also commissioned. William Stark was later thrown from his horse and killed on Long Island.

Not much is known how this treasonable conduct was handled by John Stark or the rest of the family. John was notorious for his defense of his feelings. He was an original private person. Whether William's decision elicited shame, outrage, or sorrow is unknown. It's possible that all three emotions visited the stoic John Stark, but he remained silent.

The patriots immediately rushed into the city and found conditions there wretched. After the British left, John Stark, Reed, and Wilkerson made a tour of the city after they had looked at Bunker and Breed's Hills. Wilkerson wrote:

"Arrived at the ferry stairs we discovered a canoe on shore which we launched and embarking in it crossed Charles's river to Boston and on the presumption that the enemy had taken their departure we marched through the town by a long, narrow winding street to the fortifications on Roxbury neck which had been skillfully designed and well executed; here I first saw the little military engine called cal-trops or crow-feet, [a metal device with pointed needle-like spurs which could injure horses or humans if they stepped on them] which the enemy had scattered over the street within its works. It appeared that the enemy had, very properly, forbid inhabitants to leave their houses during the embarkation and from this cause or from their ignorance of his movements or the timidity produced by their long residence with him, and the fear of reproach from their countrymen, the houses of the inhabitants continued shut up and the town presented a frightful solitude in the bosom of a numerous population. After several fruitless applications of our canes to the doors and windows we gained admittance into a house, where we were kindly treated by a well-known whig, whose circumstances compelled him to abide with the enemy. I regret I should have forgotten his name. This day was the

Sabbath and the most solemn I had seen; a death like silence pervaded an inhabited city and spectacles of waste and spoil struck the eye at almost every step."[15]

Once the British evacuation was completed, Stark was ordered to the command of two regiments, the Fifth and the Twenty-fifth under General John Sullivan. They were to proceed to New York, where they were to assist in building fortifications and strengthening the defenses of the city. General Washington was certain that General Howe was planning an assault on New York and wanted to be prepared for the onslaught. On March 16, 1776 General Horatio Gates sent new orders for Stark:

"Marching orders for Colonel John Stark, commanding the 5th and 25th regiments of foot.

"You are forthwith to march, with the regiments under your command, to Norwich, in Connecticut, according to the route indicated; and in case of extreme bad weather or other foreseen accidents you are obliged to halt a day or more, between this and Norwich, you will acquaint Brigadier general heath, who is appointed to the command of the brigade, now under marching orders, and receive and follow his directions. You will immediately apply to Commissary General Trumbull, and to Quarter master General, Col. Mifflin, for an order for carriages and provisions for your march to Norwich. Upon your arrival there, Brigadier General Heath has his excellency, the commander-in-chief's directions for the farther disposal of the brigade.

"His excellency expects you to preserve good order and exact discipline upon your march, carefully preventing all pillage and marauding, and every kind of ill-usage, or insult to the inhabitants of the country. As the motions of the enemy and the advanced season of the year make it of the utmost consequence that not a moment should be lost that can possibly be made use of on your march, the general, depending on your zeal, experience and good conduct, is satisfied that, on your part, no vigilance will be wanting.

Given at head quarters, this 16th of March, 1776.

HORATIO GATES, *Adj. Gen'l.*

Route from Cambridge to Framingham,	20
Sutton,	18
Dudley,	20
Mort Lake,	19
Norwich,	20
In all,	97

Thomas Mifflin, *Q.M. Gen'l.*"[16]

Stark arrived at New York on April 6 and soon learned that the plan was made to ship him north. If the higher command had shipped him up the Hudson-Lake Champlain corridor directly, they could have saved Stark and his men a hundred miles of walking, but such are the toils of the infantryman, yesterday and today.

9

Canada to Trenton (1776)

The decision by higher headquarters to send Stark north up the Hudson River was based on the fact that the initiatives of Brigadier General Benedict Arnold to capture Quebec via a route up the Kennebec River from the south, and Colonel Richard Montgomery's assault via Lake Champlain to Montreal and then up the Saint Lawrence River to reinforce Arnold's siege of Quebec, had failed, despite much heroism and effort from both leaders. This failure prompted a response from the Continental Congress to reinforce the Canadian effort with Sullivan's division, of which Colonel Stark was a part.

Near the end of August 1775, Colonel Richard Montgomery left Fort Ticonderoga with twenty-four hundred men. He sailed across Lake Champlain and arrived at St. John's on the Richelieu River, September 10, 1775. There he encountered a reinforced garrison of British and Canadian troops that delayed him. Montgomery decided to break off the exchange from St. John's and attacked Champly, a few miles north on the Richelieu, which quickly surrendered to him. There he replenished his ammunition and powder supply and returned to capture St. John's on November 3. Winter was beginning to grip the region when Montgomery pushed on to Montreal against light resistance. There he and his men found large stocks of warm British clothing, which was welcome, for it was getting colder by the day.

By early December, Montgomery had made his way to Quebec, where he met with Benedict Arnold at Point Levi on the southern bank of the Saint Lawrence River. Arnold's epic trek through the Maine wilderness during severe winter weather without adequate food, clothing, or shelter stands today as a testament to his skill and courage as a leader. The ordeal would have broken many men, or, at the least, dampened their enthusiasm, but Arnold remained as energetic and positive as ever, always looking for a way to fight the enemy.

As of December 31 Arnold had six hundred men, Montgomery had over three hundred able-bodied troops. That morning, Arnold gave the order to attack Quebec. He was severely wounded during the battle and had to be carried off the field. Montgomery was killed by a shot in the face. Without siege weapons, the American effort was too weak to remove the British and Canadians from their well-entrenched fortresses.

Arnold, stubborn and determined as ever, refused to leave Quebec and on April 1 was reinforced by General David Wooster, a very ineffective officer, who arrived from Montreal with heavy siege guns to relieve Arnold of his command. Shortly after the change of command, Wooster was replaced by General John Thomas.

The coming of spring also brought large numbers of reinforcements to the British forces holding Quebec in the form of men and heavily armed frigates. General John Burgoyne landed his troops in Quebec. The frigate *Surprise* shelled Arnold's position as it landed troops. In the face of overwhelming power, Arnold wisely retreated down the river toward Trois-Rivieres. He was the last man to leave Quebec. As the British were rapidly approaching his location he shot his horse, removed the saddle and blanket, and threw them in a canoe before pushing off to catch up with his retreating troops.[1]

The retreating remnants of Arnold's and Montgomery's forces, then under Thomas's command, were met by Sullivan's division at Sorel at the mouth of the Richelieu River on the Saint Lawrence. General John Sullivan, with Stark in command of the Fifth and Twenty-fifth Regiments as his vanguard, had been ordered to Canada to salvage whatever was possible from Arnold's defeat at Quebec. It was a meeting of very strong-willed military commanders.

Shortly thereafter, Thomas died of smallpox and the command reverted back to Arnold. However, General Sullivan superseded Arnold's authority and in early May was ordered to detach an expedition to Trois-Rivieres, thirty-five miles north on the Saint Lawrence.

Colonel Stark vigorously opposed the movement as being too hazardous. Because they all knew about the large army Burgoyne had brought to Canada, it was ludicrous to break up their force into smaller components that could more readily be overrun. His recommendation was ignored. The expedition to Trois-Rivieres was under General William

Thompson, Sullivan's second in command. He was a tough, boastful man who underestimated the ability of his detachment. He lost sixty men killed and three hundred taken prisoner, including himself. The survivors of the ill-fated expedition were riddled with smallpox, which spread like wildfire throughout the division. Spring always brings swarms of black flies and mosquitoes making life miserable in that portion of the continent. Some men have gone mad from unrelenting attacks of clouds of winged insects. They are especially vicious against wounded men, who are already weakened. Once the troops approached the open water of Lake Champlain, the severity lessened appreciably.

Sullivan had his men burn everything of value in Sorel while he planned his retreat to Crown Point and Ticonderoga, one hundred and sixty miles south. They passed through Chambly halfway down the Richelieu and there they replenished some of their supplies and then torched anything that would burn. Sullivan had skillfully conducted a retreat while pursued by General Burgoyne's superior force. They paused at St. John's to burn the structures. Stark and his staff were the last to leave the settlement. An advance guard of Burgoyne's army arrived just as Stark climbed into the bateau, on his way to the island sanctuary known as Isle-aux-Noix in the middle of the river, slightly north of Lake Champlain.

General Burgoyne reached Chambly to find all of the buildings burned to the ground. Temporarily abandoning his pursuit of Sullivan, he established his headquarters at the post and began to rebuild it. It was a good time for him to collect his army and plan the next move down the lake.

Sullivan was able to evacuate two thousand patients from the hospital on Isle-aux-Noix and all of the military stores in bateaus over the treacherous rapids just before entering the main body of Lake Champlain. The army that was encamped on Isle-aux-Noix left the island on June 18, 1776, successfully crossing Lake Champlain and landing at Crown Point. Stark's regiment was quartered at Chimney Point, on the eastern shore opposite Crown Point. They remained in that position until General Philip Schuyler ordered Sullivan to fall back on Ticonderoga. The first day the Americans reached Crown Point, Benedict Arnold proceeded to Skenesborough, at the southern tip of Lake Champlain, to began the construction of gondolas, sloops, galleys, and schooners to oppose a water crossing by the British who were then one hundred and twenty-nine miles to the north. His industrious efforts would result in the first naval battle of the war, and give birth to the United States Navy.

In the meantime, Stark and the other regimental commanders, Reed, Webb, and Nixon all disputed General Schuyler's order on the basis that it occupied a position that could be easily defended against a numerically superior force and that it commanded the entire lake. They also protested inadequate support of field officers and inadequate provisions. Smallpox had riddled the force with devastating consequences. Force readiness was badly weakened and the men suffered from the lack of food and medicines. On July 9, General Schuyler answered their protest from his headquarters at Ticonderoga:

"*Gentlemen*—Your remonstrance of yesterday's date was delivered at eight o'clock this evening, by General Sullivan. Previous to any observations on it, give me leave to remind you of a mistake you have made in supposing that I informed you 'that Congress had directed that the army was to be removed to Ticonderoga.' My expression was exactly in these words: 'That it be recommended to General Schuyler to form a strong camp in the vicinity of Ticonderoga or Crown Point. I observed that, as I quoted from memory, and had not the resolution with me, I could not repeat the very words of it. I rather wish to impute your mistake to misapprehension than to any intentional false repetition of what I said, which I can not suppose any gentleman can be guilty of.

"The reasons that induced the council of general officers unanimously to give their opinion to move the main body of the army from Crown Point, I can not conceive myself at liberty to give without their consent; for myself, I declare with that frankness which I wish always to characterize me, that the measure seemed not only prudent, but, in my opinion, indispensably necessary for a variety of reasons, against which those you have given do not, in my opinion, bear a sufficient weight to alter it; some of which are evidently nugatory, and all of which might be contrasted with more cogent ones in support of the resolution. I assure you, at the same time, that if I were convinced of the impropriety of the measure, I should not be in the least tenacious of supporting my opinion, but immediately give way to convictions, and rescind the resolution so far as depended on me to do it.

"I am happy, gentlemen, that you declare your readiness to obey the resolution of the general officers, although it does not meet your approbation—a sentiment that every good officer ought not to entertain, but to inculcate on others as a principle on which the preservation of every army in a great measure depends. Such a sentiment will always induce me, and I dare say every other general officer, to receive with patience and pleasure the advice of his officers and act accordingly, where I or they are concerned."[2]

Like all good soldiers, Stark and his companions obeyed orders to evacuate Chimney Point arriving at Fort Ticonderoga on July 7, 1776. There the Army was divided. A large encampment, including Stark's regiment, was stationed on the eastern shore of the lake when a copy of the Declaration of Independence arrived by courier, it was immediately read aloud to the men, and joy filled the camp as they fired thirteen-gun volleys in salute to a basic, tangible document that symbolized everything they were fighting for. It was a day they would all remember for as long as they lived. Thereafter, the camp was called Mount Independence.[3]

The sudden move to Ticonderoga displeased the Commander in Chief. He wrote a letter to Congress on July 19, 1776:

"I confess the determination of the council of general officers, on the 7th, to retreat from Crown Point, surprised me much; and the more I consider it, the more striking does the impropriety appear. The reasons assigned against it by the field officers in their remonstrance, coincide greatly with my own ideas, and those of the other general officers I have had an opportunity of conversing with, and seem to be of considerable weight, I may add, conclusive . . . the possession of Crown Point is essential to give us the superiority and mastery of the lake . . .

"I have mentioned my surprise to General Schuyler, and would, by the advice of the general officers, have directed that post should be maintained, had it not been for two causes: an apprehension that the works had been destroyed, and that if the army should be ordered from Ticonderoga, or the post opposite to it (where I presume they are) to repossessed it . . . lest it might increase the jealousy and diversity of opinions which already seem too prevalent in the army and establish a precedent for the inferior officers to set up their judgment whenever they would, in opposition to their superiors—a matter of great delicacy, and that could lead to fatal consequences if countenanced, though in the present instance I could have wished their reasoning had prevailed."[4]

The failure of American forces in the Lake Champlain-Hudson Valley corridor created a climate of fear along the northern and western frontier. On July 10, Ira Allen wrote to the New Hampshire Committee of Safety to present some interesting observations about conditions along the border:

"*Gentlemen*—I learn you are alarmed about the retreat of our army out of Canada. I can assure you the savages have killed and scalped a number of men by the river of La Cole, on the west side of Lake Champlain. When they will visit us or you, is uncertain; I advise you to look sharp, keep scouts out, but not to move, except some families much remote from the main inhabitants. Last Saturday I was at Crown Point with General Sullivan. He assured me he would do all in his power to protect the frontier settlements.

"I proposed a line of forts by this river to Cohos. He said he believed that to be the best place, and made no doubt but it would be done. He immediately ordered Colonel Waite and two hundred men to this place . . . and grant all protection in his power to the inhabitants. Before I left there, Generals Schuyler, Gates and Arnold arrived. I conclude there is a determination, before this time, in regards to the frontier . . . I had intelligence from St. Johns about twelve days ago . . . they did not appear to be in much preparation for war. At Chambly there were few men. It is thought by some that the enemy are busy in sending provisions and clothing to all the garrisons near the head of the St. Lawrence River, and in supplying the Indians with all necessities. The small-pox has almost gone through our army; they are in much better health than they were. The gondolas are building: the vessels are preparing for war . . ."[5]

Soon after General Horatio Gates took charge, Colonel Stark was given command of a brigade while he worked at improving the fortifications on Mount Independence, where he had been ever since he left Crown Point. The elevation had a commanding view of the surrounding territory. Its prominence made the position almost unassailable, hence, its value and the reason for its improvements.

Stark and his men built huts, barracks, and gun emplacements atop Mount Independence. They had cut most of the trees on the top to create a vista that stretched for miles in every direction. It was a formidable bastion for defense.

General Schuyler called the narrows between Fort Ticonderoga and Mount Independence the critical choke point for preventing the British from invading from the north. The mountain had previously been called Rattlesnake Mountain, after the heavy population of snakes found there.

That autumn, several junior colonels were promoted to brigadier general. Stark was not on the list even though he was in command of a brigade that normally warranted a brigadier general's commission. He protested that such unfair proceedings would cause discord and lack of unity within the officer corps of the army. His lengthy appeal to the Continental Congress was heartfelt and factual:

"The petition and remonstrance of John Stark humbly showeth that your petitioner served for six years in the last war, four years of which I served as Captain of Ranging service and received my commission from the Commander-in-Chief, was allowed ten shillings per day, was in every skirmish and engagement that happened in the Northern Department & never had a reprimand from a general officer during that time, although I served with each of them that was in that department.

"When Canada surrendered to the British troops I resigned my commission & returned to my family, laid up my sword in hopes never to have occasion to draw it again but when the unhappy dispute between Great Britain and the Colonies happened I heard the ministerial butchers had spilt American blood at Lexington I mustered a few of my neighbors and went to their relief at Cambridge. I waited on the Commander-in-Chief, took out orders to raise a regiment which I completed in five days & augmented to eight hundred men, was stationed at Medford until the day of Bunker Hill battle. Then I received orders to march my regiment to Bunker Hill as the regular troops were landing to attack our works. I was the first regiment that got to the lines although I received my orders one hour later than the other troops & had two miles further to go. I took my post on the left wing and could have kept it if it was not for the right wing which gave way & the left of the regulars almost surrounded me before I retreated. The execution that was done in my department I refer to General Burgoyne's letter for the proof of, & my conduct afterwards I refer you to the Generals I served under in that department & since I served in this department I have done my duty to the satisfaction of the general's that commanded me. In our retreat from Sorel I took up the rear to Crown Point, was left with a part of the stores & about thirty men only to assist me & and the regulars very often within five miles of me.

"The Commander-in-Chief in this department did me the honour of giving me the command of a brigade which I regulated to the satisfaction of my superior officers & those I commanded. But as there are so many officers in the Continental army promoted before me that neither seniority or merit intitles them to and that never was in the army until they joined the Continental service & as I am not worthy of the trust reposed in me I hope the Honorable Congress will take it into consideration and either give me my rank in the army or give me leave to retire to my family for I assure the Honorable Congress I never entered the service for the sake of ease or gain but for pure zeal for my country's cause & by enquiring into my conduct the Honorable Congress will find that what I assert is true and the petitioned as in duty bound will ever pray."[6]

Stark had laid out a litany of his achievements in the service of his country. They were as numerous and notable as those of any other officer in the Continental Army. He was sacrificed for political expediency and was justifiably angered that he was so carelessly discarded. It was unjust and uncalled for, but even today, politics frequently supersedes merit.

Stark's return to the site of his previous service in the French and Indian War must have triggered a few memories. It is probable that he remembered Lord Howe and the failed attempt to take Ticonderoga. The French and their Indian allies were strong adversaries who demanded an equivalent effort from the British and the colonists. Even the most heavily contested engagements between the British and the Americans never rose to the level of violence and depravity that took place with the Abenaki when their barbaric methods were encouraged. Now, the British used a few tribes for scouting, but the vast majority of the Abenaki were earnestly following a neutral track, not wanting to be part of the civil war then raging.

The strategic importance of the water corridor that divided New England from the rest of the colonies can hardly be overestimated. The British plan to sever New England was a strategic goal of Sir Guy Carleton in 1776. The British army in southern New York would drive north up the Hudson corridor while a larger column under General Burgoyne, already strategically poised at Fort Champly, would become the dagger that made the death thrust between the eastern and southern colonies. If that operation should succeed, there was reason to believe that the rebellion would be quickly put down, but Burgoyne pulled back to Canada for winter quarters after a heavily contested naval battle on Lake Champlain.

The invasion from the north was postponed by the audacity and sheer courage of Benedict Arnold and the brave souls who manned the gondolas, sloops, and schooners he had hastily built after retreating from Quebec. As we have seen, Stark was also an important part of that retreat and ended up fortifying Mount Independence while Arnold built the fleet of vessels he commanded. Crucial time was purchased by the suicidal attack of Arnold's small flotilla against heavy frigates of the Royal Navy.

During that summer of 1776, Arnold and his intrepid crew of militia volunteers feverishly built eight gondolas and three row galleys: they already had a sloop in their possession. Arnold was an experienced sailing master and took his midget fleet north on Lake Champlain to oppose the British fleet then assembling at St. John's. He was well aware that his tiny under-armed vessels could not match the firepower of the British, so he selected a place to lay in wait for the British as they sailed south.

The first battle took place between Valcour Island and Plattsburgh, on the New York shore. Arnold took the British by surprise. Both sides exchanged shots and the battered remnants of Arnold's navy escaped to the south in a heavy fog bank at nighttime. The British fleet eventually caught up with them and took them under fire all the way to Crown Point.

Arnold realized that his tiny fleet was doomed, and burned the boats a short distance north of Crown Point now known as Arnold's Bay. The British continued to Crown Point and took it on October 14, 1776. They half-heartedly attempted to take Fort Ticonderoga, but the American garrison resisted. The British then left the area to go into winter quarters. The invasion of 1776 had been thwarted, but it was destined to begin with renewed vigor in the spring.[7]

While the British army was making preparations for the winter at Fort St. John's, Stark's regiment and several others were withdrawn from the northern army to reinforce General Washington at Newtown, Pennsylvania. At this point, Stark left his regiment for a short furlough home, arriving in Derryfield on November 5. Stark's few moments with his beloved Molly were well-deserved.

Without a doubt, Molly and the rest of the family had worked long hours during his absence just to maintain the house and farmland. Preparations for the cold winter months must have been difficult just in preparing enough firewood for the ravenous fireplaces in the large house. Most likely

Stark found his root cellars filled with potatoes, apples, pumpkins, and squash. Subsistence living was a way of life on the frontier and it tested the most industrious of settlers just to survive. Winter dominated their lives. Much of their time was spent getting ready for winter, surviving the cold months, and recuperating from the long difficult season, but it was the changing seasons which defined the hardy and resourceful New Englander.

Stark's regiment had marched two hundred miles from Ticonderoga through Albany to Newtown and reported to headquarters a few days prior to the battle for Trenton. They were reinforcing Washington's dejected Continental army, and Stark was again assigned to General Sullivan's division. Washington had called for a council of war. Stark attended and gave his opinion to those present. Caleb Stark reported:

> "In the council of war preceding the affair at Trenton, in giving his opinion Stark observed to General Washington 'your men have too long been accustomed to place their dependence for safety on spades and pick-axes. If you ever effect (expect?) to establish the independence of these states you must teach them to place their dependence upon their fire arms and their courage'. Washington replied 'that is what we have agreed upon—we are to march tomorrow upon Trenton—you are to command the right wing of our advanced guard and General Greene the left'. Stark observed that he could not be better suited."[8]

The battered ad hoc Continental army, under Washington, had suffered failure upon failure after the British evacuation of Boston. The war in the New York area had gone badly and cost the new army dearly in both supplies and men. The small army did not have enough punch to hold New York against the powerful, well-disciplined British regiments that General Howe fielded against it. Then there was the ever powerful and aggressive Royal Navy, commanded by General William Howe's brother, Admiral Richard Howe, lending artillery support to the army up and down the Atlantic coast.

The loss of Brooklyn, Long Island, and Fort Washington on the Hudson River and the defeat at White Plains had devastated the morale of the army and threatened its very existence. Confidence in Washington's ability was waning. There was a pervasive fear among the leaders of the independence movement that all was lost. The immediate future looked bleak and many questioned the wisdom of continuing their struggle.

The severity of the situation was understood by Washington, perhaps more than anyone else. He was desperately looking for that one victory over the redcoats that would boost sinking morale. Even the Continental Congress evacuated Philadelphia for fear that the British would capture the city. Americans needed some reassurance and Washington was about to give it to them.

The bold stroke had to come before the end of the year, which marked the expiration of many of the soldiers' enlistments, and they were going home. They faced a British army of twenty thousand troops in New Jersey. The time to strike was now, but it had to be a blow the army could deliver before the British formed a defensive line, which the Americans would not be able to overcome.

Trenton was a town composed of a handful of houses on the Delaware River. It was a communication center with a good network of roads to the upper reaches of the river: a forward position for the British army and garrisoned by three crack Hessian regiments that had proved their tenacity and brutality during previous campaigns. They were arrogant troops who plundered Tory and patriot homes alike. They had a low opinion of the rebels' fighting ability and refused to build redoubts on the approaches to Trenton, defying the rebels to face their bayonets.

10

Trenton and Princeton (1777)

General George Washington didn't underestimate the strength or ability of his opponent and planned an attack to hit Trenton with three prongs. Surprise and speed were a necessity before the dreaded Hessians could form their battle lines. The Continental regiments were led by Major General Nathanael Greene, a thirty-four-year-old Rhode Island man with a slight limp. He was to cross the Delaware at McKonkey's Ferry nine miles upstream of the town of Trenton. Washington considered Greene to be one of his most trusted officers, as he would prove to be, in subsequent battles to the south.

Major General John Sullivan, the New Hampshire lawyer and politician turned soldier, was assigned the right wing with Stark's regiment to attack in the vanguard position along River Road. Greene's division would form the left wing attack on a parallel road leading to the center of town. The combined strength of the two divisions was over twenty-four hundred men. The third prong was to be Brigadier General James Ewing's Pennsylvania and New Jersey militia regiments of about seven hundred strong. They were ordered to cross over the Delaware River south of Trenton and drive north to the center of town to secure the bridge over Assunpink Creek, a small stream that ran into the Delaware from the east. Their mission was to block any retreating enemy troops to the south.

On Christmas Day 1776, Sullivan's and Greene's divisions began assembling at McKonkey's Ferry under cover of darkness, prepared to cross the river. The Fourteenth Massachusetts Militia Regiment contained within its ranks many Marblehead fishermen who manned the boats used to ferry the troops, horses, and artillery across the ice-filled water. It was strenuous and hazardous work, but the regiment successfully completed the ferrying mission by three o'clock in the morning. It had taken a little longer than Washington had expected. Now they had to travel nine miles south over snow-crusted snow to Trenton in less than four hours. They were working against time.

The redoubtable colonel Henry Knox had arranged his artillery pieces in both divisions with the vanguard (four cannons), center (three cannons), and the rear (two cannons). The line of march was inland about a mile and a half to a landmark known as Bear's Tavern, where they turned down River Road. After four and a half miles, Washington called a halt so that the men could rest and eat something.

After a short break, Washington arranged his two divisions as planned: Greene on Pennington Road to the north and Sullivan on River Road in the south. Washington rode with Greene's division. Strict silence was vigorously enforced at this point. Miller wrote:

"General John Sullivan's division was led by Colonel John Stark's 1st New Hampshire Regiment. Stark, 58, had fought valiantly at Bunker Hill, where he earned a reputation as an aggressive leader. His regiment of tough frontiersmen was probably the best in the Continental Army."[1]

Stark's orders were to push directly into the town as fast as possible before the Hessian troops had the opportunity to form a battle line. Dawn came at 7:23 as they were approaching the first enemy outpost.

The storm was still swirling and blowing snow, thus hindering visibility. A Hessian officer suddenly stepped out of the outpost and saw the Continentals and raised the alarm. The Hessians formed small lines and fired erratically at the Americans, retreating as they fired. Just three minutes after Greene's encounter with outpost pickets, they heard musketry from River Road, where Stark was rushing forward. The coordination of the attack had been near perfect despite the hardships. Washington had achieved surprise.

The outposts on River Road were at a country house called the Hermitage, with about fifty troops stationed there. Stark's men quickly scattered the outpost pickets and advanced on the Hermitage garrison, which was attempting to form a line. They saw Stark's New Hampshire men running toward them and scattered like raw recruits without firing a shot. British troopers in Trenton fled for Princeton as the Americans approached the town. The two-prong attack had succeeded in confusing the German mercenaries.

Knox's artillerymen began to fire on the open ground in the center of town. They had positioned their weapons at the junctions of roads so that they could fire down the streets, and be able to clear them in short order. The Hessians maintained a high rate of fire at the attacking Americans, but their marksmanship was faulty. So far, not an American had been killed. The Germans retreated to the open ground east of the village north of Assunpink Creek. Some artillery was repositioned to better bring it to bear on the open ground, where the Hessians were trying to organize their units. At that point, Greene's division pushed closer to the common with additional artillery.

The Hessians' position was hopeless and they knew it. Washington accepted their request for quarter and a great cheer rose from the Americans, echoing through the snow-swept air as the Hessians threw down their muskets. A few men, including Captain Baum, whom we will meet again at the outskirts of Bennington, Vermont, were able to slip away to Princeton to warn the British of their humiliating defeat. General Ewing's division failed to make contact from the south in time to prevent several hundred Hessian soldiers from escaping over the stone bridge in the center of town.

It was an important victory and one badly needed by the Americans. They had defeated some of the finest European troops without the loss of a man: only two were wounded. The Hessians lost eight hundred and sixty-eight officers and men captured, and one hundred and one wounded or killed, all within an hour. News of the victory swept the nation and refueled their resolve to complete the mission.[2]

Lieutenant James Wilkinson, of Warner, was with Stark at Trenton and described the battle in his memoirs, mentioning the performance of James Monroe, a future president of the United States, and other officers.

"While I render justice to the services of Forest, Washington, and Monroe, I must not withhold due praise of the dauntless Stark, who dealt death wherever he found resistance, and broke down all opposition before him."[3]

The battle for Princeton was a direct result of the Trenton success. Washington was not interested in having a symbolic victory. His main goal was to drive the British out of New Jersey. On December 27, 1776, he and his troops crossed the Delaware at McKonkey's and returned to Newtown on the west bank of the river, where the men rested and ate. He had ordered General James Ewing on the southern flank during the battle, to occupy Trenton. A short time later, Washington recrossed the Delaware.

On New Year's Day, General Lord Charles Cornwallis, commander of all British troops in the north, marched to Princeton with a large body of troops. Six thousand to seven thousand British and German troops prepared to retake Trenton.

Washington called for a war council on the evening of the first. Some officers urged him to retreat to Pennsylvania. He refused and the discussion of tactics (what, when, and where) proved inconclusive. Events on the ground finally dictated the tactics. Cornwallis was attacking down the road to Trenton. His military tail was still in Princeton while the vanguard was six miles from Trenton. The advance surprised Washington and he sent a one thousand man brigade under a Colonel Charles Scott of Virginia to delay the column any way it could. Scott's brigade skirmished vigorously with the column using hit-and-run tactics, destroying bridges, and felling trees across the roadways. Washington rode out to encourage and assist Scott to retard the enemy until darkness so that he could withdraw the army. Skirmishing continued until six o'clock, when darkness ended any contact with opponents.

That night, Washington again called for a council of war. Cornwallis had already blocked the road to the north. Retreating to the south would only place them in areas more difficult to defend. A retreat across the Delaware, full of ice, was out of the question. Faced with such undesirable alternatives, Washington proposed the bold move of leaving campfires burning and a small detachment behind to periodically fire at Trenton. He proposed they attack Cornwallis's army twelve miles in the rear and the small garrison left at Princeton so that they could pick up some badly needed supplies from the heavily stockpiled British military storehouse there.

Washington's six thousand men and thirty to forty cannons left their positions under the cover of darkness and marched up Quaker Road to approach Princeton from the east, an area the British had neglected to secure in the belief that they already had Washington and his army holed up with their back against the ice-clogged Delaware. They were planning a massive attack at first light to administer the final blow.

With fires burning briskly in their encampment, the colonials left the area with strict attention paid to silence. Wagon and artillery wheels were wrapped with cloth to deaden their sound on the frozen ground, and torches were forbidden. So far the ruse had worked and the vanguard had reached Stony Brook before sunrise.

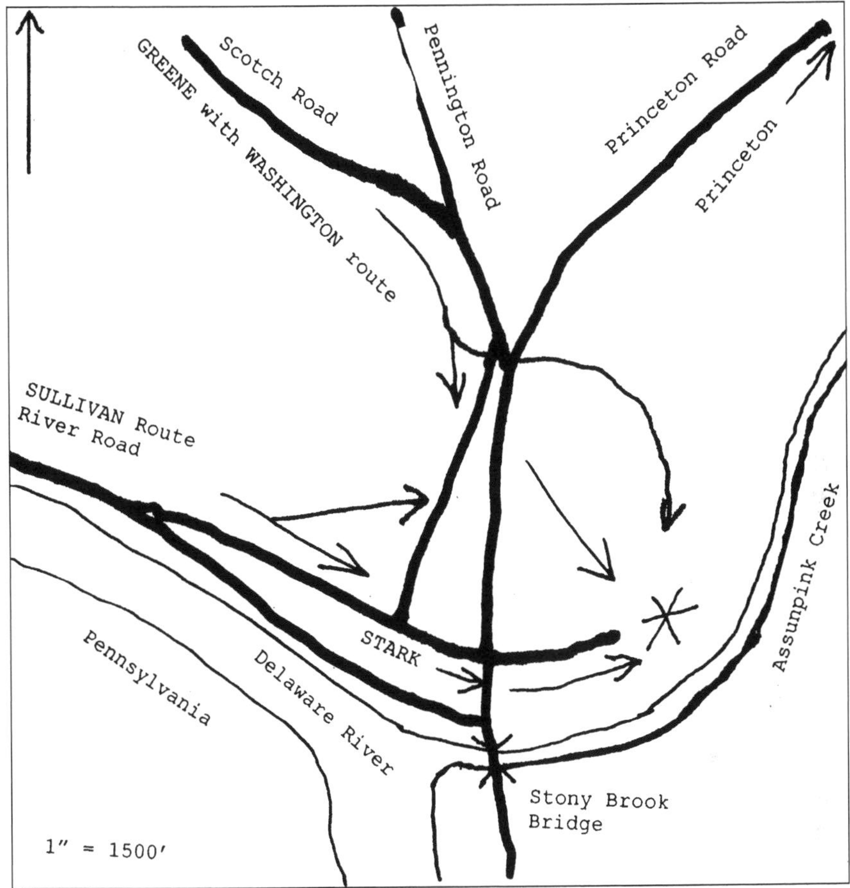

Battle of Trenton, December 26, 1776

They paused to regroup for the attack against Princeton. General Sullivan's division, composed of three brigades of New England Continentals, including Stark's First New Hampshire Regiment, turned to the northeast up Saw Mill Road, on the right flank. Greene continued north up Quaker Road, which led to the main highway Cornwallis used on his way to Trenton.

Brigadier Hugh Mercer's brigade led Greene's division and was the first to make contact with the enemy. The engagement took place in an open area around an orchard. Mercer's brigade of three men was severely mauled by concealed cannons in the orchard. He was one of the first to be killed. Pennsylvania militia under John Cadwalader quickly reinforced Mercer. The engagement was intense and the outcome was in doubt.

Washington had been with Sullivan's division and now rode to the orchard, scene of the heaviest fighting. His presence and courage under fire inspired his troops and they began to push the British troops back toward New Brunswick, leaving Princeton virtually undefended.

Sullivan's division advanced all the way to Princeton from the east, exerting pressure on two crack British regiments that shortly left Princeton. Sullivan continued through town. The troops were in a celebratory mood and paused to loot food, drink, clothing, and anything else of value. Washington, Greene, and Sullivan soon instilled order so that they could evacuate to the north. They arrived, at Morristown where they took up strong positions on the heights and prepared for winter quarters.[4]

The Americans had faced three regular British regiments and driven them from the field in hurried flight. General Sullivan had this to say after the operation, when there was friendly banter about the difference between southern troops and New England troops:

> "I have been much pleased to See a Day approaching to try the Difference between yankee Cowardice & Southern valor . . . The Day has or Rather the Days have arrived and all The General officers allowed & do allow that yankee Cowardice assumes the shape of True valor in the field & The Southern valor appears to be a Composition of Boasting and Conceit . . . General Washington made no scruple to say publicly that the Remains of the Eastern Regiments were the strength of his army though their numbers were Comparatively Speaking but Small . . . He calls them in front when the Enemy are there—he Sends them to the Rear when the Enemy Threaten that Way."[5]

The battle of Princeton was a direct result of the battle for Trenton. John Stark's contribution to the victory at Princeton is unknown, although we do know that he served as a brigade commander in both operations; therefore, he shares in their success and was partially responsible for the renewed hope that victory was possible. Trenton and Princeton were the only engagements in which Stark served with General Washington.

Prior to the battle for Trenton, the entire officer corps was faced with the fact that its army was shrinking by alarming numbers, from desertions and from the expiration of enlistments. Stark approached the men in his command in a straight-forward manner about the seriousness of the situation. He thanked them for their brave deeds at Bunker Hill and in other engagements with the enemy. He promised them that if Congress did not grant them their wages so long in arrears, he would pay them by selling off some of his own property. He proposed that they enlist for another six weeks before retiring home or to winter quarters.

It is a credit to Stark that in the veteran regiments under his command, every man reenlisted for the six weeks requested. The act exemplified their trust in his word. One of Stark's veterans elaborated on the reenlistment episode in 1822 when Stark was buried:

> "Here it may be proper to note a circumstance, not generally understood, the particulars of which were related at the funeral of the deceased general by a comrade in arms there present. It is well known that previous to this important action the American army was upon the point of being broken up, by suffering and desertion and the expiration of the terms of enlistment of a great portion of the troops. A few days previous the terms of the New Hampshire regiments expiring; Stark was the first to propose an enlistment for six weeks; He left his station as commander for the moment, took upon himself the task of a recruiting officer and not a man failed to enlist."[6]

After giving sterling performances as an officer in the service of his country, Stark was faced with one of the most discouraging periods of his life. No colonel in the army had earned the privilege of being promoted to the rank of brigadier general any more than had Stark. His dedication to the cause and his skill and courage on the battlefield elevated him to a position of merit when others had been less inclined. He was passed over for reasons that were not made public. No one knows why, but political expediency probably had more to do with the decision than his record in the field. His blunt and sometimes hasty comments and his propensity to speak the truth as he saw it did not sit well within certain social and political circles. His disdain for what he always called the "Exeter crowd" was common knowledge. The politicians probably got even by deleting him from the promotion list.

The rank of brigadier general was given to Enoch Poor, commander of the Third New Hampshire Regiment, who stayed in New Hampshire during the siege of Boston and Bunker Hill. Several other officers were promoted, including the nineteen-year-old Marquis de Lafayette, to major general. These men had no military experience but did have social and political connections. Two other fine officers with proven records of achievement were also passed over at the same time—the very able Henry

Knox and Nathanael Greene, an ex-Quaker who became one of Washington's most trusted officers. They too threatened to resign rather than accept the insult in silence. Stark, however, was the only one actually to resign from the army.

Stark had accompanied Washington's army to Morristown, then left for New Hampshire to recruit another regiment, as the enlistment of his old regiment had expired. In March 1777, Stark traveled to Exeter for instructions to take the new regiment on the campaign trail. There he learned what Congress had done. His unbending character seemed to be a barrier to promotion, yet that single virtue also defined him as one of the most successful combat commanders of the Revolutionary War. He respectfully wished Generals Sullivan and Poor success, and described the dangerous situation at Fort Ticonderoga and the importance of its reinforcement. He then said, "[A]n officer who would not maintain his rank, was unworthy to serve his country."[7]

Stark's formal resignation before the New Hampshire Court took place on March 22, 1777:

"Gentlemen—Ever since hostilities commenced, I have as far as in me lay Endeavored to prevent my country from being ravaged and Enslaved by our cruel and unnatural enemies, have undergone Hardships and fatigues of two campaigns with cheerfulness and alacrity, ever enjoying the pleasing satisfaction that I was doing my God and Country the greatest service my abilities would permit of & it was with the utmost Gratitude that I accepted the important command which this State appointed me, I should have served with the greatest pleasure; more especially at this important crisis when our Country calls for the utmost Exertions of every American, but am extremely grieved that I am bound on Honour to leave the service, Congress having tho't fit to promote Junr officers over my head; so that lest I should show myself unworthy of the Honour conferred on me & a want of that spirit which ought to glow in the Breast of Every officer appointed by this Honorable House, in not suitable resenting an Indignity, I must (though grieved to leave the service of my Country) beg leave to resign my Commission hoping that you will make a choice of some Gentlemen who may Honour the Cause & his Country to succeed.

Your Most Obedient and obliged Humble Servt

John Stark"[8]

The legislature accepted his resignation and passed the following resolve:

"*Voted,* That the thanks of both Houses, in convention, be given to Colonel John Stark for his good services in the present war; and that, from this early and steadfast attachment to the cause of his country, they make not the least doubt that his future conduct, in whatever state of life providence may place him. Will manifest the same noble disposition of mind." [9]

With the complimentary resolution still ringing in his ears, Stark returned home to Derryfield, probably a bitter man. The state court had been generous with its praise but it had no jurisdiction over national matters conducted by the Continental Congress, and therefore could do nothing about the situation. Later in life, (1810) Stark told historian Benjamin Stickney about the situation. Stickney wrote:

"At the close of the campaign Stark returned to New Hampshire upon parole. On his arrival he ascertained the truth of a report he had heard before he left the army, viz; that Congress had degraded him by the appointment of Col. Poor as a Brigadier. He went immediately to Exeter where the Legislature was then sitting and asked for a resignation. They endeavored to persuade him to withdraw his request, but in vain. He told them that an officer who would not stand for his rank would not stand for his country. However, he engaged that in case attack was made upon New Hampshire, he should hold himself in readiness for its defence. He informed them of the dangerous situation of Ticonderoga and retired to his farm as a private citizen."[10]

The command of the First New Hampshire Regiment was given to Colonel Joseph Cilley, a native of Nottingham, New Hampshire. He had been active on the Committee of Safety when the powder and military stores were taken from Fort William and Mary in New Castle. John Stark's son Caleb became Cilley's adjutant general.

March in New Hampshire is when winter releases its grip upon the land and the promise of spring is just around the corner. Muddy roads and high water in the streams and lakes make outside chores difficult, if not impossible. Maintenance of Stark's sawmill machinery and farm implements was an everyday chore. If he had any fruit trees on his land, spring was a good time to prune them. Being right on the river, Stark probably supplemented the family diet with fish year-round. He was entitled to spend some time with his family, especially his beloved Molly, who enriched his life with her love and steadfast companionship. But the call of distant drums was on the horizon.

11

Loss of Fort Ticonderoga (July 1777)

From the very early days of the American Revolution, emissaries were sent to France to try to engage the French in their fight for independence. Silas Deane, a Connecticut delegate to the Continental Congress, was one of these agents. The French were still feeling the sting of defeat from the Seven Years War and officially remained uncommitted to the solicitations for aid and assistance.

There was one prominent French businessman, Monsieur Beaumarchais, who extended credit to the young colonies in the form of twenty thousand muskets and a thousand barrels of powder of one hundred pounds each. Deane and others had stressed the need for aid without delay, so the arms and powder were sent in two shipments, one to the southern states and one to Portsmouth, New Hampshire.

The guns were shipped from Portsmouth to Fort Ticonderoga, a Mohawk word meaning "between two great rivers," to equip the soldiers manning the fortress and to other outposts in the Northern Department. There was a chronic scarcity of shoulder weapons during the first years of the war. The French muskets stimulated local manufacture of firearms by providing parts from broken or damaged weapons. Officers were quick to instruct the soldiers in the proper use of the new weapons, which were not very different from the Brown Bess models used by the British army. When Fort Ticonderoga was evacuated, the soldiers took their French muskets with them, and they played a significant role in the battles that led up to and included the battle at Saratoga, the turning point of the war for independence.[1]

Spring 1777 was a period of uncertainty and despair. The Americans were in danger of losing the war. Battle after battle except for Princeton and Trenton, was lost to the British. Those victories temporarily helped to revive and sustain the fervor, but more were needed. At times military leaders and political administrators were floundering as they gained experience in how to conduct a major war before it was lost. The inability to pay troops, and the lack of every imaginable piece of equipment, medical supplies, arms, powder, uniforms, and food plagued them to the end. Disaster was always just over the horizon.

During this period, John Stark was busy taking care of the family farm and keeping himself informed about how the war was progressing. On March 24 he wrote a letter to the New Hampshire House and Council to recommend his son Caleb and a Mr. Cogan:

> "This moment I received a letter from Major Reid which I enclose to your Honour to inform you of affairs. I am sensible that the men that are gone are not provided with sufficient arms—would be glad that you would procure the same for them. Likewise for the Companies that are raising in the West part of the state, as it will be a detriment to the officers to go to Exeter for arms and Blankets as several of them are not able to supply themselves. As for further particulars of the Majors letter concerning his march, I leave to your Honours best judgment. I likewise would inform your Honours that I expect Caleb Stark & Mr. Cogan will not be set aside on acct. of my misfortune. If that should happen I beg that you would let me know so that they may not be disappointed."[2]

Young Caleb Stark received his appointment as adjutant to his father's old regiment, the First New Hampshire, then commanded by Colonel Joseph Cilley, and was sent to Fort Ticonderoga as part of the Northern Department under General Philip Schuyler. Efforts were made to strengthen the fortress, which was crucial to the defense of the colonies.

John Stark continued to believe in the righteousness of the American cause even though he was saddened and discouraged by the significant role played by politics in the pursuit of the war effort. Politics had always offended his independent and straightforward way of doing things. Once he was back on the farm, he promptly outfitted those workers and family members who were capable of bearing arms and sent them off to join the army.

The farm and his sawmills demanded more of his time and energy than he was able to assign to the chores. Spring planting was an important part of the year. Crops could not be harvested for the winter if they were not properly seeded. However, farm and home affairs were pushed aside as secondary to the more important mission of securing for his country independence and freedom from oppression. Stark had already established his priorities when he first heard of the fight at Lexington and Concord. They were still in place, and how grateful the nation should be that he was available when that call to serve came one more time. He was the right man at the right place at the right time.

Fort Ticonderoga became an important symbol of American resistance as well as a strategic landmark during the spring and summer campaign of 1777. Its garrison included almost all of the manpower assigned to the Northern Department. It was an important communication center and provided a reassuring presence of strength sufficient to oppose any advance originating in Canada. The fort had been strengthened to defend against such an attack from the north by fortifying the ridges facing that threat.

During the late winter and early spring of 1777, the American garrison at the fort had built a wooden bridge across a narrow stretch of land between the fort and Mount Independence on the Vermont eastern shore. Approximately twenty-five hundred troops labored on the structure described by modern engineers as a marvel of eighteenth-century engineering.

Thousands of large old-growth white pine trees were cut and skidded to the site during March and April. Then they were notched together similar to the way children's Lincoln Logs are today. Large rectangular caissons (twenty-two in total) were assembled, filled with rocks, and sunk in holes chopped in the ice. Some of the caissons were fifty feet high in order to reach to the surface of the lake. Then the caissons were joined together by a deck, which allowed traffic to and from Mount Independence. When the British occupied the fort, they destroyed the bridge. The caissons remain in place under the water to this day.[3]

To those who defended Fort Ticonderoga that spring, it was never a question of whether the British would attack them: it was simply a question of when. Preparations for that event had been taking place at a feverish pace and many honestly believed that they could hold off a serious attack by General John Burgoyne. Often called the Gibraltar of the North, the fort had played a significant role during the French and Indian War. After all, the French had defeated a superior British force under General Abercromby in July 1758 when John Stark was a participant. Perhaps the Americans were too complacent behind the thick granite bastions . . .

On May 6, 1777, Lieutenant General John Burgoyne had assumed the command of all British forces in Canada, which included German mercenaries and Canadian militia units. He had previously served as second in command to Lieutenant General Sir Guy Carleton, whom Lord George Germain, Secretary of State for the colonies, disliked. Many veterans believed Carleton to be a better choice because of his knowledge of the local military situation. Burgoyne was a debonair, colorful, and ambitious officer who was well liked by his subordinates. His nickname, "Gentleman Johnny," speaks of his popularity.

Burgoyne developed a strategy not unlike the one Carleton had prepared the year before and that used earlier by Marquis de Montcalm. In its simplest form, the plan called for his Canadian, British, and German forces to push through to Albany as quickly as possible, in order to link up with a British force under the command of Colonel Barry St. Leger, who was attacking down the Saint Lawrence River to Lake Ontario and then along the Mohawk River easterly toward Albany. The merger of Leger and Burgoyne at Albany would provide the power necessary to drive down the Hudson River Valley to meet General Sir William Howe's force in New York.

Once New York and New England were isolated from the rest of the country, the British could destroy the rebellious elements one at a time with the assistance of the massive Royal Navy presence on the coast under General Howe's brother, Admiral Lord Richard Howe.

General Burgoyne's army contained more than seven thousand men as it left Montreal in early June 1777. By the thirteenth they were at St. John's ready to enter Lake Champlain. By July 13 they had abandoned their staging area at Bouquet River and climbed into their newly constructed bateaus for an assault on Fort Ticonderoga. Burgoyne's British brigade rowed down the western shore of the lake while the two German brigades, under Major General Frederick Adolph von Riedesel, sailed south on the eastern side of the lake. In the center of the two land formations were twenty-four British gunships of various sizes, including two tall-mast ships. It was a powerful force capable of delivering a crippling blow to anything blocking its path.

The American garrison had fortified the rocky cliffs of Mount Independence above the water channel across from the fort. The narrow stretch of water between the fort and Mount Independence was blocked with heavy timbers bolted and chained together to control the traffic on the water. It was located just north of the wooden bridge. The twenty-five hundred man force at the fort was commanded by Major General Arthur St. Clair, a former British army officer who was still relatively uncertain about Burgoyne's movements. Indian allies of the British had formed a strong ring around the fort. restricting St. Clair's ability to scout the intentions of the enemy. He wrote to his superior, Major General Philip Schuyler, commander of the Northern Department: "No army was ever in a more critical situation than we now are . . ."[4]

On July 1, the British advanced to within three miles of the fort before landing their troops on both shores. They silently made camp for the night while Burgoyne took note of the situation and formulated his plans to trap the Americans and cut off their path of retreat. The next morning, Mount Hope, a prominent hill northwest of the fort, was captured by British troops to eliminate that route of retreat for the garrison troops. Riedesel on the eastern shore, bypassed Mount Independence to block the road leading south toward Hubbardton, Vermont. They would contain any troops trying to retreat and prevent any relief forces from reaching the fort from the east or south.

By midday, Mount Hope had fallen to the British after a stiff resistance, possibly from the new French muskets sent earlier from Portsmouth. The Americans retreated to the old French lines to the northwest, making a difficult escape to Lake George their only salvation. Burgoyne now planned a siege of the fort and ordered his cannons forward. The Americans were already firing their cannons at British targets of opportunity.

One of Burgoyne's subordinates, General Simon Fraser, in surveying the situation, noticed a weakness in the American defenses—Mount Defiance, a hill about one mile northwest of the fort. Fraser believed it held the key to securing Mount Independence, which was a formidable stronghold thanks to John Stark's vision and labor a year earlier. An engineering officer determined that a road could be constructed to the top of Mount Defiance, which had a commanding overview of Mount Independence and the fort.

Major General William Phillips, an experienced artillery officer, told his men: "Where a goat can go, a man can go and where a man can go, he can drag a gun."[5]

Thus, two twelve-pounders were successfully wrestled to the summit and dug into position. Indian allies of the Canadians and British had been the first to climb Mount Defiance. At the summit they had built a fire, which was spotted by the Americans. St. Clair, correctly, became concerned for the safety of his army. He knew that the British could effectively pound the inhabitants of the fort into submission without losing a single soldier, and there was nothing he could do about it except to abandon the fort and save as many men as he could to fight another day.

On the eastern shore, the German troops were having a difficult time traversing the swampy ground south of Mount Independence. They had not completely blocked the so-called Great Road leading south to Hubbardton and Castle Town. A water route, South Bay, to Skenesborough was also still open. St. Clair sent his wounded men and supplies by water to Skenesborough while the main body of troops would regress overland to Hubbardton, Castle Town, and then to Skenesborough, where he planned to join the wounded men and supplies arriving by boat. Together they could travel along Wood Creek, towards Fort Edwards thirty-five miles south on the Hudson River.

The retreat was a hasty affair, but St. Clair was doing his best to maintain order among his dispirited troops. He placed the militia in the middle of the column, between the Continental troops, hoping it would restrain them from abandoning their units to go home.

The British knew that something was happening and quickly made their way across the wooden bridge between the fort and Mount Independence. There they found a cannon loaded with grapeshot and aimed down the bridge at the crossing troops. The rebels had gotten drunk and were lying on the ground, passed out, as the British troops stepped over their bodies.

By then it was evident that the Americans had abandoned the fort and were well on their way south along Great Road. St. Clair reached Hubbardston, a collection of nine houses, by one o'clock. His army was exhausted and stopped to rest, even though the British were in hot pursuit. They were about twenty miles from Ticonderoga, and St. Clair was anxious to leave the area with the main column. He left Colonel Seth Warner to stay at Hubbardston until the rear guard, the Second New Hampshire Regiment, arrived, ordering Warner to take charge. Three hours later, the

Second arrived and followed the main body of troops to Castle Town, where Warner stopped about a mile and a half from the village center.

In the meantime, Burgoyne had dispatched General Fraser after the fleeing rebels to pursue them to the point of exhaustion. The men had not eaten all day and butchered two bulls they found in the area where they had paused to rest. While they were eating, General Riedesel entered Fraser's camp to announce that Burgoyne had ordered him to support Fraser's brigade. It was agreed then that Fraser would proceed another three miles down the road while Riedsel's troops rested for the night. The plan was that by three in the morning, Fraser would attack the rebel column and the German brigade would move in to aid in the assault.

On July 7, gunfire erupted as the American pickets fired at Indian scouts. Fraser's brigade was slightly behind the scouts. They informed Fraser that a large encampment of Americans was just over a sloping knoll known as Sargent Hill. He formulated a plan of attack with two companies moving straight against the main rebel camp, a flanking force of ten companies and another ten companies of grenadiers being held in reserve.

Warner's and Colonel Francis's men had formed a column along the road to Castle Town. The weather was hot and sultry with clouds of black flies and mosquitoes drawing blood. The majority of the Second New Hampshire was forming up to continue the march. Captain Carr's company of the Second New Hampshire were still cooking breakfast when someone hollered that the enemy was upon them. The New Hampshire militiamen put up a stout and determined defense, but their position was overrun.

Warner and Francis ordered their men behind a stone wall on the top of Monument Hill, a reasonably strong position. The balance of the Second New Hampshire placed themselves on the right flank, where they repulsed a determined British charge with repeated deadly volleys that riddled the British lines. Fraser quickly brought up his reserves and swung around to the American left flank. The Americans recognized their perilous position and began to fall back to the east of the roadway, where they tried to turn the British left flank. Volley upon volley were fired by the Americans. The fight turned out to be a free-for-all with little time or opportunity to maneuver for superior position. Both sides were strafed with musket fire.

St. Clair could hear the rattle of musketry in the distance behind him, and he immediately dispatched two officers to Ransomville, to the south, and ordered the militia regiments there to reinforce Warner's troops. St. Clair had no idea what was taking place, and those at the heart of the battle knew just as little. The firing on both sides was intense and deadly. Many German soldiers imagined that they were fighting two thousand rebels. At the most, however, there were only twelve hundred Americans in the column, many of them sick and wounded.

The turning point came when the renewed attack of combined British and Hessian troops killed Francis. American militia resistance disintegrated, and many ran for the relative safety of the nearby forest. The battle had lasted less than an hour. The British casualties were approximately two hundred killed and wounded and the Americans suffered three hundred and ninety, killed, wounded or taken prisoner.

While the battle at Hubbardton raged on, the wounded men escaping from Fort Ticonderoga were carefully picking their way in bateaus toward Skenesborough, confident that the heavy chain across the narrow portion of Lake Champlain would prevent the British flotilla from pursuing them. That confidence was misplaced. The large guns on the ships quickly blasted the log chain into tiny slivers, allowing them to continue on to Skenesborough without a pause. By three in the afternoon they were a few miles from the town. They landed British troops on the eastern shore to cross over a small stream called Wood Creek that flowed past Fort Anne.

The exhausted and wounded survivors were surprised when the British opened fire on the American bateaus filled with precious supplies and sick and wounded men. It rapidly became a scene of unmerciful horror and destruction. The surviving men successfully avoided the British and burned Fort Anne as they trudged sixteen miles to Fort Edward, where St. Clair was assembling his straggling army as they came out of the jaws of death.

Fort Ticonderoga proved to be an easy capture for the powerful army General Burgoyne had assembled. Now they were poised at the southern end of Lake Champlain, master of all they surveyed. The defeat generated fear among the civilian population that they were about to be slaughtered. The Gibraltar of the North was not invincible. Now, victory seemed to be within the grasp of the British forces. Once General Burgoyne rendezvoused with General Howe on the Hudson River, the outcome of the civil war would not be in doubt.

12

Vermont Requests Assistance (July 1777)

The presence of Burgoyne's army at Fort Ticonderoga sent shock waves through the colonies, especially the newly established state of Vermont, which now occupies much of what was formerly known as the New Hampshire Grants. The American forces who evacuated the fort were fleeing to the south toward Fort Edward. Trading their muskets for axes, the Americans began a routine of cutting trees to block roads, trails, and streams. Bridges were destroyed and warnings sent out to nearby settlers to leave or at least to hide their livestock from the approaching British and German troops. Panic was in the air and there were too few forces available to stop the enemy.

The loss of Fort Ticonderoga triggered a traumatic number of desertions from militia groups that had the potential to enable General Burgoyne to continue his advance to the south with little or no resistance. The militia desertions came as the men's enlistments reached the end. On that day they left their units in droves. Whole units suddenly disappeared regardless of the efforts of concerned officers who tried to deter them. Militia units from Connecticut, Massachusetts, New Hampshire (General Enoch Poor's regiment), and New York all experienced the same thing. The men had lost confidence in their usefulness and in their officers. The chronic lack of supplies, food, medicines, and clothing to maintain some degree of health and stamina added to the feeling that their presence was not contributing to success. Their daily existence was almost unbearable, and it was difficult to blame them for leaving for their homes and families, who needed them at this crucial time of year to harvest crops and prepare for the long winter ahead.

Burgoyne remained at Skenesborough for two weeks. His rapid advance from St. John's had strained his supply line, which was now at the very end of a tenuous logistic chain. He was short of everything, including gunpowder and food. Burgoyne sent a warning to the outlying communities:

"Proclamation

To the inhabitants of Castleton, Hubbardton, Rutland, Tinmouth, Pawlet, Wells, and Granville, with the neighboring districts; also the districts bordering on White Creek, Cambden, Cambridge, &c.

"You are hereby directed to send from your several townships, deputies, consisting of ten persons or more, from each township, to meet Colonel Skene, at Castleton, on Monday, July 15, at 10 O'clock in the morning, who will have instructions not only to give further encouragement to those who complied with my late manifesto, but also to communicate conditions upon which the persons and property of the disobedient may yet be spared. This fail not to obey, under pain of military execution.

Head Quarters, at Skenesborough House, July 10, 1777.

J. Burgoyne.

By order of His Excellency, the Lieutenant General –

B. Kimpton, *Secretary.*"[1]

Burgoyne had promised vengeance, devastation, famine, and horror in an earlier proclamation issued on June 23.[2] The threat of a scorched earth policy instantly generated a countermeasure from Phylip Schuyler, major general in the Army of the United States of America, and Commander-in-Chief of the Northern Department.

"To the inhabitants of Castleton, Hubbardton, Rutland, Tinmouth, Paulet, Wells, Granville, with the neighboring districts bordering on White Creek, Cambden, Cambridge. &c., &c.

"Whereas, Lieutenant General John Burgoyne, commanding an army of the British troops, did, by a written paper, by him subscribed, bearing date at Skenesborough House, on the 10th day of July, instant, require you to send from your several townships, deputations consisting of ten persons or more from each township, to meet Colonel Skene at Castleton, on Wednesday, July 15th, at ten in the morning, for sundry purposes in said paper mentioned; and that you were not to fail in paying obedience thereto, under pain of military execution.

"Whatever, my countrymen, may be the ostensible reasons for such meeting, it is evidently intended by the enemy, then to prevail on you, by threats and promises, to forsake the cause of your injured country; to assist them in forcing on the United States of America, and under the specious pretext of affording you protection, to bring on you that misery which promises of protection drew on such of the deluded inhabitants of new-Jersey who were weak enough to confide in them. But who experienced their fallacy by being treated indiscriminately with those virtuous citizens, who came forth in defence of their country, with the most wanton barbarity, and such as hitherto hath not even disgraced barbarism. The cruelly butchered, without distinction, to age or sex; ravished children from ten, to women of eighty years of age; they burnt, pillaged and destroyed whatever came into their power. Nor did these edifices dedicated to the worship of Almighty God escape their sacrilegious fury. Such were the deeds—such were incontestibly proved to be which have marked the British arms with the most indelible stains.

"But they having, by the blessing of divine providence on our arms, been obliged totally to abandon that state they left those who were weak or wicked enough to take protection under them, to bemoan their credulity, and to cast themselves on the mercy of their injured countrymen. Such will be your fate, if you lend a willing ear to their promises, which I trust none of you will do. But lest any of you should so far forget the duty you owe to your country as to join with, or in any manner assist or give comfort to, or hold correspondence with, or take protection from the enemy: be it known to each and every one of you, the inhabitants of said townships, or any other, the inhabitants of the United States, that you will be considered and dealt with as traitors to said states; and that the laws thereof will be put in execution against every person, so offending, with the utmost rigor; and do hereby strictly enjoin and command all officers, civil and military, to apprehend , all such offenders. And I do enjoin much of the militia of said townships as have not yet marched, to do so without delay, to join the army under my command or some detachment thereof.

"Given under my hand and seal, at head quarters.

Philip Schuyler

Fort Edward, July 13, 1777.

By the general's command, Henry B. Livingston"[3]

Vermont had just recently been given the status of a state, and was still in the early stages of organizing its government; consequently, it was unable to defend itself against the sudden appearance of superior enemy forces at its western doorstep. On July 15, 1777, Vermont requested immediate and effective assistance from Massachusetts and New Hampshire:

"*Gentlemen*—This state, in particular, seems to be at present the object of destruction. By the surrender of the fortress of Ticonderoga, a communication is opened to the defenceless inhabitants on the frontier, who, having little more in store at present than sufficient for the maintenance of their respective families, and not ability immediately to remove their effects, are therefore induced to accept such protections as are offered them by the enemy.

"By this means, those towns who are most contiguous to them are under the necessity of taking such protection, by which the next town or towns become equally a frontier as the former towns before such protection; and unless we can have assistance of our *friends*, so as to put it immediately in our power to make a sufficient stand against such strength as they may send, it appears that it will soon be out of the power of this State to maintain its territory.

"This country, notwithstanding its infancy, seems to be as well supplied with provisions for victualing an army as any on the continent; so that, on that account, we can not see why a stand may not as well be made in this State as in Massachusetts; and more especially, as the inhabitants are heartily disposed to defend their liberties.

"You, gentlemen, will be at once sensible that every such town as accepts protection is rendered, at that instant, incapable of affording any further assistance; and what is infinitely worse, as some disaffected persons eternally lurk in almost every inhabited town, such become doubly fortified to injure their country, our good disposition to defend ourselves and make a frontier for your State, with our own, which can not be carried into execution without your assistance.

"Should you send immediate assistance, we can help you; and should you neglect till we are put to the necessity of taking protection, you know it is in a moment out of our power to assist you.

"Your laying these circumstances together will, I hope, induce your honors to take the same into consideration, and immediately send us your determination in the premises.

"I have the satisfaction to be your honors' most obedient and very humble servant. By order of the Council,

Ira Allen, *Secretary.*"[4]

New Hampshire was quick to recognize the urgency of Vermont's request, and immediately began implementation of a plan to send troops to defend the western frontier. The people of New Hampshire were in a difficult position. They had to defend their coastal region against British naval forces and they had sent troops out of state to serve in the Continental Army. Their western and northern frontier borders required additional resources too. In June 1777, a company of rangers under the command of Captain Timothy Bedell was raised and sent into the field to protect the Connecticut River frontier. New Hampshire's contribution to the independence of the nation was equal to or greater than that of the other colonies.

John Langdon, one of Portsmouth's most influential citizens, rose to the challenge. The New Hampshire assembly could either yield to the enemy or stand up to them. The assembly realized that Seth Warner probably had only one hundred and fifty men to hold off Burgoyne's army. Never one to avoid a fight, Langdon, the presiding officer of the New Hampshire Assembly at Exeter, and he proved himself a true patriot in every sense of the word when he addressed the assembly on July 18 with these inspiring words:

"I have a thousand dollars in hard money; I will pledge my plate for three thousand more. I have seventy hogsheads of Tobago rum, which will be sold for the most they will bring. They are at the service of the state. If we succeed in defending our firesides and our homes I may be remunerated; if we do not then the property will be of no value to me. Our friend, John Stark who so nobly maintained the honor of our state at Bunker Hill, may safely be entrusted with the honor of the enterprise and we will check the progress of Burgoyne."[5]

The New Hampshire Assembly sent a message to fetch Stark, and he immediately returned with the courier to accept the proposal, provided they give him command of a brigade with full authority to direct operations as he perceived the situation. The assembly issued him the rank of brigadier general and invested in him all the powers he requested. Perhaps Stark's demand for complete control was a little unusual, but it reflected the hard fact that the New Hampshire people had lost confidence in the general officers who had lost Fort Ticonderoga. The main fear was that the contingent being raised would be countermanded by Continental Army generals to join General Washington's command. New Hampshire and

Vermont knew that their safety was threatened; Stark and the assembly displayed wisdom, courage, and common sense when they gave Stark "full powers" separate from Congressional authority. It turned out to be a remarkably sound decision that resulted in shortening of war, even if it did ruffle the feathers of a few pompous officers when Stark rigidly maintained his own counsel, which he did with grace and dignity.

On July 19, 1777, the day after Langdon's stirring speech, President Weare sent a letter to Stark:

"You are hereby required to repair to Charles Town No. 4 so as to be there by Thuirsday next to meet & confer with persons appointed by the Convention of the State of Vermont relative to the rout of the troops under your Command, their being supplied with provisions and future operations. And when the troops are collected at No. 4 you are to take the Command of them & march into the State of Vermont and there act in conjunction with the troops of that State or any other of the States or of the United States or separately as it shall appear Expedient to you for the protection of the People or the annoyance of the Enemy; and from time to time as occasion shall require, sent intelligence to the Genrl Assembly or Committee of Safety of your operations and the manovers of the enemy."[6]

On that same day, July 19, Meshech Weare, president of New Hampshire, also acknowledged Vermont's request by sending up to twelve regiments, to form into three battalions of militia with Brigadier General John Stark in command. The enlisting process was under way as Weare wrote to Ira Allen:

"[D]ependence is made that they will be supplied with provisions in your State; and I am to desire that your convention will send some proper persons to Number Four, by Thursday next to meet General Stark there, and advice him relative to the route and disposition of our troops: and to give him such information as you may then have relative to the maneuvers of the enemy."[7]

The zeal with which New Hampshire citizens honored Vermont's plea for assistance was exemplified by Langdon's instant response and noble offer. The men who enlisted for service were promised a month's pay in advance and travel money. One member of the assembly, Colonel Gordon Hutchins, soon after Langdon's speech, saddled his horse and rode hard to Rumford (Concord) before the close of a religious service at the old North Church. Inside, a Reverend Walker was preaching to the congregation when Hutchins walked up the aisle. The preacher asked him if he was the bearer of any message. Caleb Stark relates the conversation, beginning with Hutchins reply:

"General Burgoyne with his army is on his march to Albany. General Stark has offered to take the command of the New-Hampshire men, and if we all turn out we can cut off Burgoyne's march..." Reverend Walker said: "My hearers, those of you who are willing to go, had better leave at once." At which all of the men in the meeting house rose and went out; many immediately enlisted. The whole night was spent in preparation, and a company was ready to march next day. Phinehas Eastman said, "I can't go, for I have no shoes," . . . Samuel Thompson, a shoe maker, replied, "Don't be troubled about that, for you shall have a pair before morning," which was done.[8]

Shortly after Stark's acceptance, Seth Warner, the competent and brave Vermont soldier who had fought a brilliant rear-guard action after the abandonment of Fort Ticonderoga and a well-planned battle at Hubbardton, wrote from Manchester on July 24, 1777, to bring Stark up to date:

"*Dear Sir*—I learn, by express, from the council of safety and assembly of your State, dated the 19th instant, and directed to the council of this State, that it is expected that one fourth part of twelve regiments are to be immediately drafted, formed into three battalions, and put under your immediate command, and sent forthwith into this State, to oppose the ravages and coming forward of the enemy; and also to desire the convention of this State to send some person or persons to wait on you, at No. 4, this day to advise with you relative to the route and disposition your troops are to take, as also the present disposition and manoeuvres of the enemy.

"By Major Tyler and Captain Fitch I send you an extract of a letter from General Schuyler, relative to the situation of the enemy. And from what intelligence I have been able to collect since that date, I judge there is not less than 2,000 at different places in Castleton and Rutland, and a large number at Skenesborough; part of which are (by their motion) making preparations for a speedy movement toward this camp, which is at present so thinly inhabited that I can by no means be able to make a stand without assistance. It is, therefore, of the most pressing importance that your troops be forwarded to this place with as much expedition as possible. Provision will be made here for their subsistence, on their arrival. The council of safety of this State are present, and join me in urging the necessity of your speedy assistance.

I am, sir, your very humble servant,

Seth Warner"[9]

On July 30th Meshesh Weare sent word to Colonel Samuel Folsom to proceed to Fort Number Four to meet with Stark in order to determine the condition of the men and their supplies, which had been promised by Vermont. Some supplies had already been sent to the fort, and another shipment was on its way to Stark. It included forty-three bushels of salt, a thousand pounds of assorted sizes of musket balls, four hundred flints, and a cask of medicines. Tin kettles were unavailable and could not be sent. Folsom was ordered to deliver two hundred pounds to Stark for his use in case he needed the money for brigade expenses. Folsom was also ordered to talk with Mr. Grant and Colonel Hunt about the availability of military stores at Bennington and report back to the New Hampshire Assembly.[10]

Within a week after Stark agreed to take the command, he had twenty-five companies, almost fifteen hundred men signed up to serve, a remarkable accomplishment. The urgency of the situation also contributed to the high rate of enlistment. In one town thirty-six percent of the eligible male population had joined up. Collecting men was much easier than assembling the quantities of supplies such a formation needed in the field. Cannons, bullets, gunpowder, wagons, horses, tin kettles, medicines, and food, all proved to be in short supply. It was an old story that was being retold in every state, and it would continue until the end of the war.

Stark immediately sent two hundred men to Manchester, Vermont, in advance of the main body, to join Seth Warner's force. An additional three hundred men were promised on the next day to reinforce the command. They were fighting the battle of time and the clock was ticking.

Stark must have found the old Fort Number Four somewhat different from when he first passed through the stockade doors years past. Captain Phineas Stevens, the very popular commander of the fort during the French and Indian Wars, had been killed in Nova Scotia. After 1763, the inhabitants of Charlestown had torn down the fort using the boards and timbers to construct and improve their homes once the danger of Indian raiding parties had passed. All that was left now was the large meadow that ran from the fort proper to the Connecticut River and a few dilapidated outbuildings. The location was still an important jumping-off place for the western and northern frontiers. A steady flow of supply trains from New Hampshire destined for the Northern Department passed through Charlestown.

Stark wrote a letter to the New Hampshire Assembly from Charlestown, Number 4, on July 30, 1777:

"I received yours of the 22nd inst. With the inclosed informing me of the situation of the enemy and of our frontiers; but previous to your letter I had received an Express from Col. Warner informing me of their situation and I forwarded the 250 men to their relief on the 28th; I sent another detachment of this day and as fast as they come in I will send them. I expect to march myself to-morrow or next day; we are detained a good deal for want of Bullet molds as there is but one pair in town and the few Balls you sent goes but a little way in supplying the whole.

"I am afraid we shall meet difficulty in procuring Kettles and utensils to cook our victuals as the Troops has not brought any. If such articles can be procured I believe it would be of the utmost importance to the safety and welfare of the troops. I am informed this day by a man from Otter creek that the enemy has left Castletown and is gone to Skeensborough with an intent to march to Bennington but I rather think they do it by way of a faint to call the attention of General Schuyler from Fort Edward or to Fatigue the troops. There is four pieces of small cannon at this place that looks good but wants to be cleared out and put on Carriages; if you think proper I will order it done as there is people here that says they can do it; as there is but very little Rum in the Store here if some could be forwarded to us it would oblige us very much as there is none of that article in them parts where we are going. I inclose you a Copy of a letter I this moment received from Col. Williams and as you informed me when I saw you last that you had not received any account from any gentleman in the army since the desertion of Ticonderoga I liklewise inclose a copy of a letter from Mr. Coggan and by the best information is as near the truth as any you may receive. I have showed it to Col. Bellows and a number of other officers that was present and they say they could all sign it.

I am, Sirs, your Honours most Obedt humble servt

John Stark."

He added, "I would take it kind if the Brigade Major's Commission could be forwarded to me, as being present with me; his name is Stephen Peabody; likewise adjt. Edward Evans of Col. Stickney's Regt."[11]

Stark left Fort Number Four on the third of August and the next day was in Peru, Vermont, twenty-five miles away. When he arrived at Manchester, his brigade was on parade having been ordered to join Schuyler's Continental Army at Albany by Major General Benjamin Lincoln, a forty-four year old Massachusetts farmer who was liked and trusted by General Washington. Lincoln and Major General Benedict Arnold had been sent to strengthen Schuyler's Northern Department after hearing of the loss of Ticonderoga. Stark immediately demanded to know what was going on. Lincoln told him he was acting under orders from General Schuyler and had sent Stark's formation to march to the confluence of the Mohawk and Hudson Rivers. Stark instantly informed Lincoln that he was capable of commanding his own troops and that he could tell Schuyler his New Hampshire troops were his alone to command. He then handed Lincoln a copy of his commission. Stark had not been on good terms with Schuyler since his opposition to abandoning Crown Point a year earlier.

Captain Peter Clark, a farmer and justice of the peace from Lyndeboro, wrote to his wife describing how the orders Lincoln gave the brigade were quickly countermanded after Stark's arrival in Manchester. Lincoln was a heavy, two hundred and forty pound man, several years younger than Stark, with little combat experience, yet he outranked Stark.

Stark was warned by Lincoln that his refusal of Schuyler's orders was wrong, to which Stark replied that he was used to taking responsibility for his actions and would do so in the future, all in the cause of his country. He was there in answer to a request for assistance from Vermont he said and he intended to act on that mission. His intransigence was viewed by many as irresponsible and cantankerous at best. It is no wonder that Stark was furious that orders had been given to his command without his knowledge. It was a serious breach of military protocol and Lincoln was quick to see the error he had committed. He wrote to Schuyler that Stark was " . . . exceedingly soured and thinks he hath been neglected and hath not had justice done by him by Congress . . . he is determined not to join the Continental Army until Congress gives him his rank"[12]

Stark was resolute in his refusal to take orders from any officer in the Northern Department. The differences were not of Stark's making even though it was a crucial period of the war, when harmony among the differing factions should have prevailed. General Schuyler was wise enough and gracious enough to realize that Stark should not be mistreated and quickly ordered Lincoln to patch up their differences. Schuyler had not been aware of the unique status Stark was granted by the New Hampshire Congress.

The tiny community of Bennington was comprised of a meetinghouse and a dozen houses when Stark marched his men to the center of town. There he met with the Council of Safety, which strongly opposed the Continental army's order for him to join Schuyler, and Stark agreed that if his men departed, it would leave the people naked to the ravages of several hundred Indians that Burgoyne used as the vanguard of his army. The Vermonters were frontier people who had experienced the terrors of Indian raids for years, so it was only natural that they feared what might happen to them if left unprotected. Even if they were not molested, the enemy would be in a position to confiscate food, livestock, and any military stores. They were aware that Burgoyne was short of everything his army needed to conduct a long campaign in the field.

It must be remembered that Burgoyne was intent on using any measure at his disposal that would draw manpower and supplies away from the Continental army. His campaign of terror was an integral part of his overall strategy. Once he started south on Lake Champlain, the terror increased in intensity. He used the Six Nations of the Iroquois and supplemented them with British provincial regulars and notorious Tories such as the feared and despised father-son team of Walter and John Butler.

Lincoln soon left Bennington for Stillwater, on the west bank of the Hudson River. He met with Schuyler and probably convinced Schuyler that it would be wise to leave Stark alone and let him do his thing. The two officers came up with a scheme of maneuver whereby Lincoln would join Stark and Seth Warner with five hundred men, and a supply of desperately needed camp kettles and ammunition. They could link up with Warner then at Cambridge, just west of the New York-Vermont boundary, and from there mount an attack against Burgoyne's rear while he was stalled at Skenesborough. (It should be noted that the militia under Stark's command was essentially a task force enlisted for one month. There had been no time to train or organize them, yet, Stark was able to handle the men with apparent ease.)

Schuyler and Stark began communicating with each other on a more amicable basis. Stark laid out his plan to intercept and cut off supplies by removing livestock and stores beyond Burgoyne's reach. At the same time, he planned to attack and destroy any targets of opportunity such as foraging parties and scouting patrols. An attack against the main body of men was never an option. Schuyler was pleased with Stark's plan and was in the process of implementing it when Generals Burgoyne and Riedesel provided a diversion of their own!

When Washington sent Generals Arnold and Lincoln to aid Schuyler in the Northern Department, Arnold had gone to Fort Stanwix, on the Mohawk River, to help lift the siege taking place there. St. Clair's men from Ticonderoga had retreated south to join Schuyler's force at Fort Edward. After capturing Ticonderoga, Burgoyne decided to march on foot through Skenesborough to Fort Edward. He could have returned to Ticonderoga and mounted his troops and supplies into boats, safely floating down Lake George to the Hudson and Fort Edward with only a short portage. It was a major mistake that contributed to his surrender.

Fort George, on Lake George, contained a large supply depot Burgoyne could have used if he had selected that route to Fort Edward. The extensive swampland brought his progress to a crawl. A small legion of rebel axemen had traded their muskets for axes and felled trees and destroyed bridges hampering his way south. Three weeks later, on July 29th, Burgoyne reached Fort Edward as Schuyler retreated south to Stillwater on the Hudson. Burgoyne's men were exhausted by the time they arrived. Stark's rapid advance from Number Four to Manchester, a distance of fifty miles, was made at the same time as Burgoyne traveled the twenty-eight-miles from Skenesborough to Fort Edward.

Burgoyne anxiously checked the progress Lieutenant Colonel St. Barry Leger was making in the west along the Mohawk Valley. St. Leger had under his command a force of one thousand redcoats, Hessian mercenaries, and a mixture of Canadian and Tory troops. He had traveled from the Saint Lawrence River to Lake Ontario and landed at Oswego, on the New York shore. After a march to the southeast, he was near Fort Stanwix, which he had been told was lightly garrisoned by inexperienced militia troops. Instead, he found the fort had seven hundred and fifty New York Continental troops commanded by Colonel Peter Gansevoort, an able leader, who was determined to delay or stop Leger's rendezvous with Burgoyne regardless of the cost.

Foster and Streeter had this to say about the independent command:"Stark's independent command was in historic harmony with the unfortunate but inevitable conditions which he had to meet; with the task he had to perform, and with the characteristics of the man and his contemporaries. Personal dependence and self-assertiveness were the distinguishing characteristics of the frontiersman and Indian fighter and his troops whom he so aptly described as 'undisciplined free men'. . . "[13]

Statue of Major Caleb Stark located on the common at Dunbarton, New Hampshire. The plaque reads as follows: "In 1759, Major Caleb Stark, the first child of General John and Molly Stark, was born in Dunbarton at the home of his grandfather, now known as the Molly Stark House. At age 15, he left this house and his grandfather, Capt. Caleb Page, on the eve of the battle of Bunker Hill to join in the American Revolution. He represents Dunbarton's own minutemen and his likeness is embossed on the Town Seal. He was wounded at the Battle of Saratoga and, during the closing stages of the conflict, served as an adjutant to his famous father. After the war he married Sarah McKinstry and built the Stark Mansion where he entertained General Lafayette in 1825. He was tireless in his pursuit to arrange for payments for services of Revolutionary War officers and his efforts succeeded when lands in Ohio were granted as compensation. He died in Ohio in 1838 and is buried at the Stark Cemetery on Mansion Road in Dunbarton." Author's collection.

Above: General John Stark's gravesite in Stark Park, Manchester, New Hampshire. Author's collection.

Below: Stark home built in 1736 on the east bank of the Amoskeag Falls, Manchester, New Hampshire. The structure was moved to Elm Street, and is administered by the Molly Stark Chapter, Daughters of the American Revolution. Author's collection.

Above Statue of Brigadier General John Stark (1728-1822), Victor of the Battle of Bennington, 1777. "There they are boys! We beat them today or Molly Stark sleeps a widow tonight." Author's collection.

Below: Home of John and Molly Stark at the top of the hill, River Road, Manchester, New Hampshire. When they built their home most of the land was cleared and they had a beautiful view of the Uncanoonic Mountains to the west. The house was burned in 1858 by inmates after it was taken over by the State Industrial School. The DAR have placed a plaque at the site. The original well and front step is intact. Courtesy Manchester, New Hampshire Historical Association.

Molly Stark. Courtesy of the New Hampshire Historical Society.

Diorama of General John Stark at the Battle of Bennington. Courtesy of New Hampshire Historical Society.

Statue of John Stark at Stark Park, Manchester, New Hampshire. Courtesy New Hampshire Historical Society.

Portrait of General John Stark. Courtesy Manchester, New Hampshire Historical Association.

13

Fear on the Frontier (Summer 1777)

After the loss of Fort Ticonderoga, the Americans ran out of steam. Burgoyne had partially completed his strategy to fractionalize the colonies when he moved into Fort Edward, yet his army was desperately in need of supplies and horses. Washington had confided to his brother: "[T]he game is up. You can form no idea of the perplexity of my situation. No man, I believe, has a greater choice of difficulties than I, and no means to extricate himself."[1]

During the dark days of 1777, Thomas Paine wrote harshly of what he termed "Sunshine Patriots" who fought only when the situation suited them. "What we need is an American Joan of Arc."[2]

The Adirondack and Green Mountain frontier was the scene of an incident that immediately launched a rallying cry for Tories and Whigs alike. The spirited and beautiful Jane McCrea lived near Fort Edward. She had fallen in love with a neighbor, David Jones, who was a British officer in Burgoyne's army, and they had planned to marry. The two families had lived together in peace and friendship regardless of their different political ideologies.

David had written to Jane immediately after the American evacuation of Fort Ticonderoga:

"Dear Friend, I have the opportunity to send you this... hoping. . . it will come safe to hand. . . Since last writing, Ty [Fort Ticonderoga] has been taken, and we have had battle [at Hubbardton]. . . Through God's mercy I escaped destruction, and am well at this place, which thanks to Him. The rebels cannot recover from the blow [we] have struck and no doubt the war will end soon. . . Dear Jenny . . . In a few days we will march to Fort Edward, for which I am anxious, when I shall have the happiness to meet you, after a long absence. I hope if your brother John goes [to Albany], you will not go with him, but stay at Mrs. McNeil's . . . There I will join you."[3]

Jane frequently visited the cabin of Mrs. Sara McNeil, a stout, middle-aged Tory and a cousin of British General Simon Fraser, where she could receive news about her betrothed. By July 25 Fort Edward was rapidly being evacuated by both militia and Whigs. Jane secretly remained behind with Sara McNeil. Jane had been staying with her brother in order to be closer to the McNeils. Burgoyne, to his credit, had warned his Indian allies against any mistreatment of civilian or military personnel. His attempt to restrain them failed. On their march to Fort Edward, the Wyandots killed and scalped a family (the Allens) in a most brutal fashion. Lieutenant David Jones was alarmed when he heard of the outrage and ordered Chief Duluth, a Huron, to bring Jane and Sara McNeil to the British camp, where they would be safe from the bloodthirsty Wyandots under Chief LeLoup. Before the Christian Hurons could reach the McNeils' cabin, the painted Wyandots had already broken into the cabin and dragged Jane and Sara out of the storm cellar, in which they had been hiding. The captives were informed that they would be taken to the British camp, where they would meet General Fraser and Lieutenant Jones.

The capture of the women was witnessed by a rear guard of Continental soldiers who immediately reported the incident to their superiors. LeLoup met Duluth, who had been charged to escort the women by Jones, on the crest of a hill. There an argument developed about which group would claim the reward for the women. What took place after the disagreement may never be known. Either Jane was killed by one of the Indians or she was killed by friendly fire from a group of Continental soldiers who had rushed to her rescue. Either way, she was dead. Chief LeLoup then scalped her lifeless body and threw it in a ravine. Her blood-stained chestnut hair was hanging from the belt of the Wyandot when they returned to the British camp to collect their reward. He forcefully argued that he did not kill her, claiming that she was already dead when he removed her scalp.

Burgoyne was enraged with their performance and vowed to exact justice, but his staff and other officers talked him out of it for fear of Indian alienation. The tragic death of Jane McCrea has been tightly woven into the fabric of the War for Independence. Her death inflamed the country, igniting a fervor of patriotic feelings. Many loyalists joined the ranks of the Whigs (patriots) after the tragedy. Patriotic fever and a sense of outrage was spreading across the land as John Stark was leading his New Hampshire men into Vermont.[4]

On July 13, Alexander Hamilton wrote a letter to John Jay pertaining to the pessimistic mood of the country with the loss of Ticonderoga and Burgoyne's seemingly unstoppable drive south. His casual prophecy was on the mark:

> "All is mystery and dark conjecture. But we must not be discouraged by misfortune. We must rather exert ourselves to remedy the ill consequences of it. If the army gets off safe, we shall soon be able to recover the face of affairs. I am in hope that Burgoyne's success will precipitate him into measures that will prove his ruin. The enterprising spirit he has credit for, I suspect, may easily be fanned into his rashness."[5]

Burgoyne was experiencing some doubts about his position deep in enemy territory with a long supply trail, fully aware that Howe would not be able to reinforce him from the south because he was committed in Rhode Island. If the strategy of delineating the colonies was to be completed, he would have to be the person to do it. At that point, he was thinking of the prestige and honors that would be his if he was successful. His vanity may have fueled that fantasy, but with Howe's failure to assist and the fact that Leger was having difficulties along the Mohawk River, his dreams of glory were disintegrating.

Burgoyne's subordinate position to Howe made him uncomfortable enough that he contemplated changing directions for an expedition to the east to the Connecticut River. Such a move, he rationalized, would isolate New England just as effectively as the original strategy down the Hudson. The scheme withered on the vine and he followed his orders to march to Albany. However, his eastern flank was vulnerable to attack by rebels from New England, and that was a threat he could not ignore. Therefore, he organized the Baum task force to protect his east flank, which would facilitate his progress to Albany. Major General Frederick van Alfred Riedesel, commander of the German troops, agreed with the proposal, believing that a force in the wilderness moved easier and quicker with packhorses than with supply wagons over roads that were excruciatingly slow to build.

Riedesel had been in Castleton and knew about Seth Warner's command, which had been badly treated at Hubbardton, and that rebels were gathering in Vermont. The desperate need for horses overshadowed everything else, however. Every few miles the army advanced, it had to stop and wait eight to ten days for supplies to be moved forward. The fifteen horses they had brought from Canada could be assigned to haul artillery and military stores. Horses purchased or taken from the Connecticut Valley could be used to mount troops as cavalry and as packhorses, giving the army more mobility than it now had. He was most anxious to mount his Hessian dragoons.

Riedesel and Burgoyne reviewed the plans on August 4. It was a major operation instead of the hit-and-run strike originally envisioned by Riedesel. Baum was expected to accomplish many things, including the acquisition of large numbers of cattle, horses, and carriages while he was testing the local population's loyalty to the Crown. The dragoons were especially hopeful that they could find mounts early on in the operation so that they could facilitate the remainder of their mission. Baum's force was expected to travel to Rockingham, on the eastern shore of the Connecticut River, where they would establish a post and send scouting details to Brattleboro. Then they were to travel over the Green Mountains toward Albany. It was a formidable two-hundred-mile excursion that Burgoyne expected to be carried out within two days!

Riedesel disagreed vehemently, arguing that Baum should go as a foraging force looking for supplies or as an armed force prepared to take on the enemy. He argued successfully that it was foolhardy to combine both missions with the same force. Besides, Manchester and Rockingham were too far away for the troops available. Burgoyne was disappointed and reviewed his plans, surprised at the resistance they met from Riedesel. It was an unrealistic proposal that indicates some ineptness.

Within a few days, events on the ground altered Burgoyne's eastern expedition when he learned that a sizable cache of military stores was at a Bennington supply depot and that it was lightly guarded. The prospect of obtaining horses at Bennington was appealing, so Burgoyne canceled his grandiose plan for the Connecticut River Valley much to the relief of his staff.

Fredrich Baum was a fifty-year-old professional soldier with several years experience in the Seven Years War, but he had no experience with troops in heavily forested regions like northern New England. His primary failing was that he could not speak a word of English. He and his force left Fort Edward on the August 9 and started south toward Fort Miller. Cambridge was sixteen miles east of the Hudson. Between Cambridge and Bennington, some of the Indians in the van of his column came in with several horses demanding cash payment. Baum was unable to meet their demands so the Indians destroyed several of the horses and drove the others away, to the disgust of his dismounted dragoons. Baum encountered a party of fleeing loyalists who informed him that some fifteen hundred to eighteen hundred rebel militia troops were in the area. It was disturbing news, and Baum moved ever more cautiously toward Bennington.

On August 7 Stark wrote to his New Hampshire Committee of Safety with a progress report:

"I arrived at this place yesterday afternoon, awaited on the commanding officer, Gen. Lincoln, who informed me that it was Gen. Schuyler's orders to him, to take command of the militia; and march them to Stillwater, where he is retreated to—-I informed him that my orders was not to put myself under the Command of the Continental Troops, But was to meet and Consult with the Committee of the State, and to act in Conjunction with the States troops or those of any other—or in conjunction with the Troops of the United States, but was not to be commanded by either of them.

"The inhabitants that do Reside on this side of the river apprehend themselves in great danger by reason of the near approach of the enemy, in their late moments, and do Universally declare, they will Retire with their families from that part of the Grants that lays above Bennington. Gen. Burgoyne and his troops are at Stillwater—The savages have killed and scalped several women and Children, which very much frightened and damped the Spirits of the remainder of the Inhabitants. I have met and conferr'd with the Committee of this State, they are of opinion that if my troops is ordered to join the Continental troops, on the west side of the North river that the inhabitants are in imminint danger and determin'd to withdraw, into our State, or into the Massachusetts State—and thereby leave ours the Frontier. I am much of a similar opinion, as all the Troops are drawn from this place except what under my command, and about one hundred of Col. Warner's regiment also mine are not all as yet arrived. I shall tarry here until Sunday and hope that by that time they will all join, and then I will march to Bennington, and there shall wait for further orders—

"But must beg it as a favor, in addition to the many already conferred on me by your Honours—not to put me under the Command of those officers on whose account I quitted the army, Lest the remedy should prove worse to me than the disease.

"I have this moment Rec'd Intelligence, by two persons who made their escape from Ticonderoga, belonging to our State, who was captivated at the time of the evacuation of that fortress, except a few is employed in Transporting their stores to Lake George—I understand they take but very little care of the Prisoners as they leave them every day, more or less.

"The strength of Gen. Schuyler's army I cannot ascertain. But I'm affraid he will retreat to Albany, as he has forfeited the people's confidence in him, entirely—I am Gentlemen with great Respects, your most obdeint And most Humble Servant, John Stark B.D.G.

"PS With respect to Stores, I cannot see how it will be of any Consequence to us at this juncture, to so forward any to this place as it is impossible they can arrive here in season. Rum at this place is Twenty Shillings a quart, from them you can form a Judgment Gent. How much we can afford to drink."[6]

General Lincoln's letter to General Schuyler on the same day that Stark wrote the above letter sheds some light on how Stark received word that his command was being hijacked:

"Yesterday General Stark from New Hampshire came into camp at Manchester. By his instructions from that state it is at his option to act in conjunction with the continental army or not. He seems to be exceedingly soured and thinks he hath not had justice done him by Congress. He is determined not to join the Continental army until the Congress have given him his rank there in; his claim is to command all the officers he commanded last year, as also those who joined the army after him. Whether he will march his troops to Stillwater or not I am quite at a loss to know. But if he doth it is a fixed point with him to act as a separate corps and take no orders from any officer in the northern department, saving your honor, for he saith they were all either commanded by him the last year or joined the army after him. It is very unhappy this matter is carried by him to so great a length, especially at a time when every exertion for our common safety is so absolutely necessary. I have good reason to believe that if New Hampshire were informed of the matter they would give new and very different instructions to Gen. Stark. The troops from Massachusetts are collecting here. I don't know what number may be expected. I suppose the rear will be up tonight at farthest."[7]

John Stark felt an intense dislike for Schuyler, who took the matter to Congress. Schuyler's letter did not arrive in Philadelphia until after the Battle of Bennington. Some called it insubordination, but a censure of Stark was voted on and failed to pass. Congress sent a copy of Lincoln's letter to the New Hampshire Congress. Finally, Stark and Lincoln were able to come together with a plan that designated Cambridge, New York as a staging area for future operations. On August 12, 1777, Schuyler (at his headquarters at Stillwater) sent Stark the following message with a conciliatory note:

"Dear General. As the route through Schaghticoke to this place will save at least twelve miles march you will please to come that way. It gives me great pleasure to find that you are coming on with your troops. Be assured that I would not wish you to do anything inconsistent with your Honor, but in this critical conjuncture, if a Gentleman, while he asserts his Rights, sacrifices his feelings to the good of his country, he will merit the thanks of his country.

"On your arrival you will be informed that I have also been injuriously treated, but until the country is in safety and that I have done my duty as a good citizen, I will stifle my resentment. Adieu. I am yours, Ph: Schuyler."[8]

Stark reported from Bennington to Lincoln at Stillwater on the following day:

"Dr General

I this moment received your express just as I was beginning to march my brigade from hence. The reason of my setting out yesterday was because my brigade could not be supplied with provisions or carriages to transport the same together with our baggage, I presume General from your letter that our plan has effectually taken place. I have consulted with the Committee of Safety of this place as well as Colonels Warner and Wms. They all agree that it would be detrimental to my troops to march to the camp as it would cause them to march fifty miles to gain fifteen. We imagine that the order was given on the supposition that I with my troops was on my march and had advanced a good part of the way. Col. Warner is to meet with his at the same place. Ammunition will be wanted as there is very little at this place—Balls in a particular manner. But if it is thought best that I should march to the camp I will immediately acquiesce with it. I have this moment received Intelligence that a party of Indians fifty in number have this day been seen in Cambridge. I have sent two hundred men to intercept their progress. I am sir your friend & Humble Servant. John Stark

"NB This moment information came to hand that a large body of the enemy are on the march to Cambridge."[9]

Lincoln replied to Stark on the fourteenth to confirm that their plan was adopted and to say he was pleased that Stark detained his troops at Bennington. He notified Stark that he was bringing ammunition, kettles, axes, and flints and a surgeon from Albany.

On August 13 Stark reported to Schuyler that he was meeting Warner and Lincoln at the designated place in Cambridge:

"I join with you in Sentiment and shall throw away all private Resentment, when put in Balance with the Good of the Country. . . think that the present plan will give the Army in general present Satisfaction and stop the progress of murmuring . . . Another Express 4 oclock in the afternoon informs that a large party are on the march to Cambridge. . . "[10]

When Stark arrived at Bennington, he found that several militiamen from surrounding communities had concentrated in the village. Each man was equipped with a musket, powder horn, bullet pouch, and a flask primarily filled with rum. A few had hand-forged swords hanging from their belts, and they looked not much different from Stark's New Hampshire men. General Schuyler had appealed to the Massachusetts General Court for able-bodied men between the ages of sixteen and fifty years to reinforce his Northern Department's army. Volunteers from Hampshire and Berkshire Counties answered the call, for they too were susceptible to attacks by Burgoyne. Men from nearby Vermont and New York also answered the desperate call for help. By the 13 Stark had about a thousand men in his immediate command, excluding Seth Warner's badly mauled regiment at Hubbardton.

Stark and his New Hampshire brigade were on the road between Manchester and Bennington when Baum left for the same destination.

Stark was twelve miles from Cambridge when he received word of Indians at Cambridge, which turned out to be Baum's forward scout element. Stark immediately sent word to Schuyler that he had sent a two-hundred-man reconnaissance force under Lieutenant Colonel William Gregg to intercept the approaching enemy.

Gregg traveled to a gristmill at Sancoick (now North Hoosick, New York), about nine miles from Bennington, where they destroyed a bridge over a small creek called Owl Kill. They decided to wait there until Baum's force showed itself. At about eight o'clock the next morning, Gregg was shocked to see Baum's force enter the bivouac. They fought a delaying action and Gregg withdrew into the forest to the east, toward Bennington. Baum discovered that the abandoned gristmill contained seventy-eight barrels of flour and twenty barrels of salt and assigned several loyalists to guard the valuable stores while he continued toward Bennington on the north side of the Walloomsac River. Along the way, loyalists were flocking to his force requesting arms, prepared to take the oath of allegiance. They were vouched for by Colonel Skenes, who owned the large estate and shipbuilding facility in Skenesborough.

Baum and his men crossed the bridge they had just repaired at Sancoick and shortly after stopped to rest. It was hot and humid and the dragoons, with their heavy boots and headgear, were bothered by the heat. Baum was also having trouble controlling his Indian detachment. They looted, scalped, and destroyed property at will. The chief of the Mohawk detachment was killed in the skirmish with Gregg's patrol. The Indians were so filled with grief that Baum ordered a makeshift funeral service. Sixteen dragoons fired three volleys over his grave site. The rebel columns heard the gunfire and thought an attack was under way.

Gregg had sent word to Stark that he was abandoning the mill site, withdrawing back to the main body. Stark had learned that a large body of enemy troops was behind the Indians already reported, and quickly sent word to Seth Warner and other militia units in the area for immediate assistance. Stark observed Gregg's troops rushing forward with enemy troops about a half mile behind them. Baum was as surprised to see the militia as Stark and Gregg were to see his force so close. Baum immediately halted his detachment and stationed his men on a piece of high ground north of the river.

Baum was located at a stronger defensive position on a hill overlooking the bridge and the road to Bennington. He positioned his two three-pounders to dominate the bridge and road. For the balance of August 14 he methodically fired shot into the area. Baum was worried about the fifteen hundred to eighteen hundred enemy troops against his eight hundred men. He decided to hold in place and send for reinforcements.

Stark called for a council of war at which he announced that they would attack the next morning at first light. Hamilton's prophecy turned out to be accurate. The vicious battle that would soon take place was the instrument of destruction, and New Hampshire's John Stark was about to deliver the decisive blow.

The two armies had accidentally bumped into each other. Neither commander had adequate intelligence of the presence or the strength of his opponents. Stark, unsure of what he faced, wisely declined a precipitate fight he might not be able to win and pulled back to avoid an accidental collision. Both sides sent out patrols to gather intelligence and skirmishers exchanged fire to maintain the distance between the two camps.

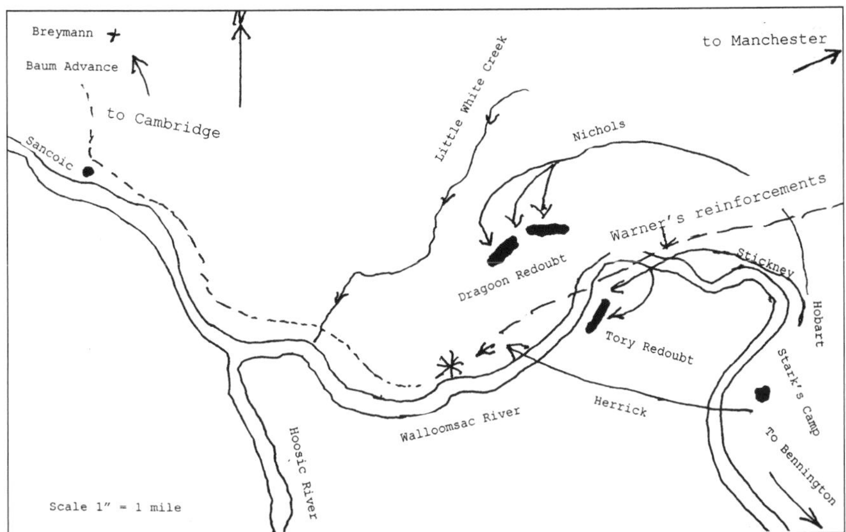

Battle of Bennington, August 17, 1777, Battle took place in Hoosic, New York

14

The Battle of Bennington (August 16, 1777)

The planned attack on August 15 against Baum's entrenched force was called off. It was another rainy day, with heavy downpours that made it difficult to see very far and to keep gunpowder dry. It had been a wet summer, one that turned roads and cart tracks into muddy rivers. Stark's small patrols and skirmishers continuously harassed the enemy and gathered intelligence. The British force strengthened its positions without venturing far from its protective enclosures. The Americans kept them inside their perimeter with sporadic sniper fire. On August 14, Baum sent a letter from Sancoick, by express rider to Burgoyne:

"*Sir:*—I have the honor to inform your Excellency that I arrived here at eight in the morning, having had intelligence of a party of the enemy being in possession of a mill, which they abandoned at our approach, but in their usual way, fired from the bushes; and, took their road to Bennington; a savage was slightly wounded. They broke down a bridge which has retarded our march above an hour. They left in the mill about seventy-eight barrels of fine flour, one thousand bushels of wheat, twenty bushels of salt, and about one thousand dollars worth of pearl and potashes.

"I have ordered twenty provincials and an officer to guard the provisions and pass of the bridge. By the five prisoners taken here, they agree that from 1,500 to 1,800 men are in Bennington, but are supposed to leave at our approach. I will proceed so far to-day as to fall on the enemy to-morrow early, and make such disposition as I think necessary from the intelligence I may receive. People [Loyalists] are flocking in hourly, but want to be armed; the savages cannot be ruled. They ruin, and take everything they please.

"I beg your Excellency to pardon the hurry of this letter, it is wrote on the head of a barrel."[1]

The intermittent sniping and skirmishes on the 15 of August were responsible for the death of thirty enemy combatants, including two Indian chiefs. Within the British compound a three-sided redoubt was constructed at the top of the highest hill, positioned to secure Baum's rear. Fifty dragoons were stationed there. South of the redoubt, near the foot of the slope where Little White Creek flowed into the Walloomsac River, was covered by light-infantry soldiers. The two three-pounders were located south of the hill closest to the river, with sixty or more grenadiers and infantrymen. The strongest position was astride the roadway at the center of the secured perimeter. Baum stationed himself here with the best troops: British marksmen, Brunswick jaegers, and most of the elite dragoons, with their awkward headgear, wool uniforms, and heavy boots. The latter were fighting as infantry but retained their heavy broadswords. Several hundred Loyalists had built and manned a third redoubt on the south side of the Walloomsac River closest to Stark's camp.

One strange feature of Baum's defensive position was that local inhabitants entered and exited the compound at will, giving rise to the possibility that their position would be given away to the rebels surrounding them. Stark had sent small groups of civilians into the camp disguised as loyalists. They were dressed in shirtsleeves and wore white paper badges attached to their hats to signify that they were Tories willing to take the oath of allegiance to the British cause. Colonel Philip Skenes, a notorious self-promoter attached to Baum's expedition because he was familiar with the area, told Baum that the people were considered loyalists or Tories, even though he had no way of knowing for certain. They were able to observe Baum's camp, on an hourly basis, and get up-to-date information out to Stark, who was staying at the Catamount Tavern in Bennington. It was an efficient fifth-column operation that supplied crucial data that Stark and his officers used to formulate plans for the enemy's defeat.

Burgoyne instructed Baum to strengthen his position if he was unable to attack the rebels, a vital step Baum had already taken on his own. Burgoyne then added that he should await further orders and that he was sending a reinforcement column to him under the command of Lieutenant Colonel Heinrich Breymann. Riedesel strongly disagreed with Burgoyne's decision, and suggested that he should have had Baum withdraw. Burgoyne was violating a basic military law by breaking his command into small detachments which could be destroyed one unit at a time by smaller enemy forces, and should have listened to Riedesel's advice. If Breymann and Baum had been allowed to proceed as a larger command, they would have been able to withstand much greater enemy pressure. Burgoyne ignored the advice and ordered Breymann into the field to assist Baum. The order gave no hint of an emergency.

Breymann's corps was known throughout the army as being slow marchers. The hot, humid August weather added to the men's discomfort. The corps consisted of a company of riflemen, a battalion of light-infantry, and grenadiers with two six-pounders, consisting of six hundred and fifty men. They were on the road by nine o'clock in the morning of the fifteenth. It was not an easy march in the heat over hilly terrain which frequently slowed the column to a near halt. They traveled an average of one mile per hour. Baum had been informed that a relief column was on its way, yet there was no sense of urgency anywhere up or down the chain of command.

The column had planned to march to Cambridge and then to Baum's encampment, but the guide got them lost and they made camp that night several miles short of Cambridge. Breymann sent notice to Baum of his location. The message reached Baum at eleven o'clock. Baum sent Colonel Skene, who knew the area and the people, with horses and wagons to facilitate Breymann's movement to his camp.

The Stark camp received some reinforcements from Berkshire volunteers at one o'clock the morning of the sixteenth, under the able command of Colonel Symonds. Another group of volunteers, from Pittsfield, Massachusetts, came into the camp that morning, commanded by Reverend Thomas Allen, a descendant of Cromwell's Burnsides. He reported at the log house where Stark was living: "The people of Berkshire have often turned out to fight the enemy, but have not been permitted to do. We have resolved that if you do not let us fight now, never to come again."

"Would you go now," Stark observed. "In this dark and rainy night? No, go to your people; tell them to take rest if they can; and if God sends us sunshine to-morrow, and I do not give you fighting enough, I will never call upon you to come again."[2]

❦

Allen and Symonds were not the only ones to arrive at Stark's camp. Throughout the night, a steady stream of motivated volunteers marched grimly into the encampment, determined to drive the British from their land and out of the country. They were a reflection of the many militia units that had come together in a common cause. Some were undisciplined and uneducated and most of them carried a distinct hatred of the loyalists or Tories in their midst, which frequently was more pronounced than their hatred for the British army. Soldiers taken prisoner were given much better treatment than civilian loyalists whom they branded as traitors. The loyalists, in turn, thought of the rebels as the ultimate traitor.

The war councils Stark convened gave him a chance to discuss the latest intelligence received from his spies in Baum's camp. With that information available, he devised a scheme of maneuver that would defeat Baum just as soon as the sun broke out of the heavy low-lying clouds that blanketed the area. Stark must have been reminded of the situation that confronted Abercromby, who suffered a humiliating defeat at Fort Ticonderoga back in July 1758. Stark decided, wisely, that he had to use different tactics to rout the enemy from its trenches and breastworks. Maneuver tactics were his choice.

Stark visualized a large pincer movement against the strongest redoubt with the dragoons. Lieutenant Colonel Moses Nichols was given the task of marching his two hundred and fifty men to the rear of the enemy's left wing. Nichols, a physician from Amherst, New Hampshire, was a strong advocate of the American cause. It is probable that Stark knew him well; the two had worked on county affairs together. Colonel Samuel Herrick, of Vermont, was to cross the small Walloomsac River and the road to Bennington, where he was to fan out in a semicircle to the south. He was protected and screened by a wooded ridge to the south. Then he had to recross the river and quietly make his way up the valley formed by Little White Creek, which flowed into the Walloomsac. That would place him within earshot of Nichols' assault force at the rear of the enemy.

Stark cleverly assigned two forces, under Colonel Thomas Stickney and Colonel David Hobart to attack the redoubts within the area of the pincer arms. Stark planned to lead the rest of his force, about three hundred men, in a frontal assault after the initial strike by Nichols and Herrick to draw the enemy's attention to their flanks. This gave Stark three divisions to attack the enemy simultaneously. None of the units involved had trained together, and that gave some concern that any unforeseen element could upset the best of plans. Discipline, timing, and a favorable nod from Lady Luck would determine the success or failure of the attacks.

Just before the plan was put into motion, Stark gave his men a short pep talk as he had done at the battle of Breed's Hill. He was wearing his old Continental army uniform of blue and buff, with a single silver star attached to each shoulder that stood out from the beige and brown homespun hunting shirts of most of his militia. Lean and tan from long periods of exposure to the elements, he moved about with ease, projecting an air of confidence. His deeply set light blue eyes shrouded by heavy brows reflected the seriousness of the occasion. His affection and respect for every man in his command was evident in his demeanor, and there was a hint of sadness, even melancholy, as he surveyed the militia groups. He was a veteran of numerous campaigns and knew that when the time came to attack, many of the fine men would die. It is a truism of command, and most leaders suffer from that burden all their lives.

He spoke in a firm voice, impressing the importance of the operation they were about to implement, and wished them success. His last solemn words were: "There are the redcoats and they are ours, or Molly Stark sleeps a widow tonight." (Another version: "Now my men, yonder are the Hessians; they were bought for seven pounds tenpence a man. Are you worth more? Prove it. Tonight the American flag floats over yonder hill or Molly sleeps a widow.")

With those few words, John Stark was at his best. The experienced campaigner knew what he was asking his men to do. He was sober and taciturn while preparing for combat, yet once it started, he had that rare gift of being able to think quickly and coherently regardless of the chaos around him, fearless and mindful of the risks involved. General John Stark had that illusive quality of inspiring men to maximum effort. Honesty and respect for the men he sent into battle were a large part of his character. Leadership, especially inspiring leadership, starts at the top and filters down to the troops. The American soldier, be he a Continental or a rebel militiaman, could spot a phony in a heartbeat. Stark was the genuine article. The men followed him with enthusiasm and affection. Leadership is defined by character and Stark was richly endowed with that virtue. At forty-nine years he was at the pinnacle of his military career.

The militia units under Stark totaled about two thousand men. Baum's brigade had five hundred men and Breymann's division of 650 men made a total of one thousand two hundred and fifty enemy troops.

Immediately after Stark had ordered Herrick and Nichols to begin their flanking attack, he took several companies and had them parade back and forth in full view of the enemy so as to make them believe that he had more troops than he really possessed. His simple ruse worked.

At the last minute, Colonel Nichols had expressed to Stark a worry that he might need more troops to do the job, so Stark gave him another one hundred men. Nichols had six miles of woodland to travel before he ended up at Baum's rear, but he arrived without incident and waited for the signal, two musket shots, to start his attack.

Baum had relied heavily on his Indian component to be his eyes and ears because he realized that his command was widely dispersed for mutual defense. He brought a cannon into the redoubt when he had word that rebels had been seen in the woods, and was anxiously awaiting the arrival of Breymann's division, which would increase not only his manpower, but his firepower as well with the addition of two six-pounders.

The moment the assault columns were in place, Nichols launched the attack. At three thirty, he sent the troops forward. The dragoons saw the rebels coming and suddenly a loud volley of fire erupted from both attacking columns. Herrick and Nichols had positioned their forces with perfect timing. Their coordinated rapid fire and movement tactics shattered the morale of the dragoon defenders. The militia fired and reloaded quickly and the cannons roared, adding to the noise rising above the pastoral countryside. The salvos had an intensity and volume that Stark, no stranger to battlefield scenes, had never heard before. He called it "the hottest engagement I have ever witnessed resembling a continuous clap of thunder."[3]

Early in the attack on the redoubts, a wagon containing the spare German ammunition exploded, partially destroying the structure. The Americans stormed the structure as the dust was falling. Perhaps that was "the clap of thunder" Stark referred to.

The dragoons displayed their traditional discipline and offered stiff resistance, firing by platoons, inflicting a heavy toll on the assaulting militia troops. Baum's Indian detachment fled the battlefield shortly after the fighting started. The Americans had carried the redoubt with their first charge and were now inside. Men were screaming and the dragoons abandoned all discipline. They struggled to get out of the enclosure before the wild Americans caught them with rifles wielded as clubs or with bayonets at the end of empty muskets. The ferocity of the clash in the redoubt spelled death and destruction to the Germans. It was impossible to stop the onslaught.

Even as the Hessians left the redoubt to run downhill, the Americans followed and outrun them. The scene resembled a free-for-all. Troops were too intertwined to make any order out of the situation. Some of the veterans likened the battle to Bunker Hill except that fewer cannons were being fired. Stark found one of the three-pounders left by Baum and told some of the men to charge the piece. They did not know how, so he dismounted and loaded the gun himself, then leaped back on his horse and ordered them to fire.

Julius Fredrich Wasmus, a surgeon serving with the Baum brigade, tried to attend to the wounded soldiers and was overwhelmed by the numbers of injured men. At times, he had to seek cover to save himself until the battle had swept past. He heard bullets all around him as he slipped and fell in the soupy morass. Two Americans approached him as he lay on the ground and asked if he was German or British. He tried to explain that he was a friend by extending his hand. The Americans acknowledged his gesture and proceeded to search his pockets, taking his watch, purse, and knife and a pad of paper.

Upon hearing of a surgeon nearby, a father sought him out and asked him to treat his son, who was wounded in the thigh. At that moment, General Stark rode to the scene astride his beautiful young brown mare and ordered Wasmus to treat Americans too, which he had been doing anyway. He noted that the Americans were liberally supplied with rum and many sipped from a wooden flask they carried around their neck. Some appeared to be drunk.

At the loyalist redoubt near the southern bank of the Walloomsac River, about two hundred and fifty men huddled behind the earthworks. It was here that neighbors of opposite political views, acquaintances and friends of earlier times, and fought to the death. Their encounters were perhaps some of the most violent of the battle.

Once the dragoon and loyalist redoubts had been breached, Stark was able to concentrate on the main objective, Baum's central position on the roadway. He had relocated his last remaining cannon to protect his left flank. If he had left it in its original position, covering the bridge the Americans were now running across, it might have bought him some time by stopping the flow of rebels into his compound. Just as the Germans ran out of ammunition, large numbers of Americans stormed the area. Baum ordered the Germans to sling their muskets and use their broadswords to defend themselves. Within minutes after the Americans gained the earthworks, those Germans able to do so fled the scene in disarray.

Throughout the battle, Stark was on his horse at the center of the fighting, encouraging, cajoling, and directing the troops. He was worried that Colonel Seth Warner's regiment had not arrived, and kept checking his watch, remarking, "It was time they were here."[4]

Several of the dragoons, including Baum, escaped to the meadow south of the bridge where the Walloomsac makes a sharp turn to the west. There they were quickly surrounded and captured. Baum had received a serious wound in the abdomen. The captured surgeon, Wasmus, later wrote that the river was filled with dead bodies, and captured loyalists were tied together with rope to be led away from the battlefield toward Bennington. Wasmus's guards also began leading him to Bennington. Two miles from the bridge, they found Baum lying in a wagon complaining that the drivers were traveling too fast. The fact that he could speak only German contributed to his agonizing ordeal. The American guards carried him to a nearby house and laid him on the dirt floor. They shook his hand and ushered Wasmus out the door after he had listened to Baum's farewell and his last message for Riedesel. Baum died shortly after.

The much anticipated Breymann relief force was still on its way when organized resistance between the Americans and Baum's brigade ceased. Breymann's abysmally slow progress is difficult to understand, even though his men were heavily burdened with cannons and supply wagons that were difficult to haul over the hilly terrain. He felt no sense of urgency. His orders contained nothing to indicate that Baum's situation was critical, and his unimpressive rush to relieve his comrade spelled disaster to Baum and his men. About two o'clock in the afternoon, Colonel Skene sent word to the column to detach a small force to guard the valuable supplies at the gristmill at Sancoick before it was captured by the rebels.

Advance elements of Breymann's division were at the mill by four-thirty. They reported that there was no sound of battle, which is surprising because it was still taking place at that time. The mill was only two miles from Baum's position. Breymann continued, unaware that Baum's brigade was being destroyed, even though musketry could be heard that far away. He asked Skene to guide the column to Baum's camp. A short distance from the mill, they encountered a group of Americans with white pieces of paper tucked into their hats. Once again, Skene assumed they were loyalists and went on his way. The civilians were not loyalists, however, and they fired a volley into the column and ran for the safety of the forest. It's amazing how often this ruse worked. Breymann instantly established a skirmish line and brought up his two cannons (six-pounders), which he positioned near a log house, and began firing at the Americans.

Colonel Herrick had spotted Breymann's approach and quickly rode back to warn Stark. The troops had been fighting for two hours and were exhausted. Many were diligently looking for booty. It was a stifling hot day and many had already drunk too much rum. The Americans had been surprised by Breymann's presence near the field of battle, and Stark had trouble getting his men into a suitable skirmish line. They were scattered over the disputed landscape, resting, celebrating their victory, and searching for plunder and souvenirs. When Breymann and a detachment of his regiment rode against the militia, the Americans slowly gave ground and escaped to the forest. They continued to shoot from behind trees, conducting a fighting withdrawal.

A small detachment of Seth Warner's regiment under Major Samuel Saffords arrived near Bennington the night before the battle. The next morning they dried themselves and their equipment. They were short on ammunition. Late in the day they heard gunfire west of Bennington and rushed toward the battlefield. Passing through Stark's camp, where they stored their knapsacks and coats. They also received four ounces of rum and water before continuing to the river, where they met wounded men walking to the rear. Baum's men could be seen running down the hill with Americans close behind them. At that point, Seth Warner rode up to explain that the militia was in trouble and asked that Safford's men hurry to their aid.

Breymann's line of grenadiers continued to shoot although the Americans pulled back out of range of their muskets. But their six-pounders were continuously firing grapeshot into Stark's weak blocking detachment. He was in trouble and knew that the six-pounders were capable of obliterating his thin line. Retreating stragglers from all over the battlefield began to come to the aid of their comrades just as the Brunswick infantrymen were about to outflank them. There was great confusion as the two lines became entangled.

The sudden appearance of Warner's regiment and a small command under Major John Rand, who had brought his volunteers from Worcester County, Massachusetts, began to fill the open spots in Stark's line. The battle then became one of the most fiercely contested engagements at Bennington. Rand, an elderly man, was riding his black mare when it was killed. The doughty elder leaped off the horse and climbed up on a stump, directing his men forward with a large broadsword.

Warner, who was a tall, well-proportioned man, brought the battle to a quick climax when he yelled in a booming voice for the Americans to fix bayonets and charge. He had been at Bennington with Stark when the battle started. His regiment was on its way from Manchester but he entered the battle with Stickney's regiment directly behind Stark's frontal assault troops. (Warner was ill at the time of the battle.) Major Rand also ordered his men to follow Warner's example and to attack. The German line was rushed and overcome. One of the six-pounders was loaded and captured before it could be fired. A burly militia sergeant had hit the gunner and turned the cannon around, and poured the grapeshot into the retreating enemy. The Germans had run out of ammunition when Warner's men hit them, forcing their retreat into a complete rout with the Americans in hot pursuit, shooting or capturing them. Except for sporadic firing, the battle was over.

As darkness approached, Stark ordered his men out of action to prevent accidentally shooting their comrades. The flight of the Germans continued into the night, leaving the battlefield in the hands of the citizen-soldiers who had met some of the best troops from Europe and defeated them with skill and great courage. As darkness descended, exhausted militiamen looked for the most comfortable place to spend the night and rest their exhausted bodies.

One veteran of the battle, Thomas Mellon of Francestown, New Hampshire, recalled the battle in his later years. He spoke to Reverend J. D. Butler, who, related his story to the Vermont legislature in 1848 when Vermont accepted the two three-pounders captured from Baum. Excerpts from his experience follow:

"... I enlisted at Francestown, New Hampshire, in Colonel Stickney's regiment and Captain Clark's company as soon as I learned that Stark would accept the command of the State troops; six or seven others from the same town joined the army at the same time. We marched forthwith to Number Four, and stayed there a week. Meantime I received a horn of powder and run two or three hundred bullets; I had brought my own gun. Then my company went on to Manchester [Vermont], soon after I went, with a hundred others, under Colonel Emerson, down the valley of Otter Creek; on this excursion we lived like lords, on pigs and chickens in the houses of tories who had fled. When we returned to Manchester, bringing two hogsheads of West India rum, we heard the Hessians were on their way to invade Vermont. Late in the afternoon of rainy Friday, we were ordered off for Bennington in spite of rain, mud and darkness. We pushed all night, making the best progress we could; about daybreak I, with Lieutenant Miltimore, came near Bennington, and slept a little while on a hay mow . . . then hurried three miles west to Stark's main body.

"Stark . . . rode up near the enemy to reconnoitre; were fired at by cannon, and came galloping back. Stark rode with his shoulders bent forward, and cried out to his men, 'Those rascals know that I am an officer; don't you see they honor me with a big gun as a salute.' We were marched round and round a circular hill till we were tired. Stark said it was to amuse the Germans . . .

"Between two and three o'clock the battle began . . . The first time I fired, I put three balls in my gun; before I had time to fire many rounds, our men rushed over the breastworks, but I and many others chased straggling Hessians in the woods; we pursued until Breymann with 800 fresh troops and larger cannon, which opened up with grape shot; some of the grape shop riddled a Virginia fence near me . . . We skirmishers ran back till we met a large body of Stark's men and then faced about. I soon started for a brook . . . but the enemy outflanked us, and I said to a comrade, 'we must run, or they will have us'. . . In a few minutes we saw Warner's men hurrying to help us; they opened right and left of us, and one half of them attacked each flank of the enemy, and beat those who were just closing in on us. Stark's men then took heart and stood their ground. My gun barrel was at this time too hot to hold, so I seized the musket of a dead Hessian, in which my bullets went down easier than my own. Right in front were the cannon, and seeing an officer on horseback waving his sword toward the artillery, I fired at him twice; his horse fell; he cut the traces of an artillery horse, mounted him and ride off. I after heard the officer was a Major [Colonel] Skene. We might have mastered them all, as they stopped within three miles of the battlefield; but Stark, saying 'he would run no risk of spoiling a good day's work,' ordered a halt, and return to quarters.

"I was coming back, when I was ordered by Stark himself, who knew me, as I had been one of his body guards in Canada, to help draw off a field piece. I told him 'I was worn out'. His answer was, 'don't seem to disobey; take hold, and if you can't hold out, slip away in the dark.' Before we had dragged the gun very far, Warner rode near us. Someone pointed to a dead man by the road-side, said, "Your brother is killed,' 'Is It Jesse? asked Warner?' And when the answer was 'yes,' he jumped off his horse, stooped and gazed in the dead man's face, and then rode away without saying a word."[5]

The living slept in close proximity to the bodies of friend and foe. Earlier in the day, the air was filled with the deafening rattle of musketry and the thunder of cannons. Now the guns were silent, and from all corners of the lonely battlefield the mournful cries of wounded men echoed across the battered landscape. Some called for relief from pain, others called out for their mothers or their loved one's names. Those who experienced it would carry those sounds with them for the rest of their lives. The jubilation of the survivors was truly earned, but it was tempered by the sad and sobering cries wafting across the battlefield.

Freedom and liberty are not free.

The plaque erected by the State of New Hampshire at Bennington Battlefield, Hoosic, New York:

"Erected in honor of Brigadier General John Stark and the 1400 New Hampshire men who came to the defense of Vermont in August 1777. Assembling at Fort Number Four in Charlestown, New Hampshire, Stark and his troops crossed the Green Mountains to aid in the defense of the newly-established State of Vermont as the Commander in Chief of all the American Forces from New Hampshire, Vermont, Massachusetts, and New York. General Stark had approximately 2000 men in all in the first phase of the battle. General Stark's army defeated and captured a British detachment led by Lt. Col. Frederich Baum. Shortly after this triumph, with the timely assistance of Col. Seth Warner and his "Green Mountain Boys," a relief column under Col. Heinrich Von Breymann was repulsed. By thus denying the enemy sorely needed supplies these twin victories near Bennington on August 16, 1777, contributed notably to the total British surrender at Saratoga two months later, and to the subsequent military alliance with France, the turning point in the war for American independence." Presented to the State of Vermont by the New Hampshire American Revolution Bicentennial Commission, August 16, 1977."

15

The Aftermath (August–September 1777)

General Burgoyne's habit of acting with detachments from his main force had been predicted by General George Washington. The loss of Fort Ticonderoga was worrisome to the Americans, but Burgoyne's early success had precipitated his ruin. After John Stark's victory at Bennington, Burgoyne had only five thousand men for his drive to Albany, deep in enemy territory, and suffered from severe supply shortages, especially horses. This gave pause to the British commander, who had lost much of the popular support from the loyalists in the surrounding communities. His status as a victor was now in question. Those who were unopposed to the war were inspired and invigorated by the magnitude of Stark's victory, and were more ready than ever to take up arms for their own defense.

Burgoyne's losses at Bennington drastically reduced his ability to forge south through the American lines to Albany. He was at a crossroads, and the enemy had robbed him of favorable tactical options. After the battle, Burgoyne's Indian detachment believed they had been poorly treated and found no reason to remain with the British. Perhaps the Indians had a feeling that the Rebels just might win the war and they did not want to be on the losing side. Burgoyne was somewhat relieved because they were frequently more trouble than they were worth. With the Jane McCrea episode so fresh in everyone's mind, the departure of the Indians actually lessened his anxiety.

On August 16, the day of the Battle of Bennington, Burgoyne completed a flotation bridge across the Hudson River that would enable his horses and wagons to cross easily to the west bank. He had planned to move south to Albany on the west side of the river and also contemplated, that his German foragers would be driving large numbers of horses and cattle over the bridge into his encampment. German General Simon

Fraser established a post on the west bank in preparation for the thrust to the south. Stores, troop baggage, and other equipment began to be moved from Skenesborough to Fort Edward as soon as the bridge was completed.

Burgoyne was constantly evaluating his options. The disaster that befell Leger at Fort Stanwix removed another arrow from Burgoyne's tactical quiver. Later, Leger made an attempt to retrace his steps back into Canada to follow Burgoyne's trail down Lake Champlain to Ticonderoga. It was a brave effort but of little value. Burgoyne pulled all of his dragoons from Ticonderoga when he learned that Lieutenant General Sir Henry Clinton would be working his way up the Hudson River from New York to attack Fort Clinton and Montgomery. This effort had the potential of drawing some of Gates's troops south to counter Clinton's movement. Burgoyne was delighted at the prospect of Gates's blocking force being diminished if he moved south on the west bank of the Hudson. He could have used the eastern bank where there was less rebel resistance, but the river at Albany was wider and deeper with steep banks, on the western shore, offering an ideal location for the rebels to oppose the crossing. The other option available to Burgoyne was to fall back on Ticonderoga, which he dismissed because it would demoralize his troops. Retreat was not in his plans.

❧

Prisoners taken at Bennington were treated fairly by the militia. The loyalists or Tories (the colonists called them Tories and the Canadians called them loyalists), however, were given a rough time by their neighbors and former friends. That capture by the rebels could mean physical abuse and public humiliation was enough of an incentive not to join Burgoyne's ranks to fight the rebels. Burgoyne had planned on recruiting them in large numbers to supplement his force, knowing that the upper New York region was heavily populated with citizens loyal to the Crown. The lack of volunteers to his army could probably be blamed on the American victory and their subsequent maltreatment of the loyalists taken prisoner. The repercussions from Stark's victory reached far beyond the site of the battle.

Prisoners were rounded up and marched to Bennington, where they were quartered in a church. The Tories (about one hundred and sixty) were tied to a lead rope with a horse attached. The Hessian soldiers were marched in close-order ranks with flank guards, an indication of the respect the militia had for the German soldiers.

The German surgeon Julius Wasmus was taken with other prisoners to a house for the first night after the battle. His opinion of the average rebel was not very high. Their "simplemindedness" seemed to irritate him. The next day the prisoners were given a meal consisting of pork, potatoes, and punch. Colonel Seth Warner even joined them for the meal. After he had eaten, Warner brought in a metal box filled with lancets that had been stolen by the militiamen who captured Wasmus. Warner opened the box and removed six of the instruments for his own use before returning it to Wasmus.

Stark also visited the prisoners in the morning to assure them that their personal possessions would be returned to them if they could be found. He told them they would be moved to Bennington. The officers would be lodged at the Catamount Tavern, a landmark inn where Stark had frequently stayed during the French and Indian War. Midday of the nineteenth, the prisoners were lined up to sign a parole that they would not desert or talk to the inhabitants of the countryside about the war while they were marched to Boston for shipment back to England. For the Germans and the British, the war was over. Wasmus, however, was a special case. He was neither soldier nor civilian, and being a physician did not give him the right to be exchanged. He was ultimately sent to Canada and arrived home at Brunswick in 1783!

Lieutenant Caleb Stark, General Stark's oldest son, was at Horatio Gate's headquarters (Gates was replacing Schuyler) when word came of the Bennington victory, and he witnessed the euphoria the news caused. He was then allowed to accompany a group of officers from his camp to open a line of communication with Stark's militia. Before leaving Gate's headquarters, General Gates told Caleb to tell his father that he wanted the artillery taken at Bennington for the battle that was imminent with Burgoyne.[1]

Gates had informed Stark that he was sending two officers and twenty artillerists to take charge of the four fieldpieces captured at Bennington. There was a scarcity of fieldpieces in the Continental Army and they were badly needed in the coming battle.

On August 19, at the American camp at the junction of the Mohawk and Hudson Rivers north of Albany, Major General Philip Schuyler handed over the command of the American Northern Department to

Major General Horatio Gates. Gates inherited an army of four thousand five hundred men riddled with sickness and low morale that gave rise to daily desertions. Major General Benedict Arnold arrived with an additional twelve hundred men including a superb corps of riflemen led by the muscular, raw-boned frontiersman, Colonel Daniel Morgan. Morgan was cut from the same cloth as John Stark, and shared his values as an experienced wilderness campaigner. Morgan's frontier riflemen from Pennsylvania, Maryland, and Virginia equaled the original Rogers' Rangers in their handling of difficult operations.

Burgoyne's only obstacle between the Saint Lawrence River and Albany was the Continental army's Northern Department. The loss of Fort Ticonderoga demoralized the department and Congress, and the bitter quarrel that developed between Schuyler and Gates only made matters worse. To his credit, Schuyler, a native of New York, did everything in his power to delay the British advance. He warned the countryside to remove and hide their livestock and stores of supplies, and to impede Burgoyne's passage through the swampy woodland south of Lake Champlain by destroying bridges and felling trees along the way. He had assisted Benedict Arnold in the delaying naval action at Valcour Island in Lake Champlain.

Gates was a former British army officer and had served with General Braddock on the Monongahela, where he was wounded. He married a wealthy Virginia woman, which placed him in the same social circles as George Washington, and became Washington's adjutant general. Gates had a long nose and a skinny neck and had a tendency to command from a distance. Many found him timid and vacillating. He had successfully cultivated the allegiance of the New England congressional delegations and had warned them that Schuyler would never hold on to Ticonderoga, the only military sentinel on the western frontier.

By early September, Gates's army had swollen to seven thousand men, and he moved them to Stillwater on the west bank of the Hudson, fifteen miles north of Half Moon. Three miles farther north, at Bemis Heights, so called after a nearby tavern owned by Jotham Bemis, where the road to Albany passes through a defile between the Hudson and wooded land to the west, he found a forested plateau with excellent views of the surrounding landscape. It dominated the road to Albany and was perfect for defense.

On September 13, Burgoyne and his entire army crossed the Hudson on his temporary boat bridge, which he destroyed after their crossing. That act severed his line of communication to Canada. He had intentionally isolated his army and had come to the conclusion that his only chance to save his army was to advance on Albany as originally planned, even if General Howe was not going to assist him from the lower Hudson. His last hope for relief died when he received word from Colonel Leger that he was unable to secure Fort Stanwix (later called Fort Schuyler), and was retreating back to Canada via Lake Ontario. Burgoyne was destined to face the unpleasant task of opposing the Americans alone.

As expected, a number of letters passed to and from Stark's camp immediately after the battle, which became a source of great joy and thanksgiving across the land. When General George Washington learned of the success at Bennington, he exclaimed, "One more such stroke, and we shall have no great cause for anxiety as to the future designs of Britain."[2] The news squelched all negative reactions by politicians in Congress and irate officers in the Continental army about Stark's firm refusal to place his militia under their control. Success had validated his obstinate refusal to violate his authority for an independent command. The first letter Stark wrote after Bennington was a report to the New Hampshire Council. Dated August 18, 1777, he wrote:

"*Gentlemen*—I congratulate you on the late success of your troops under my command, by express. I propose to give you a brief account of my proceedings since I wrote you last.

"I left Manchester, Vt., on the 8th instant, and arrived here on the 9th. The 13th I was informed that a party of Indians were at Cambridge [New York] which is twelve miles distant from this place on their march thither. I detached Col. Gregg, with two hundred men under his command, to stop their march.

"In the evening I had information, by express, that there was a large body of the enemy on their way, with field pieces, in order to march through the country, commanded by Governor Skene. The 14th I marched with my brigade, and a portion of the State militia, to oppose them, and cover Gregg's retreat who found himself unable to withstand their superior numbers. About four miles from this town I accordingly met him on his return, and the enemy in close pursuit of him, within a half mile of his rear; but when they discovered me, they presently halted on a very advantageous piece of ground.

"I drew up my little army on an eminence in view of their encampment,—but could not bring them to an engagement. I marched back about a mile, and there encamped. I sent a few men to skirmish with them, who killed thirty of them, with two Indian chiefs. The 15th it rained all day; [It was a very rainy summer and fall that year.] I sent out parties to harass them.

"The 16th I was joined by this State's (Vt.) militia, and those of Berkshire county. I divided my army into three divisions, and sent Lieut. Col. Nichols with two hundred and fifty men on the rear of their left wing, Colonel Herrick on the rear of their right, ordered, when joined, to attack the same. In the meantime I sent three hundred men to oppose the enemy's front, to draw their attention that way. Soon after I detached Colonels Hubbard [Hobart] and Stickney on their right wing with two hundred men, to attack that part; all which plans had their desired effect. Colonel Nichols sent me word that he stood in need of reinforcements, which I readily granted, consisting of one hundred men; at which time he commenced the attack at precisely at three o'clock in the afternoon, which was followed by all the rest. I pushed the remainder with all speed.

"Our people behaved with the greatest spirit and bravery imaginable. Had they been Alexanders, or Charleses of Sweden, they could not have behaved better.

"The action lasted two hours; at the expiration of which time we forced the breastworks, at the muzzle of their guns; took two pieces of brass cannon, with a number of prisoners; but before I could get them into proper form again, I received intelligence that there was a large reinforcement within two miles of us, on their march, which occasioned us to renew our attack; but, luckily for us, Colonel Warner's regiment came up, which put a stop to their career. We soon rallied, and in a few minutes the action began very warm and desperate, which lasted until night. We used their cannon against them, which proved of great service to us.

"At sunset we obliged them to retreat a second time; we pursued them till dark, when I was obliged to halt for fear of killing our men.

"We recovered two pieces of their cannon, together with all their baggage, a number of horses, carriages, &c.; killed upward of two hundred of the enemy in the field of battle.

"The number of wounded is not yet known, as they are scattered about in many places. I have one lieutenant colonel, since dead, (Colonel Baum), one major, seven captains, fourteen lieutenants, four ensigns, two cornets, one judge advocate, one baron, two Canadian officers, six sergeants, one aid-de-camp, one Hessian chaplain, three Hessian surgeons, and seven hundred prisoners.

"I enclose you a copy of General Burgoyne's instructions to Colonel Baum, who commanded the detachment that engaged us. Our wounded are forty-two—ten privates and four officers, belonging to my brigade; one dead. The dead and wounded in the other corps I do not know, as they have not brought in their returns yet.

"I am. Gentlemen, with the greatest regard, your most obedient and humble servant, Brigadier General John Stark.

P.S. I think in this action we have returned the enemy a proper compliment for their Hubbardston engagement."[3]

General Schuyler was quick to announce the good news to John Hancock, president of the Congress, even though his replacement had already arrived in the theater. From Van Schaik's Island, August 18, 1777, Schuyler wrote:

"*Sir*—I have the honor to congratulate Congress on a signal victory obtained by General Stark, on account whereof is contained in the following letter from General Lincoln, which I have this moment had the happiness to receive; together with General Burgoyne's instructions to Lieut. Col. Baum, a copy whereof is inclosed.

"I am in hopes Congress will very soon have the satisfaction to hear that Gen. Arnold has raised the siege of Fort Schuyler. If that takes place, I believe it will be possible to engage two or three hundred Indians to join the army, and Congress may rest assured that my best endeavors shall not be wanting to accomplish it.

"I am informed that General Gates arrived at yesterday. Major Livingston, one of my aids, will have the honor to deliver this dispatch. Your obedient servant,

PH SCHUYLER"[4]

General Schuyler also sent a personal note of congratulations to Stark on the nineteenth of August. It was one of his last duties as commander of the Northern Department:

"*Dear Sir*—I do myself the pleasure to congratulate you on the signal victory you have gained. Please accept my best thanks. The consequence of the severe stroke the enemy have received can not fail of producing the most salutary results. I have dispatched one of my aids-de-camp to announce your victory to Congress, and the Commander-in-chief. Governor Clinton is coming up the river with a body of militia; and I trust that, after what the enemy have received from you, their progress will be retarded, and that we shall yet see them driven out of the country. General Gates is at Albany, and will this day resume the command.

PH. SCHUYLER."[5]

Meshesh Weare, the Chairman of the New Hampshire Committee of Safety acknowledged Stark's report:

"Dear Sir—The committee received yours, of the 18th instant, with the greatest pleasure, and have directed me to present their very sincere thanks to you, the officers and soldiers under your command, for their brave and spirited conduct manifested in the late battle, and for the essential service done to the country at this critical period. I hope, sir, that this success may be a prelude to greater things of the same kind; and that heaven will yet bestow many blessings upon our country, through your hands.

"Fervantly praying that the God of armies may protect you in the day of battle, and be a shield and buckler to our countrymen under your command, and that he may give success and victory to all your undertakings, I do, in behalf of the committee, subscribe myself. . . [6]

General Burgoyne wrote a letter announcing his peril to Lord George Germain, exaggerating the number of militia opposing him. Germain failed to appreciate his tenuous situation. Excerpts from Burgoyne's letter of August 20, 1777 follow:

"The consequences of this affair [the battle of Bennington], my Lord, have little effect upon the strengths or spirits of the army; but the prospects of the campaign in other respects is far less prosperous than when I wrote last . . . Fort Stanwix holds out obstinately.

"I am afraid the expectations of Sir Johnson greatly fail in the rising of the country. On this side I find daily reason to doubt the sincerity of the resolution of the professing Loyalists. . .The great bulk of the country is undoubtedly with the Congress, in principle and in zeal; and their measures are executed with a secrecy and dispatch that are not to be equaled.

Wherever the King's forces point, militia, to the amount of three or four thousand, assemble in twenty-four hours; they bring with them their subsistence, etc., and, the alarm over, they return to their farms. The Hampshire Grants in particular, a country unpeopled and almost unknown in the last war, now abounds in the most active and most rebellious race of the continent, and hangs like a gathering storm upon my left. [Stark and the men with him would be flattered with this description of them.] In all parts the industry and management of driving cattle and removing corn are indefatigable and certain . . .

"Another most embarrassing circumstance is the want of communication with Sir William Howe . . . only one letter is come to hand, informing me that his intention is for Pennsylvania . . . Washington has detached Sullivan, with 2,500 men, to Albany; that Putnam is in the highlands with 4,000 men; that after my arrival at Albany . . .

"No operation, my Lord, has yet been undertaken in my favor . . . Putnam has detached two brigades to Mr. Gates, who is now strongly posted near the mouth of the Mohawk River, with an army superior to mine in troops of the Congress and as many militia as he pleases. He is likewise far from deficient in artillery, having received all the pieces that were landed from the French ships which got into Boston.

"Had I the latitude in my orders, I should think it my duty to wait in this position, or perhaps as far back as Fort Edward, where my communication with Lake George would be perfectly secure. . .but my orders being positive to 'force a junction with Sir William Howe'. . . I am not at liberty to remain inactive longer than shall be necessary to collect twenty-five days of provisions . . . the hour I pass the Hudson's River and proceed towards Albany, all safety of communication ceases. I must expect a large body of the enemy from my left will take post behind me.[Stark's force]. . .

"Whatever may be my fate, my Lord, I submit my actions to the breast of the king, and to the candid judgment of my profession, when all the motives become public, and I rest in the confidence that, whatever decision may be passed upon my conduct, my good intent will not be questioned . . ."[7]

General Stark stubbornly refused to report directly to Congress or to the Continental army. His main obligation was to the State of New Hampshire, and once that was fulfilled, he voluntarily submitted the following letter to Gates. It is more detailed than the one he sent to New

Hampshire and, seems to give the best point of view of the Battle of Bennington available. General Lincoln had previously notified Gates of the victory at Bennington. It should be noted that Stark gave Colonel Baum a military funeral with full honors. The letter of August 22, 1777 to Gates follows:

"Dear General—Yours of the 19th was received with pleasure and I should have answered it sooner, but I have been very unwell since. [We do not know what kind of illness Stark had, but it's unlikely that he was wounded.] General Lincoln has written to you upon the subject, with whom I most cordially concur in opinion. [The above introduction is taken from Moore's version of the letter on page 333. The balance of the letter is an exact duplicate of the one General Gates received from Stark.] I shall now give your Honour a brief account of the action on the 13th inst. I was informed that there was a party of Indians in Cambridge on their march to this place. I sent Lieut. Colonel Greg of my brigade to stop them with 200 men. In the night I was informed by express that there was a large body of the enemy on their march in the rear of the Indians. I rallied my brigade and what Militia was at this place in order to stop their proceedings. Likewise sent to Manchester to Colonel Warner's regiment that was stationed there; also sent expresses for the Militia to come in with all speed to our assistance, which was punctually obeyed. I then marched in company with Colonel's Warner, Williams, Herrick and Brush, with all the men that were present. About 5 miles from this place I met Colonel Greg on his retreat and the enemy in close pursuit after him.

"I drew up my little army in order of battle, but when the enemy hove in sight, they halted on a very advantageous hill or piece if ground. I sent out small parties in their front to skirmish with them, which scheme had a good effect. They killed and wounded thirty of the enemy without any loss on our side, but the ground that I was upon did [not] suit for a general action, I marched back about one mile and incamped. Called a counsel, and it was agreed that we should send two detachments in their rear, while the others attacked them in front. But the 15th it rained all day; therefore, had to lay by, could do nothing but skirmish withy them.

"On the 16th in the morning was joined by Colonel Simmons with some Militia from Berkshire County. I pursued my plan, detached Colonel Nichols with 200 men to attack them in the rear. I also sent Colonel Herrick with 300 men to attack in the rear of their right, both to join, and when joined to attack their rear. I likewise sent the Colonels Hubbard and Whitney with 200 men on their right, and sent 100 men in their front, to draw away their attention that way, and about 3 o'clock we got all ready for the attack. Colonel Nichols began the same, which was followed by all the rest. The remainder of my little army I pushed up the front, and in a few minutes the action began. In general, it lasted 2 hours, the hottest I ever saw in my life. It represented one continued clap of thunder. However the enemy was obliged to give way, and leave their field pieces and all their baggage behind them. They were all environed within two breastworks, with their artillery. But our martial courage proved too hard for them.

"I then gave orders to rally again, in order to secure the victory, but in a few minutes was informed that there was a large reinforcement on their march within two miles of us. Lucky for us, that moment Colonel Warner's regiment came up fresh, who marched on and began the attack afresh. I pushed forward as many of the men as I could to their assistance. The battle continued obstinate on both sides till sunset. The enemy was obliged to retreat. We pursued till dark. But had daylight lasted one hour longer, we should have taken the whole body of them. We recovered 4 pieces of brass cannon, some hundred stands of arms, 8 brass barrels, drums, several Hessian swords, about seven hundred prisoners, 207 dead on the spot. [Collections of trophies were sent to New Hampshire, Massachusetts and Vermont] The number of wounded is as yet unknown. That part of the enemy that made their escape marched all night, and we returned to our camp.

"Too much honor cannot be given to the brave officers and soldiers for gallant behaviour. They fought through the midst of fire and smoke, mounted two breastworks that was well fortified and supported with cannon. I can't particularize any officer as they all behaved with the greatest spirit and bravery.

"Colonel Warner's superior skill in action was of extraordinary service to me. I would be glad he and his men could be recommended by Congress.

"As I promised in my orders that the soldiers should have all the plunder taken in the enemy's camp, would be glad your Honour would send me word what the value of the cannon and the other artillery stores above described may be. Our loss was inconsiderable, about 40 wounded and thirty killed. I lost my horse, bridle and saddle in the action."[8]

On September 6, 1777, the State of Vermont Council of Safety wrote to General Stark. It is self-explanatory:

"The council's compliments most cordially wait on his honor, Brigadier Gen. Stark, with their sincere thanks for the honor the general has been pleased to do them, by presenting a Hessian broad-sword, taken by a number of troops from the State of New Hampshire and elsewhere, under his command, in the ever memorable battle fought at Walloomschaik, near this place, on the sixteenth day of August last; and also for the honor the general has pleased to do them in applauding their exertions as a council."[9]

Many historians and writers have assumed that General Stark's horse was killed out from under him during the battle. It was not killed, it was stolen, and Stark was furious about it. He ran the following ad in the Hartford, Connecticut *Courant*:

"TWENTY DOLLARS REWARD. Stole from me, the subscriber, from Wallumsciok, in the time of action, the 16th of August last, a Brown Mare, five years old, had a star in her forhead. Also, a doe skin-seated saddle, blue housing trimmed with white, and a curbed bridle. It is earnestly requested of all Committees of Safety, and others in authority, to exert themselves to recover said thief and Mare, so that he may be brought to justice, and the mare brought to me; and the person, who ever he be, shall have the above reward for both, and for the Mare alone, one half of that sum—How scandalous, how disgraceful and ignominious, must it appear to all friendly and generous souls, to have such sly, artful, designing villains enter into the field of action, in order to pillage, pilfer, and plunder from brethren when engaged in battle!"[10]

Historical scholars Foster and Streeter summed up their opinion of Stark:

"Stark showed quiet insight and decision, followed by deliberate action. At Bennington, Bunker Hill and Trenton, he was quick to use the importance of flanking movements and cool in carrying them out . . . He was as active in attack as he was obstinate in defense."[11]

16

Saratoga (September-October 1777)

The British were convinced that 1777 was going to be the year they triumphed over the rebellious colonists. The traditional passage of enemy troops through the Champlain-Hudson River corridor appeared to be working, and the means to confront such a strong force was beyond the floundering Continental army under General George Washington to oppose it. Fear and despair that their cause was lost was universal. The newly founded state of Vermont was unable to persevere in the face of such a powerful army so they had sent out letters requesting assistance to their New Hampshire, New York and Massachusetts neighbors.

New Hampshire could not refuse and Brigadier General John Stark with a brigade of New Hampshire militia answered the call. While they were rushing to the region, Burgoyne pushed beyond Ticonderoga down Champlain to the southern extreme of the lake to Skenesboro, where he began his overland march along Wood Creek to Fort Anne. The rugged wilderness and sporadic sniping by the Americans who had left Ticonderoga had whittled away at Burgoyne's strength and supplies, delaying his progress. The local militia denied him access to cattle and other food supplies and, most of all, to horses for his German dragoons.

Stark's defeat of the Baum and Breymann detachments further eroded Burgoyne's strength. He had high hopes of gaining aid from Colonel Leger, who was fighting his way east along the Mohawk toward the Hudson. Those hopes were dashed when word came that Leger was retreating from Fort Stanwix after the aggressive General Benedict Arnold had mounted a relief expedition from Albany to reinforce the fort. The American victory on the Mohawk, accompanied by success at Bennington, reversed much of the defeatism that had permeated the Americans outlook. Now, victory seemed more plausible even though a lot of hard fighting lay ahead. Bennington was a moral victory that delivered a crippling blow to Burgoyne's shrinking army. Morale among the fighting troops and the general population soared.

As he noted in his reports to Gates and the New Hampshire Congress, John Stark was ill, possibly during and after the battle. Administrative measures and the problems of securing care and adequate supplies for the wounded delayed him for a month. After the battle, he received warm congratulations from every portion of the country and he must have felt vindicated for his determined independent stance against those who would undermine his authority. There is no evidence that he was bothered by the bruised egos of his superiors. His triumph over his political opponents, was complete. The fact that he maintained exclusive authority over his independent command was the key to his brilliant victory at Bennington. Stark wore the crown of success with modest dignity, always giving credit to the men who served under him.

On September 18, Stark and his brigade marched into Gates's camp to offer his services. It was a gallant show of solidarity on Stark's part and it pleased Gates, who was anxious to assemble as many troops as possible. The feeling was that Burgoyne was positioning himself for an imminent fight. He had less than a month's supply of food on hand, and that fact limited his options.

Enlistment time of one month for Stark's brigade had expired and he returned to New Hampshire to make his report in person. Gates had offered the men an additional ten dollars apiece if they would stay for the battle about to take place, but they were determined to head home when their time was up. It proved to be one of the limitations associated with militia troops during the entire Revolutionary War. The New Hampshire Assembly had recognized the limitations of the brigade then under Stark and had set in motion plans to secure another brigade to serve under him. Once his new, New Hampshire brigade of three thousand troops was assembled and provisioned, Stark headed back to the Hudson Valley to assist in the defeat of Burgoyne's army. Stark was somewhat hampered with illness throughout the fight at Bennington and Saratoga. We have no information on the nature of his illness, but it was probably arthritis or rheumatism, which severely plagued him for the rest of his life.

The Hessian prisoners of war were well treated by Stark's troops. They were veterans of the Seven Years War and came from a mountainous region in Germany that produced sturdy, well-disciplined soldiers. They were brave and efficient and Stark admired them. When he returned to New Hampshire to obtain a new regiment, Stark brought several Hessian soldiers with him. They soon formed the nucleus of a prosperous farming colony. One Henri Archelaus was a body servant to Colonel Baum and tended to him in death. Archelaus lived a long life and died in Weare, New Hampshire.

Early in October, Stark received a letter from John Hancock, President of the Congress of the United States, authorized by the delegates from all thirteen states.

"To General Stark, Esquire

We, reposing especial trust and confidence in your patriotism, valor, conduct and fidelity, do, by these presents, constitute and appoint you to be brigadier general in the army of the United States, raised for the defense of American liberty, and for repelling every hostile invasion thereof. You are, therefore, carefully and diligently to discharge the duty of brigadier general by doing and performing all manner of things thereunto belonging; and we do strictly enjoin, charge, and require all officers and soldiers under your command to be obedient to your orders, as brigadier general. And you are to observe and follow such orders and directions, from time to time, as you shall receive from this or a future Congress of the United States, or committee of Congress, for that purpose appointed, or the commander-in-chief, for the time being, of the army of the United States, or any other, your superior officers, according to the rules and discipline of war, in pursuance of the trust reposed in you. This commission to continue in force until revoked by this or a future Congress. Dated October 4, 1777.

By order of Congress—

JOHN HANCOCK, *President.*

Attest. CHAS. THOMPSON, *Secretary.*"[1]

The above resolve was accompanied by another letter from Hancock dated October 5, 1777:

"To General Stark, from President Hancock.

Sir—It is with the greatest pleasure I transmit the enclosed resolve of Congress, expressing the thanks of that body to you, and to the officers and troops under your command, for the signal victory you obtained over the enemy in the late battle of Bennington.

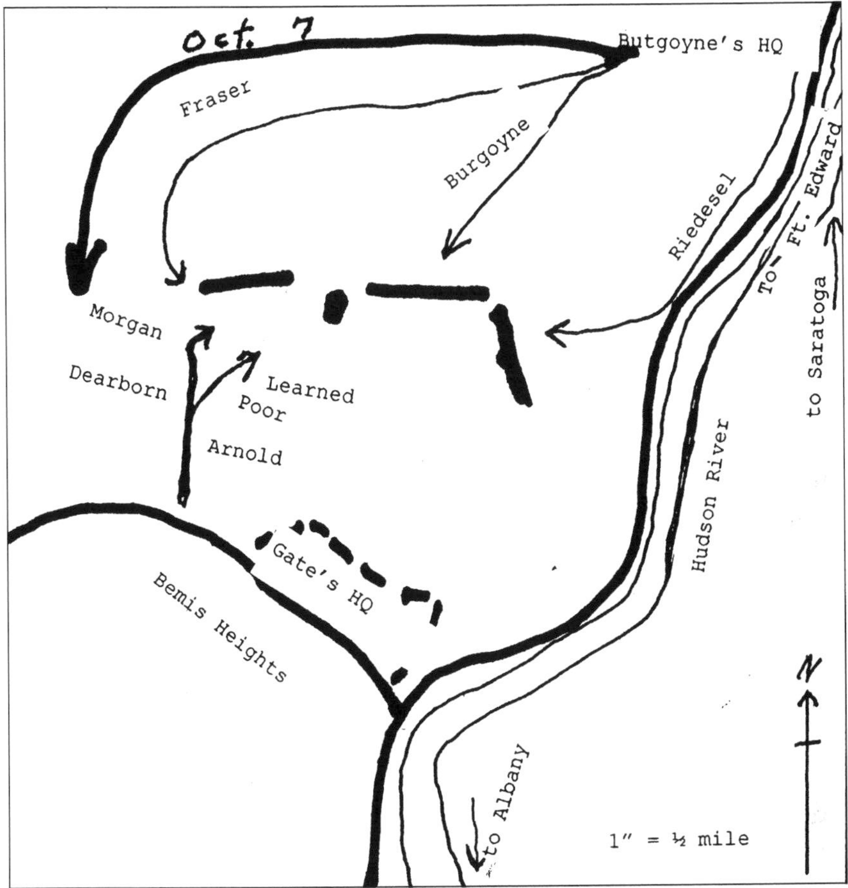

Battles of Saratoga, September 19, 1777 and October 7, 1777

"In consideration of your distinguished conduct on that occasion, and the service you rendered the cause of freedom and your country, the Congress have been pleased to appoint you a brigadier general in the army of the United States. Be pleased to communicate to the officers and troops, under your command, this marks of the approbation of their country for their exertions in defence of American liberty.

"I inclose your commission, and have the honor to be, with the greatest esteem and respect, sir, your most obedient and very humble servant,

JOHN HANCOCK, *President*

In Congress, October 4, 1777

Resolved, That the thanks of Congress be presented to General Stark, of the New Hampshire militia, and the officers and troops under his command, for their brave and successful attack upon, and signal victory over the enemy, in their lines at Bennington; and that Brigadier Stark be appointed a brigadier in the army of the United States.

By order of Congress—

JOHN HANCOCK, *President.*"[2]

John Stark's oldest son, Caleb, was wounded in the left arm during the action at Saratoga on October 7. He had been an adjutant to Colonel Cilley's First New Hampshire Regiment. Because a commission as brigadier general allowed a full-time aide, the general picked his son for the job. Lieutenant Caleb carried out his duties as aide, brigade major, and adjutant general when his father was head of the Northern Department from 1778 through 1781. Caleb was a good writer, and possessed good penmanship. He wrote all of his father's letters for the duration of the war. It was an ideal arrangement and we can assume that it was enjoyable for both parties, especially young Caleb, who was able to observe the higher echelons of power from a strong vantage point.

Events on the Hudson were racing to an explosive encounter. The British walked over their temporary bridge across the Hudson to the west bank on September 13, and headed for Saratoga with four weeks of food supplies. Burgoyne dismantled the bridge and floated his baggage and all of the supplies from Fort Anne and Fort Edward, down the river in large bateaus to a protected area known as Dovegate (now Coville). The British army was now cut off from its line of supply in Canada. That first night, Burgoyne sent out small patrols to locate the Americans; his intelligence was limited then because most of his Indian scouts had deserted. The patrols did not make contact with the Americans, but they did hear their evening guns being fired in the distance.

That autumn of 1777 in the Champlain Valley was a wet one and roadways were easily churned into rivers of mud by the heavy supply wagons. Days were warm, but the nights were getting colder and in the morning light frosts covered the ground. The leaves were beginning to change from green to red and yellow. Winter in the northern portions of New York was always long and severe. Burgoyne knew he had to reach Albany before its onset. He could not survive a winter where he was.

The American camps were filling daily with more troops. The country had generously responded to Gates's urgent request for troops from New England, New York, and Pennsylvania. The destruction of Burgoyne's army was their main goal. Morale was high, and the troops were anxious to finish the job. By early September Gates had nine thousand men in his command and it was growing larger every day.

Gates had ordered a bridge built across the Hudson slightly north of the Fishkill River. This enabled him to communicate with the Massachusetts regiment, which was in a blocking position on the eastern bank of the Hudson. At the same time, work began in earnest at Bemis Heights, a wooded plateau three miles north of Stillwater, overlooking the road to Albany. The brilliant Polish engineer Colonel Tadeusz Kosciuszko had designed and directed the construction of redoubts on the elevations overlooking the river, continuing north and west to include Neilson's house, which was embraced at the northern extreme of the redoubt. The fortifications were strongly built and adequately manned. The artillery and infantry positions on the higher elevations near the river effectively closed the Hudson Valley escape route to the British, and forced them to fight the Americans much as Gates had planned.

From September 13 through the nineteenth, the opposing forces sent out regular patrols to locate their respective enemy. Gates strategy was to wait within the confines of his fortifications and let Burgoyne come to him. It was a logical plan because he was blocking Burgoyne's passage south to Albany and time was on Gates's side. He set up his headquarters a half mile south of Neilson's house.

Benedict Arnold had a passion for being at the front of his troops so he could influence the action. He had brought with him a regiment of Continental soldiers from Connecticut, troops raised by the Continental Congress to serve as federal troops for two or three years. He and Gates were constantly feuding over military matters. Gates was spitefully determined to keep Arnold from leading troops so as to not be "outclassed" by the energetic and courageous general.

September 19 dawned with a drizzling rain and a heavy mist that hampered visibility. Burgoyne left his headquarters near Saratoga north of Bemis Heights at eight in the morning with three columns of troops. Brigadier General Fraser was on the right flank, Brigadier General Hamilton brought up the center, and Major General William Philips with Major General Riedesel's Hessians in support were on the left flank covering the Albany Road and the riverbank. Burgoyne's plan was to locate the Americans' left wing with Frazer's troops while he and Hamilton's center column followed a cart track westward north of Freeman's farm, so called after the Tory owner, who had fled the scene. Philips and Riedesel would remain in strength on the road, which Burgoyne knew was heavily barricaded.

By nine o'clock the mist was burned off by the sun, highlighting the red uniforms of the British as they marched through the forest. Burgoyne halted his center column near Freeman's farm house and waited for Fraser to complete his right hook to Gates's left flank. By one o'clock, the signal gun was fired to alert the columns to move forward until contact was made with the Americans.

Arnold's regiment was covering Gates's left wing with Brigadier Ebenezer Learned fortifying the center line. Arnold had successfully badgered Gates to allow him to go forward to support his own Connecticut regiment, with Colonel Daniel Morgan's riflemen, Major Henry Dearborn's elite light-infantry and his own Connecticut regiment in support. At 12:45 Morgan's men clashed with a detachment of Canadians and Indians, killing all of the officers. As they pursued the fleeing Canadians, Morgan ran into the main column of Fraser's infantry, scattering Morgan's men in a rout. At that moment the battle became a slugfest. Soldiers on each side fought bravely. Brigadier General Enoch Poor's New Hampshire and New York brigade reinforced Morgan's riflemen and tried to turn the British right flank, but failed.

Hamilton's center had borne the majority of the fighting. Arnold's troops on the left flank had also suffered heavy casualties, but they still had a lot of fight left. Arnold needed more troops for a final push. Gates denied his request, afraid of Arnold's impulsive behavior.

Darkness was descending on the battlefield as Burgoyne ordered Riedesel to attack with his regiment and two six-pounders loaded with grapeshot. The Germans cleared the field as the Americans retreated into the security of their entrenchments, leaving the British masters of the battlefield, even though they had paid a heavy price without breaching any of Gate's redoubts. The British lost one hundred and sixty dead, three hundred sixty-four wounded and forty-two missing. Thirty-five of the casualties were officers. Gates had sixty-three killed, two hundred and twelve wounded and thirty-eight missing.

That night, Burgoyne had some difficult decisions to make and postponed the attack for the next day. On September 21 he received a letter from General Henry Clinton, dated the eleventh, that he planned to attack Forts Montgomery and Clinton on October 3, a detachment of troops would continue up the Hudson to Aesop (now Kingston), forty-two miles from Albany. Eventually, his force was recalled on October 22. He was too far away to influence or reduce the pressure on Burgoyne anyway.

During the lull following the first engagement, both sides worked feverishly to improve their positions. Burgoyne's became even more tenuous with no hope of relief from Lord Clinton's southern column. His troops constructed three heavy redoubts on the ground between the Hudson River and the higher elevations near Freeman's farm. On October 3 he cut food rations to conserve his supply. Throughout the pause, reinforcements from the region continued to flow to Gates's headquarters, and he tracked Burgoyne's movements with constant patrols. Burgoyne now had about five thousand men. His horses were dying from starvation.

On October 4, Burgoyne called for a council of war and planned another reconnaissance in force to test Gates's positions. If they found them to be insurmountable, then Burgoyne suggested they retreat to Batten Kill. On October 7 he ordered his three-pronged attack in motion with him and his staff at the center column under Riedesel. The right wing was still under Fraser's command and the left was commanded by Brigadier General Acland. The mobile columns were picked for their proven mobility and their artillery firepower, including two eight-inch mortars.

Burgoyne again halted the attack force beyond their redoubts and north of the Great Ravine. Gates was warned of their presence and ordered Morgan's riflemen and Dearborn's infantry, both seasoned fighters with high mobility, to outflank the British right wing. Poor was ordered to attack the left wing and Learned was prepared to absorb the main thrust from the enemy's center.

Poor's brigade was the first to make contact, on the left. Major Acland put up a spirited resistance but had to give ground. He was wounded and taken prisoner early in the operation. Minutes after Poor's initial contact, Morgan and Dearborn opened fire on Fraser's flank and rolled it back. Fraser was mortally wounded during this engagement. As he was a much respected officer, Fraser's loss took some of the fight out of his brigade.

When Lady Harriet Acland, wife of Major John Acland, received word that her husband was wounded and taken prisoner, she was given permission by General Burgoyne to go to his side. She climbed into a boat with her maidservant, her husband's wounded valet, and the Reverend Edward Brudenell. They sailed down the Hudson until they were hailed by Major Henry Dearborn, who ordered them ashore. He noted that the determined lady was pregnant and immediately escorted her to his house. A fire was laid and her luggage placed inside the house. She carried a note from General Burgoyne, who entrusted her to Gates's care so that she could be with her husband. She was introduced to General Gates, who was taken in by her beauty and title. He called her, "the most amiable, delicate piece of quality you ever behold"[3]

Burgoyne's center became seriously exposed and vulnerable when his left and right wings were pressed hard. Riedesel's three hundred Germans faced ten times as many Americans from Learned's brigade. The battle continued with great ferocity on both sides. Burgoyne knew he had to withdraw behind his recently built barricades after suffering four hundred casualties. His last hope was to hang on to the breastworks so that he could extricate his army to safety. Those hopes were dashed when Benedict Arnold arrived on horseback to take command of the situation. Gates had been quarreling with Arnold since Schuyler's departure, and had removed him from his command. That did not stop Arnold from riding into the crucible, rallying scattered units and bringing an aggressive sense of purpose to the American combatants. He correctly recognized that the redoubt that Burgoyne had withdrawn to was too strong to take in a frontal assault, so he concentrated on the northernmost redoubt at the top of the hill, commanded by Breymann. His Hessians put up a strong resistance with their customary courage. Breymann was killed shortly after the redoubt was abandoned.

Arnold's horse was shot out from under him during the assault. He fell, breaking his wounded leg. As the battle was waning, Burgoyne broke off the fighting and withdrew to the redoubt on the highest elevation, overlooking the road to Albany and the Great Ravine. He had lost one hundred and seventy-six killed, two hundred wounded and two hundred and forty captured. Gate's suffered about two hundred casualties.

The next day, Burgoyne recognized that his position was untenable and withdrew even farther toward Saratoga. His retreat was difficult with wagon wheels axle-deep in mud. The troops were exhausted and demoralized. The lowly rebels had shown that they too were capable of standing up to the best the British had to offer. Perhaps a new admiration displaced their scorn for the unconventional army of rebels. They were also thankful that Gates did not immediately pursue them.

Gates was perfectly content to stand off at a safe distance to pound their positions with cannon fire and wait for starvation to defeat the enemy for him. On October 12, Burgoyne called for a council of war. He and his officers planned to break away in the dead of night without their baggage and artillery. Their main concern was to save the army. It might have worked except that Fort Edward had just been taken by Stark's new brigade. Ketchum described Stark's major contribution to the Saratoga battle:

> "The northern escape corridor had been sealed off during the night by the mercurial hero of Bennington, John Stark, who had suddenly appeared with more than a thousand New Hampshire militia, led them across the Hudson near the mouth of the Batten Kill, and erected a battery on the west side."[4]

On October 13, Burgoyne asked Gates for terms and surrendered his army on October 16. This surrender was the turning point in the Revolutionary War, and Stark's performance at Bennington had set the stage for Gates's success at Saratoga. Therefore, General Gates requested General Stark to fire the salute at the surrender ceremony. After igniting the charge in thirteen cannons, Stark then exclaimed, "Now one more for Vermont," and proceeded to do so.[5]

17

Post-Saratoga (1777-1778)

The surrender of Burgoyne's army at Saratoga was a pivotal moment in the War for Independence. Coming on the heels of Stark's stunning victory at Bennington, Saratoga lifted the hearts from the despair that had gripped the country after a long chain of defeats, at Philadelphia, Brandywine, Long Island, Germantown, in addition to Ticonderoga. Now, there was a feeling among the colonial officers that General Arthur St. Clair's decision to evacuate the fort and save his men to fight at a later date was tactically wise, even though he was severely chastised at the time.

One of New Hampshire's most prominent citizens, John Langdon, Speaker of the New Hampshire House, had led a voluntary militia company to Saratoga, where he witnessed the surrender of Burgoyne. He immediately had a copy of the Treaty of Convention (demanded by Burgoyne instead of a Treaty of Capitulation). He rode his horse hard to Portsmouth, and there handed it over to John Paul Jones, captain of the newly built and commissioned USS *Ranger*, a twenty-gun sloop-of-war built in John Langdon's shipyard on Rising Castle Island (now called Badger Island) in the middle of the Piscataqua River east of Portsmouth.

On November 1, Captain Jones eased the *Ranger* into the swift current of the Piscataqua River for her maiden voyage. He was ordered to carry the news of Saratoga to France, with the hope of gaining assistance for the war. Soon after the *Ranger* unfurled her new sails for the first time, a severe northeaster hit the region and Jones had to strike the sails and secure the vessel. The next day the ship sailed down the river to the Atlantic with its new American flag snapping proudly in the wind. It was Captain Jones's desire to get the information to Benjamin Franklin, the American commissioner in Paris, as soon as possible. The *Ranger* anchored at Nantes on December 2nd· He immediately sent the documents inland to Paris, where he discovered that another American ship, the *Penet,* a brigantine from Boston, had beaten him by two days. They had left Boston on October 31.[1]

Great expectations were contemplated for French assistance in conducting the war against England. The fledgling thirteen colonies that had the audacity to rise against one of the world's great powers were seeking official and international recognition for their independence. Although many sought that recognition, there was still within the colonies a lingering remembrance of the French cruelties during the French and Indian War. There was little sentiment to have France reconstitute its demand for Canada. Too much blood and treasure had been expended evicting the French from the New World so the request for assistance came with some reservations.

France responded to the appeal with two documents, the Treaty of Amity and Commerce and the Treaty of Alliance, signed on February 6, 1778. France soon became the primary source of American military supplies and equipment. The following year Spain entered the war as an ally of France. This forced England to fight on several fronts, thus weakening her ability to concentrate on the wayward colonies. This turn of events, triggered by the Saratoga victory, would not have been possible without Stark's success at Bennington. Now, ultimate victory was in sight even if temporary setbacks occasionally clouded the vision for the future.

When the two armies lined up for the surrender ceremony at Saratoga on October 17, the exhausted and defeated British and German troops were impressed with the demeanor of the Americans. Historian Ketchum wrote:

> "[N]ot a single man gave any evidence or the slightest impression of feeling hatred, mockery, malicious pleasure or pride for our miserable fate . . . it seemed rather as though they desired to do us honor . . . they behaved with the greatest decency and propriety . . . which circumstance I really believe would not have happened had the case been reversed."[2]

Stark and his son Caleb had the opportunity to meet the leading British officers at Gates's Headquarters. Caleb wrote:

> "After the surrender he [Caleb] accompanied General Stark on a visit to General Gates's at his headquarters and was introduced to all the British officers of rank who were there assembled as the guest of the American

General-in-chief of the Northern army. He said that Major Acland and General Burgoyne were in personal appearance two of the best proportioned and handsomest men. General Burgoyne held a long conversation with General Stark, apart from the other company, on the subject of the French war, of which the former then stated that he intended to write a history."[3]

After the ceremony, the war in the northern regions was winding down for the winter, and Stark planned to return to New Hampshire. On October 18 General Gates forwarded an exact copy of the convention signed by Burgoyne to Stark:

"Dear Sir—Inclosed I send you an exact copy of the Convention, signed by Gen. Burgoyne, and ratified by me. I will forward everything necessary for your assistance. Colonel Warner had my verbal instructions last evening. Let me very frequently hear from you by express, and be sure to keep a sharp look out upon Lake George and South Bay, and between Fort Ann and Fort Edward. HORATIO Gates."[4]

Stark's replied to Gates from Bennington on October 25th:

"Dear General, I arrived at this place to-day but cannot hear anything northward. I have wrote to Col. Herrick at Pollet [Pawlet] to send a skout to Tyconderoga and see what the enemy are about thare. When they return I have ordered them to make return to you and if it should be thought most necessary to Tyconderoga pray send word to the council at this place and they will give me notice which order I will punctually obey. If that nest is not broken up they may give us some trouble. I am Sir your most obd. Humble Servt, JOHN STARK."[5]

The British troops whom Burgoyne left behind at Fort Ticonderoga and Mount Independence evacuated the installations early in November. They carried away or destroyed and burned anything of use at either place, leaving them in shambles. Their departure to Montreal left the entire Hudson Valley and Lake Champlain free of British troops. The winter brought a close of military operations to the area. Most of the American troops left to join General Washington at Valley Forge near Philadelphia. It would turn out to be as bad as any of the other winter encampments the Americans had experienced. Food, clothing, and medical supplies were scarce or nonexistent and desertions were taking place in large numbers.

On December 12, 1777, the Massachusetts Senate sent the following commendation to Stark:

"That the Board of War of this State be and they are hereby directed in the name of this Court to present to the Honorable Brigadier General Stark a complete suit of clothes becoming his rank, together with a piece of linen, as a testimony of the high sense this Court have of the great and important services rendered by that officer."[6]

That winter of 1777-78 Stark became embroiled in a far-fetched scheme conceived by Gates, who now headed the National War Board. It involved a secret invasion into Canada via Lake Champlain and St. John's, on the Richelieu River, to destroy shipping and dock facilities. At first it was intended as a raid, until on December 3, 1777, Congress ordered General Stark to prepare for a winter operation by gathering men and supplies, and to proceed to Albany for a meeting with James Duane, Esq., a member of Congress from New York. Stark was sworn to secrecy. He was authorized to raise volunteers, and a sum of five thousand dollars would be advanced to purchase supplies. On December 16 Duane wrote Stark:

"Manour Livingston, 16th Dec., 1777.

"Sir—Congress, from a high sense of patriotism, activity and valor, have conferred upon you the chief command of an important enterprise, which they have very much at heart, as, under divine providence, its success entirely depends upon your expedition and secrecy.

"I am enjoined to meet with you, as soon as possible, at Albany, and there deliver your commission and instructions; and, in a personal conference, fully explain their views. . .

"I left your friend, General Folsom, in good health and spirits the 5th instant. He desired me to present you with his respectful compliments.

"It is with singular pleasure that I congratulate you and your brave militia on the honor which you have acquired at the important battle of Bennington. I feel it the more gratefully, as it has eminently contributed to rescue this devoted State (New-York) from the dangers with which it was surrounded.

"Waiting for your speedy answer, by return of the express, whom you will order to take the shortest route to this place, I have the honor to be, &c.,

JAMES DUANE."[7]

Stark wore his new uniform for the first time when he met Mr. Duane in Albany. The primary goal of the expedition was to induce Canada to join with the thirteen states. The operation became complicated when a commanding officer was being considered. Gates notified Stark of changes on January 24, 1778:

"Dear General—The honorable Congress having thought proper to direct an irruption to be immediately made into Canada, and their design being in part communicated to you by Hon. James Duane, Esg., I am directed by that honorable body to acquaint you that, for wise and prudent reasons, they have appointed Major General the Marquis de Lafayette, first in command, and General Conway, second in command, who will act in concert with you in promoting the interest and political views of the United States in Canada . . .

Horatio Gates"[8]

It is impossible to determine precisely what Stark thought of this bizarre arrangement. On the surface, common sense might have told him that Lafayette, an inexperienced twenty-year old officer, and Conway, an overly ambitious officer who had attacked the competence and integrity of General George Washington with Gates's support, were not suitable for such an enterprise. If things went well, they would get all the credit, and if they went sour, Stark would be the logical one to shoulder the blame. Stark replied February 7 in a letter to Lafayette in a rather cool tone:

"Sir,

Being informed by the Honorable General Gates that you are appointed to command an expedition against British troops in Canada & that I am to go on the same expedition should be glad to know as soon as possible what number of troops you expect I shall bring with me, what states I shall raise them in, the place of rendezvous and when to be rendezvoused and I shall leave no method untried to meet your expectations. I am, dear General, your most obedient humble servant,

JOHN STARK."[9]

Lafayette never answered this letter. By the spring of 1778, the scheme had fallen apart from lack of interest and political ineptness. Secret forays may be intriguing, but they frequently die on the vine. Stark probably shrugged his shoulders with a sigh of relief when informed that the project was stillborn. The proposed chain of command would have made it unworkable. It is interesting to note that Conway, a selfish troublemaker who never stopped criticizing Washington, was challenged one day to a duel by General John Cadwalader, a close friend of Washington, who put a bullet through Conway's mouth and neck, thereby "shutting his lying mouth." Conway was exiled to France and died seven years later.[10]

General Stark arrived in Albany on May 18 to accept the command of the Northern Department with Caleb as an aide and major of brigade. Young Caleb was a likeable young man with an engaging personality. Father and son stayed at one of the best taverns in town. It was the elder Stark's first independent Continental army command with Gates as his immediate superior. On May 18, Gates sent him a letter that arrived the first day Stark reported in at Albany.

"To Brigadier General Stark.

Fishkill, May 18, 1778.

Dear Sir—This instant I received your favor of the 19th of April last. I hope that this letter will find you in Albany, from whence I have desired General Conway to remove, the moment he has embarked the troops and stores to be sent down the river. As the committee at Bennington have offered to recruit Colonel Warner's regiment with three hundred men, I desire you will immediately transmit them the inclosed requisition for that number. I will write to Congress for the commission of your son [General Stark's eighteen year old son Archibald], and shall, the instant I receive it, transmit it to your hand.

I am, dear Sir, your affectionate humble serv't,

HORATIO GATES."[11]

Early in June, Stark wrote to General Washington to inform him that he would have been willing and happy to serve under General Sullivan in his campaign if that was the general's wish. The two New Hampshire generals got along well, even though they were of opposite personalities. Stark spoke of the disagreeable situation at Albany and how he had little opportunity to serve the country or himself to any advantage. Being a dedicated soldier that he was, Stark wrote that he "would cheerfully obey any orders that are entrusted to me, and proceed wherever Congress shall think I may be of most service. I have no will of my own; the good of the common cause is all my ambition . . ."[12]

Stark's tour of duty at the isolated post in Albany was frustrating. Very few troops were available to maintain basic law and order, even though he was authorized to call for additional men from New Hampshire, Vermont, and Massachusetts. To adequately secure and patrol such an unlimited wilderness would require ten times the manpower he had available. Surrounded by Tories, spies, speculators, and common criminals, the frontier was a very unsafe place. Stark administered the region with a firm hand, meting out just punishment that included several hangings. On June 28, he sent an accurate assessment of his situation in a detailed report to New Hampshire Congress:

"Dear Sir—I take this opportunity, by express, to inform you of my situation at this place. I arrived on the 18th of May, and found the greatest irregularity in the army. There were then two regiments here, and both ordered away. I detained one of them for the security of the city and stores, as I could place no dependence upon the militia; such a set of poltroons is not to be found on the face of the earth. When their all is at stake, they rather chose to see it destroyed than to hazard anything in its defence. On the 13th of May, a party of continental troops, who were stationed at a place called Schoharie, about thirty or forty miles from this place, being informed that a party of the enemy were advancing to destroy it, marched out, but could not induce the militia to follow them, except seven or eight; and in a short time were engaged with a party of the enemy, in which action the captain, and the lieutenant, and fifteen men were killed, while the militia coldly looked on, but did not go to their assistance. Such is their conduct; and when I applied to them for a guard for their state prisoners, they told me there were so many tories among them that they could not be depended upon.

"The Indians and tories are making depredations daily at the westward. They have burned many houses, killed and driven away a great number of cattle.

"The enemy have been very still at the northward, but I expect they will break out soon, as they visit Crown Point sometimes. If they should appear in that quarter, none can be depended upon for the security of the country but you.

"Gen. Bayley informs me that he has sent one Major Wright, of Peter's corps, to Number Four, but could not get the people of that place to take him into custody, which is similar to their conduct last year. I wish their conduct to be inquired into. He was obliged to send him to you. I would take it kind if he were secured, as he is an arrant poltroon.

"It is reported here that General Howe has left Philadelphia, and gen Washington is on his march for New-York. That may be, I do not pretend to say; but it is certain they have put their baggage on board some time ago. Gen. Gates is on his march to new-York. They (the people) do very well in the hanging way. They hanged nine on the 16th of May; on the 5th of June, nine; and have one hundred and twenty in jail, of which, I believe more than half will go the same way. Murder and robberies are committed every day in this neighborhood. So you may judge by my situation, with the enemy on my front, and the devil in my rear.

I am your obedient humble servant,

JOHN STARK."[13]

Stark had a small network of patrolling rangers and bordermen who systematically reported back to him. In that respect he was well informed about events in his sphere of responsibility, but he was almost powerless to intervene where intervention was necessary. He participated in a heavy volume of correspondence with Gates and Washington. All of Stark's letters were now being composed by Lieutenant Caleb Stark, who did a better job than his father. On the 24 of July, Stark wrote to General Washington:

"Dear sir—The Pennsylvania regiment, and a detachment of the second rifle corps arrived here the 27th inst., but in a very miserable condition for want of clothing. I inclose a return of what is wanted by them at present, without which they will not be fit for scouting, which appears the only business on hand. I shall send them immediately to the frontiers to protect the affrighted inhabitants, whose fears are not but well grounded. I think the western frontiers will never be at peace until we march an army into the Indian country, and drive these nefarious wretches from their habitations, burn their towns, destroy their crops, and make proclamation that if ever they return they shall be served in the same manner . . .

With due respect, &c.,

JOHN STARK."[14]

Stark's recommendation in 1779 was a valid one, and Washington ordered General Sullivan into the field to defeat the Indians under Brant, the infamous Tory Butlers, and the sons of Sir William Johnson, of New York. Sullivan's forces eliminated the hostile Indian settlements between the Susquehanna and Genesee Rivers in New York and Pennsylvania. The

British still controlled Crown Point on September 24, 1778, when Stark sent an interesting letter to the commander:

"To the British Commander at Crown Point.

Sir—I am not a little surprised to think of the conduct of the master of your vessels on the lake at Crown Point, who says that, by your order, he has detained Captain[unknown], whom I sent with a flag of truce, in order to carry over to you a number of people in your interest. If that was not the case, you must be sensible that it is contrary to the law of nations to detain such a flag; but also the laws of humanity forbid it; and as I have a number of prisoners in my custody, it is in my power to make retaliation. You may depend upon it I shall not let that piece of broken faith pass unnoticed.

I am, Sir, your most humble servant,

JOHN STARK."[15]

In September, 1778 Stark received intelligence that William Brant, the powerful renegade chief of the Mohawks and the illegitimate son of Sir William Johnston, was gathering a force of Tories and Indians at Unadilla on the Susquehanna for the purpose of laying waste to the New York frontier. Colonel William Butler was detached with a coalition force of Continentals and militia to oppose Brant. On October 23, Stark reports an account of the operation to General Washington:

"Dear Sir—I have just returned from Schoharie, and find that the enemy have been driven too far from the frontier for me to overtake them this season, as it is so far advanced. Too much honor cannot be given to Colonel Butler and his brave officers and soldiers, for their spirited exertions in this expedition against the Indians. [William Butler was a spirited Patriot and he should not be confused with the Tory father and son team of Walter and John, whom terrorized the frontier.] They have put it entirely out of the power of the enemy to do our frontier any serious injury for the remainder of the campaign. I beg your excellency that they may be relieved, as soon as the nature of the service will admit, as both officers and men are much fatigued.

I must beg also that clothing may be sent them, for want of which they are neither fit for duty where they are, nor in condition to be removed. It grieves me to the soul to see such brave troops in so miserable a condition.

I am, sir, &c.,

JOHN STARK."[16]

Few commanders of the period had as much experience in campaigning in the frontier wilderness as John Stark. When he praised Colonel William Butler and his men, he spoke from long experience on the deadly and lonely trail of renegades, be they Indian or white men. His experience with Rogers' Rangers made him a better general officer and his compassion for his men's suffering was genuine for having experienced it himself.

There had been some displeasure about Stark's performance in supplying and equipping militia units within the sphere of his responsibilities. He had found it impossible to satisfy all requests for supplies when he had none to give. General Hand inherited the same frustrating situation and found it as difficult.[17]

Orders came to Albany in October 16, 1778 for Stark to turn over his command at the Northern Department to General Hand. Gates needed Stark at Rhode Island. He was glad to be relieved, as was his replacement a few months later.[18]

Upon arriving at Gates' Headquarters in Providence, Stark was assigned a post in East Greenwich, on the northwestern shore of Narragansett Bay. Winter arrived and the season for action had ended, so Stark traveled back home to the arms of his beloved Molly. Caleb accompanied him via Boston to Derryfield. That winter they campaigned for additional recruitments and supplies. Recruiting support to keep the war functioning was a never-ending task.

18

Rhode Island to the Northern Department (1779-1780)

In the spring of 1779, John Stark rejoined the army at Providence. General Gates ordered him to survey the coastline from Providence along Narragansett Bay to Point Judith. Stark had a small number of men at his disposal and was kept busy intercepting British espionage detachments trying to infiltrate the area. The Royal Navy ruled the waters along the eastern coast, with the exception of small and fast privateers that preyed upon English shipping lanes. It was possible for the British to establish coastal strongholds anywhere they desired to service their fleets of warships and merchant vessels. The Americans were stretched very thin in manpower and supplies to guard against such intrusions, for the British were difficult to dislodge once they had established themselves ashore.

The most destructive defeat of an American fleet in our history took place that summer of 1779 in Penobscot Bay at Majabagaduce, now called Castine, Maine. After suffering years of shipping losses in the North Atlantic to privateers, who played a large role in supplying General Washington's army, England established a fort at Majabagaduce, called Fort George. It would provide some defense against the privateer trade and serve as a safe haven for Tories fleeing from the colonies. Brigadier Francis McClean, of the British army, and Captain Henry Mowatt, of the Royal Navy, brought seven hundred men and three sloops-of-war with fifty-six cannons to build the fort at a prominent peninsula. They called it New Ireland and planned to establish a loyalist colony.

Knowledge of the fortress reached Massachusetts and a fleet of ships to dispose of it was assembled from Massachusetts, New Hampshire, and the Continental navy, with Massachusetts financing the operation. Commodore Dudley Saltonstall was in command, with Brigadier General Solomon Lovell in charge of the twelve-hundred-man militia. Lieutenant Colonel Paul Revere commanded the artillery detachment assigned to the expedition.

The fleet sailed from Boston Harbor on July 25. The American fleet of forty-four ships, including nineteen of them armed with three hundred forty-four cannons headed for Penobscot Bay, one hundred seventy miles away. The warships entered the Bay and immediately opened fire on Fort George. The British returned fire from the fort and the three sloops, and for two hours the bombardment continued, with little damage to either side.

The Americans assaulted and overran Nautilus Island, due south of the fort, where Colonel Revere placed some of his artillery. General Lovell urged Saltonstall to close with the enemy and destroy the sloops. The commodore refused to budge. As incredible as it sounds, the Americans remained passive for two weeks. Troop morale plummeted, yet Saltonstall steadfastly refused to confront the sloops, their most serious antagonists. He had received a message from the Massachusetts Naval Board that a powerful British squadron was leaving New York to relieve Fort George. The same communication ordered Saltonstall to attack and destroy the enemy before the arrival of reinforcements. He still refused to budge!

Finally, on the thirteenth of August, Saltonstall's fleet prepared to attack while Lovell stormed the fort. The enemy fleet was sighted entering Penobscot Bay just before the operation got under way.

The Americans had a more powerful fleet than that of the British, yet when the British opened fire, Saltonstall retreated up the river in disorder and ran most of his ships aground. When he began burning them, men jumped overboard and climbed to safety on the western bank of the Penobscot. Amid the confusion, Colonel Revere lost contact with his men. It was a rout with every ship burned or run aground. Five hundred Americans were killed, wounded, or taken prisoner. Some made their way through the wilderness to Fort Western (now Augusta) and Falmouth (now Portland). Many perished in the harsh environment.

Saltonstall was court-martialed for cowardice. Revere was charged with unsoldierlike behavior and cowardice. He fought the charge for years and eventually cleared his name, but the stigma followed him to his grave.[1]

By early fall, there were indications that the British were getting ready to leave Rhode Island, in preparation for General Howe's offensives south of New England. On November 10, Stark relocated his headquarters to Point Judith. The next day he watched the British ships leave Newport, clear the harbor, and turn south. The next morning he crossed Narragansett Bay and occupied the city of Newport, setting up patrols to prevent looting and to maintain law and order. He was functioning primarily as a policeman instead of as a soldier.

General Washington was concerned that the naval force that had left Newport would attack New York, which was vulnerable. He immediately ordered Stark and Gates to leave a small garrison force at Newport and to proceed to New Jersey. Gates left Rhode Island first; Stark followed with his brigade to Morristown, New Jersey, where Washington had gone into winter quarters.

On December 28 Stark took his turn as commandant of troops at Morristown, composed of two regiments each from Maryland, Pennsylvania, and Connecticut, plus General Hand's brigade and his own. He inspected the troops and fulfilled the role with his usual efficiency, praising good work and punishing violations of the soldier's code of life. One of Stark's most admired characteristics was his accessibility and willingness to listen to what his men had to say. He had that knack of being authoritative without putting on airs of superiority. At the same time, he never struggled to make the hard decisions his position demanded. As one example:

"At a division Court Martial held in Camp Morristown by order of Brig. Gen. Stark, commandant, Dec. 28th, 1779, Lt. Col. Huntington, President. John McClane and Wm. Harper of the 4th N.Y. Regiment, tried for desertion and being absent above twelve months. Guilty: McLean [McClane] 100 lashes on his naked back to be inflicted four several times. Harper to run the Guantlope through the brigade to which he belongs. The Commander-in-chief approves each and every of the aforegoing sentences."[2]

That winter, Stark was sent to New Hampshire to recruit and arrange for supplies. He was anxious to leave Morristown for the sanctuary of his home on the Merrimack. Conditions for the men he left behind were atrocious. The longer the war lasted, the worse things seemed to get for the common soldier. Basic necessities were never adequate to sustain a robust fighting force. Over-winter locations were the most terrible ordeal considering the lack of food, clothing, and shelter.

Stark returned to the army in May 1780. He participated in the Short Hills Battle of Springfield in June, commanding a brigade of about one thousand men. The British believed that there was much discontent within the American ranks, primarily within the militia formations, and that many were anxious to join the British. This miscalculation was drawn from the extreme levels of malnutrition that plagued the Americans for the duration of the war. The main reason Stark was urged to return to his home was to generate the men and goods necessary to pursue the war effort.

Washington had detached a brigade toward Albany to control an Indian outbreak. This decision gave General Wilhelm Knyphausen a good opportunity to move into New Jersey. With six thousand men, he crossed from Staten Island into Elizabethtown on June 23, 1780.

They advanced to the small village of Connecticut Farms. There they set fire to some buildings including a church, accidentally killing Reverend James Caldwell's wife. The British advance guard was engaged by Colonel Maxwell's troops under General Greene. Maxwell was outnumbered and began a slow withdrawal. Stark reinforced Maxwell and a brisk firefight took place for about an hour. The British continued to burn the village during the engagement, then began to make a fighting withdrawal. General Nathanael Greene ordered Stark and Maxwell to pursue the enemy. They harassed the retreating columns for a few miles, capturing several prisoners and a large amount of baggage abandoned by the enemy.[3]

After the Springfield battle, Stark was sent back to New Hampshire to obtain another militia brigade. He took it to West Point, on the Hudson River, relieving General Le Clair at West Point. The pleasant warm days and cool evenings of September did nothing to dissipate the discouraging atmosphere of betrayal and treachery. Benedict Arnold was scheming to hand over the strategic fortress of West Point to the British, whom he had labored long and courageously to defeat. His vile act came as a shock to those who knew and admired him as an extraordinary military leader, as he had proved in Quebec, Fort Ticonderoga, and Saratoga. His reasons for betraying his country and his honor require more explanation than we can go into here. It is sufficient to say that Arnold had been poorly served by the political elements of the country, and by his new wife, Peggy Shippen, who had supported, even encouraged her husband's deceit from the beginning of their relationship.

Major John André, a British soldier in charge of the British Intelligence Service in the colonies, had acted as a liaison between Arnold and the British. He had been, at one time, a suitor of the lovely Peggy Shippen. André was a consummate soldier of fine character, respected by all who knew him. Arnold had agreed to hand over West Point to General Clinton for the sum of twenty thousand pounds. He had been ordered to West Point as its commandant by Washington on August 3, 1780.

André and Arnold conferred on the night of September 21-22, 1780 on the west bank of the Hudson River near Haverstraw, New York. When André left Arnold, he had five documents in his possession. He left for Peekskill via Kings Ferry and headed south to Tarrytown, where he was captured by alert American sentries on the twenty-third. When Washington arrived, on September 25 he was given the packet of five documents that André had unsuccessfully concealed on his body. He recognized Arnold's handwriting and exclaimed in alarm to Henry Knox at his side, "Arnold has betrayed me. Whom can we trust now?"[4]

Arnold had escaped from West Point on board the *Vulture,* sailing down the Hudson on the twenty-sixth. He recognized the magnitude of his deed and wrote a letter to Washington while on board:

> "*Vulture*, September 25, 1780
>
> Sir: The heart that is conscious of its own rectitude cannot attempt to palliate a step which the world may censure as wrong; I have ever acted from a principle of love to my country since the commencement of the present unhappy contest between Great-Britain and the Colonies; the same principle of love to my country actuates my present conduct, however it may appear inconsistent to the world, who very seldom judge right of any man's actions.
>
> "I have no favor to ask for myself. I have too often experienced the ingratitude of my country to attempt it; but from the known humanity of your Excellency, I am induced to ask your protection for Mrs. Arnold from every insult and injury that the mistaken vengeance may expose her to. It ought to fall only on me; she is as good and as innocent as an angel, and is incapable of doing wrong. I beg she may be permitted to return to

her friends in Philadelphia, or to come to me as she may chose; from your Excellency I have no fears on her account, but she may suffer from the mistaken fury of the country.

"I have to request that the inclosed letter be delivered to Mrs. Arnold. And she be permitted to write to me.

"I have also to ask that my cloaths and baggage, which are of little consequence, may be sent to me; if required their value shall be paid in money."[5]

John Stark was selected to be one of the thirteen general officers to sit on a military tribunal to pass judgment on André's actions. It was a sad and difficult duty to perform. All of the officers, having had intimate contact with the prisoner, shortly determined that he was an honorable soldier who became the willing collaborator with a traitor. Stark and his brother officers surely understood the gravity of the decision they were asked to make. The liberty of the country was at stake and they would be setting a standard of performance that would guide future boards. Their findings:

"JUDGEMENT OF THE BOARD OF GENERAL OFFICERS, IN THE CASE OF Major John Andre.

The Board, having considered the letter of His Excellency, General Washington, respecting Major Andre, adjutant general to the British army, the confession of Major Andre, and the papers produced to them:

Report to His Excellency, the commander-in-chief, the following facts which appear to them relative to Major Andre:

First—That he came on shore from the Vulture, sloop-of-war, in the night of the 21st of September instant, on an interview with General Arnold, in a private and secret manner.

Secondly—That he changed his dress within our lines, and, under a feigned name, and in disguised habit, passed our works at Stoney and Verplank's Points, on the evening of the twenty-second of September instant, and was taken the morning of the twenty-third of September instant, at Tarry Town, in a disguised habit, being then on his way to New-York; and when taken, he had in his possession several papers which contained intelligence for the enemy.

"The Board, having maturely considered these facts, DO ALSO REPORT TO HIS EXCELLENCY, General Washington, That Major Andre, adjutant generals to the British army, ought to be considered as a spy from the enemy; and that, agreeable to the law and usage of nations, it is their opinion he ought to suffer death.

NATH. GREENS, M. GEN'L., President.
STERLING, M.G.
AR. ST. CLAIR, M.G.
LA FAYETTE, M.G.
R. HOWE, M.G.
STEUBEN, M.G.
SAMUEL H. PARSONS, B.GEN'L.
JAMES CLINTON,, B.BEN'L.
H. KNOX, BRIGR. GEN'L ARTILLERY.
JNO. GLOVER, B.GEN'L.
JOHN PATTERSON, B.GEN'L.
EDWARD HAND, B. GEN'L.
J. HUNTINGTON, B.GEN'L.
JOHN STARK, B.GEN'L.
JOHN LAWRENCE, J.A. GEN'L.

"In regards to the execution of Major Andre, six members were in favor of his being shot; six members were of the opinion that he ought to be hung as a spy. General Greene, the president, decided the question in favor of the latter."[6]

After the trial Major André wrote the following letter to General Washington:

"Tappan, October 1, 1780

Buoyed above the terror of death by the consciousness of a life devoted to honourable pursuits, and stained with no action that can give me remorse, I trust that the request I make to your Excellency at this serious period, and which is so often my last moments, will not be rejected.

"Sympathy towards a soldier will surely induce your Excellency and a military tribunal to adopt the mode of my death to the feelings of a man of honour.

"Let me hope, Sir, that if aught in my character impresses you with esteem towards me, if aught in my misfortunes marks me as a victim of policy and not of resentment, I shall experience the operation of these feelings in your breast, by being formed that I am not to die a gibbet."[7]

Excerpts from the journal of Dr. James Thacher describe the kind of man Major André really was:

"October 2d, 1780—Major Andre is no more among the living, I have just witnessed his exit. It was a tragical scene of the deepest interest. During his confinement and trial he exhibited those proud and elevated sensibilities which designate greatness and dignity of mind. Not a murmur or a sigh ever escaped him, and the civilities and attentions bestowed on him were politely acknowledged.

" . . . when the hour of his execution was announced to him in the morning, he received it without emotion, and while all present were affected with silent gloom, he retained a firm countenance, with calmness and composure of mind. Observing his servant enter the room in tears, he exclaimed. 'Leave me till you can show yourself more manly!" His breakfast being sent to him from the table of General Washington, which had been done every day of his confinement, he partook as usual, and having shaved and dressed himself, he placed his hat on the table and cheerfully said to the guard officers, 'I am ready at any moment gentlemen, to wait on you.'

"The fatal hour had arrived, a large detachment of troops was paraded, and an immense concourse of people assembled; almost all of our general and field officers, excepting His Excellency and his staff, were present on horseback . . . Major Andre walked from the stone house, in which he had been confined, between two of our subaltern officers, arm in arm, The eyes of the immense multitude were upon him, who rising superior to the fears of dearth, appeared as if conscious of the dignified deportment which he displayed. He betrayed no want of fortitude, but retained a complacent smile on his countenance, and politely bowed to several gentlemen whom he knew, which was respectfully returned.

"It was his earnest desire to be shot, as being the mode of death most conformable to the feelings of a military man, and he thought he had indulged the hope that his request would be granted. At the moment, therefore, when suddenly he came in view of the gallows, he involuntarily started backward and made a pause.

"'Why this emotion, sir?' said an officer by his side.

"Instantly recovering his composure, he said, 'I am reconciled to my death but I detest the mode.'

"While waiting and standing near the gallows, I observed some degree of trepidation . . . choking in his throat as if attempting to swallow . . . he stepped quickly into the wagon, and at this moment he appeared to shrink, but instantly elevating his head with firmness, he said, 'It will be but a momentary pang,' and taking from his pocket two white handkerchiefs, the provost-marshal, with one, loosely pinioned his arms, and with the other . . .and aged his own eyes with perfect firmness, which melted the hearts and moistened the cheeks . . . of the throng of spectators.

" . . . he slipped the noose over his head and adjusted it to his neck, without assistance of the awkward executioner. Colonel Scammel now informed him that he had an opportunity to speak, if he desired it. He raised the handkerchief from his eyes, and said, 'I pray you to bear me witness that I met my fate like a brave man.' The wagon being now removed from under him, he was suspended, and instantly expired. . .He was about twenty-nine years of age. . .till by a misguided zeal he became a devoted victim."[8]

Major Caleb Stark and his younger brother, Lieutenant Archibald Stark had often accompanied their father on visits to André's cell. The three Stark officers witnessed his execution. Major André was a handsome and charming soldier. His capture and eventual hanging turned him into a legendary character admired by all.

While at his quarters on Peekskill Hollow Road, General Stark composed a letter to Washington:

"The impaired state of my health and the unsettled state of my accounts with the State of New Hampshire renders my presence in that State the ensuing winter highly necessary. I have never as yet settled my depreciation or received any cash from that source. Without an arrangement of these matters it is impossible for me to subsist in the army. The many favors I have received from you and the zeal you have manifested for the interest of the officers under your command, induces me to ask leave until spring. The brigade I have the honor to command is under orders to join its several states; therefore it is not probable it will be in my power to render the country any essential service until the next campaign."[9]

Washington had been planning an attack against Staten Island for some time and ordered Stark and his brigade, organized as a task force, to recover all the grain, cattle, and forage that he could find. Stark's force pillaged the area for several days until one stormy night, Colonel Humphrey, Washington's aide-de-camp, rushed the boiling Hudson to tell Stark that the attack for Staten Island had been called off and he should return to Peekskill.

When Stark returned, he received from Washington approval to set out for New Hampshire as soon as his health permitted. Stark replied on January 1, 1781:

"Sir—Your letter of the 31st ult . . . If my health permits, I shall endeavor to pursue my journey by the last of this week. But my finances are exhausted; neither do I know where they can be replenished unless by application to your excellency. I believe five thousand dollars may answer my purpose . . . I have not drawn a single farthing of cash since the last of December, 1778 . . . Therefore as my demands have not been great and my present necessity is urgent, I flatter myself that your excellency will furnish me with the cash . . . I shall return as soon as my health will permit . . ."[10]

Washington replied that he did not have the funds; the military chest was empty! Stark, feeling the desperation of trying to function without finances, had confided to General Sullivan in a letter dated November 28, 1780:

"Long service in the defence of my country has at length so far impaired my constitution as to render it necessary that the remainder of my days should be spent in domestic retirement.

"But, sir, knowing you to be my confidential friend, a friend of the rights of the army I think I may more properly apply to you for advice than to any other man within the circle of acquaintance...

"For my own part should any provision be made suitable to my rank, or should I be under the necessity of retiring without provision, my life and services shall always be in readiness to answer my country's call, and whenever the wishes of my fellow citizens or the exigencies of the public require me to take the field for short periods. I shall cheerfully exert my influence to encourage and by personal hazards endeavor to stimulate my countrymen to actions worthy of free born Americans. These services my shattered constitution will yet permit me to perform.

"I cannot think of resigning at this hour especially after having been induced to continue in service by no other motive than an ardent zeal for my country, hoping that every new campaign would be the last, until I am in manner unable to leave it.

"The conclusion of the war appears altogether uncertain and my health strongly urges me to retire for a time at least to my farm now in ruinous state for want of proper management and cultivation, during my long engagements in the service of my country, for that difficulty a remedy may be provided, but the decay of nature are irreparable."[11]

While General Stark was home, he had his sons help him petition the legislature in Exeter for some settlement of his accounts; he was broke and needed some assistance. They were able to persuade the legislature to give each officer home on furlough twenty-five dollars in new currency. The General received eighty dollars while Caleb and Archibald got twenty-five each. That winter of 1780-81, Stark wrote to Sullivan, was "one of the most severe winters we have had these ten years and it is exceedingly cold."[12]

His rheumatism was so debilitating that he could not ride for any distance, so he waited patiently for the blessed warmth that spring brings to New Hampshire.

19

The Last Post (1781-1783)

In June 1781, Stark was ordered, by General Washington, to assume command of the Northern Department at Saratoga. Washington wrote:

"Upon finding it necessary for the operations of the campaign to recall the continental troops from the north, I have ordered six hundred militia from the counties of Berkshire to that quarter, in addition to the militia and State troops of New York and I have now to request that you will assume the general command of all the troops in that department, as soon as convenient may be. I am induce to appoint you to this command on account of your knowledge and influence among the inhabitants of that country.

"You will be pleased, therefore, to repair to Saratoga and establish your headquarters at that place retaining with you four hundred of the troops from Massachusetts, and sending the other two hundred to Col. Willett, who will remain in command upon the Mohawk River, as his popularity in that country will enable him to render essential services there.

"In case of an incursion from the enemy, you will make such dispositions, as you shall judge most advantageous, for opposing them and protecting the frontier, not withdrawing the troops from the Mohawk River. I rely upon it you will use your utmost exertions to draw forth the force of the country from the Green mountains and all contigious territory. And I doubt not your requisitions will be attended with success, as your personal influence must be unlimited among these people, at whose head you have formerly fought and conquered with so much reputation and glory.

"I request you will be particular in keeping up proper discipline and preventing the troops from committing depredations upon the inhabitants.

"Be pleased to let me hear from you from time to time and believe me, dear sir, Your most obedient humble servant, Geo. Washington."[1]

Three days later, Washington followed up with another letter to Stark, this one requesting that he check with General Schuyler before making any major decisions—meaning that Washington had second thoughts about giving Stark full authority to do anything he wanted. The Northern Department included a vast frontier area of responsibility. Fort Edward was fifty miles away, Fort Schuyler one hundred twenty miles, and two regiments under the commands of Butler and Alden were in northern Vermont. The area was overrun with spies, traitors, and other criminals. There was very little trouble from the Abenakis Indians in Canada, northern Vermont, and New Hampshire. Not much had changed from his last posting to the position, except that violence and disorder was even more widespread and intense. Vicious depredations by Joseph Brant and John Butler and their followers were at their peak in the Wyoming Valley and Cherry Valley of New York. Even General Schuyler's house was robbed and vandalized. Stark reviewed his situation in a letter to General Washington dated August 9, 1781:

"Dear Sir—In compliance with your orders, I arrived at Bennington on Friday last, and on Saturday made a visit to their governor, who, together with the leading men of the country, have promised me every assistance in their power to repel the common enemy. I have reason to believe, from their conduct, that their promises are not fallacious; for, before I came to Bennington, Major McKinstry, who has command of troops at Saratoga, sent an express to apprise them of the enemy's advance for his post. The alarm was spread, and in a few hours one hundred and fifty men on horseback, marched to his assistance. The alarm proved false, and then next day they returned, but not until they had visited Saratoga.

"On Monday last, at sunrise, a party of eleven was discovered in the south-east part of Bennington, supposed to be a party of tories from Hoosac, passing to Canada. The people were instantly in arms, pursued them until 1 o'clock, when three of the pursuers came up and made them prisoners. They were instantly marched to Bennington. Upon examination, I found them to be a party from Canada which first consisted of six. . . I inclose you their instructions. For my part, I think they ought to be considered as spies, and beg your excellency's opinion on the subject.

"Perhaps you will be surprised when I inform you that the militia from Berkshire and Hampshire have not yet arrived at Saratoga. Upon being apprised of it at Bennington, I wrote to Gen. Fellows by express, begging that they might be hastened without loss of time. I likewise wrote Major Mckinstry to send me a return of the garrison at Saratoga, and find it to consist of but ninety men, including officers; for which reason, I thought it most prudent for me to return to Albany and wait until a larger number can be collected; but be assured that when a number arrives that will render my presence necessary, I shall lose no time in repairing to my post.

"I should be remiss in my duty not to inform your excellency that it was with greatest difficulty I procured an express to Saratoga, for want of something to pay his expenses; and in a department that requires so much intelligence to be communicated, if possible, some provision ought to be made. Knowing that your excellency will do all in your power for the public good, your directions on this, and every other subject, shall be my invariable and certain guide.

". . . There is not a drop of public rum in the department. I wish that a quantity may be ordered this way, as large as would amount to our portion. Your excellency must know that, if I do my duty, I must keep scouts continually in the woods, and men in that service ought to have a little grog in addition to their beef and water.

"Every intelligence worthy of your excellency's notice shall be regularly communicated, if in my power.

"Wishing your operations against our enemies all the success that the virtue of our cause deserves,

"I have the honor to be, Your excellency's most obedient and humble servant,

JOHN STARK."[2]

While Stark was busy at Saratoga administering the Northern Department, he carried on a voluminous correspondence with General Washington, Governor George Clinton, (a distant cousin of the Tory Henry Clinton), General Schuyler, and other officials. Important events were taking place along the Atlantic seaboard.

Washington met in Connecticut for a war council with French General Jean-Baptiste Rochambreau. They agreed on a joint French-American naval and ground attack against New York. Earlier, British General

Charles Cornwallis abandoned plans to conquer North and South Carolina after suffering heavy losses at Guilford Courthouse in North Carolina. He revised his strategy to defeat Virginia.

For months Cornwallis had chased General Nathanael Greene's army, trying to bring it to a decisive battle but without success. He then set up a British base of operations at the small port of Yorktown at the mouth of the York River on Chesapeake Bay, and established a sea link with General Henry Clinton's forces in New York.

By August 14 Washington had changed plans to attack New York after receiving information from French Admiral Count de Grasse that he had a fleet of twenty-nine ships and three thousand soldiers and was heading for Chesapeake Bay. Washington and Rochambreau coordinated to rush their best troops to Virginia to destroy British positions at Yorktown. Admiral de Grasse's fleet arrived off the coast on the 14 and began to unload troops. They linked up with General Lafayette's American troops to cut off any opportunity for Cornwallis to retreat overland.

In the meantime, Stark was still trying to bring order out of chaos within his department. It was the same sorry situation that created most of his problems; lack of supplies of every description. His position at the Northern department required the collection, assessment, and dissemination of important intelligence, but in order to function, he had to be able to feed and clothe his people. The government failed to provide supplies or funds for Stark to carry out his orders.

Stark wrote to Colonel Henry Laurens from Albany on August 27, 1781:

"Dear Sir—By a spy, who has been on board the enemy's ships at Crown Point, we learn that their intention is to make a push upon this place, to alarm the New-Hampshire Grants by way of Castleton, and gather all the tories in this quarter, who are to be met by General Howe's army near this place. Therefore I should advise you to keep your men in readiness.

Your obed't serv't,

JOHN STARK."[3]

Stark had asked the Governor George Clinton, of New York, for permission to send a flag of truce to Canada to exchange prisoners and the authority to provide transport and provisions for the operation. The governor responded from Poughkeepsie on August 28, 1781:

"Dear sir—Your letter of the 11th instant is this moment received. I can have no objections against your sending a flag to Canada, to negotiate an exchange of the inhabitants who are prisoners with the enemy, as their liberation is an object I have frequently attempted, although in vain, and most ardently wish.

"I need not mention to you, sir, the great care that ought to be taken, especially in our present situation, in an appointment of an officer to conduct this business, as your own good sense will dictate that he ought to be a man of address and firmness; and no person should be permitted to accompany him but such as merit the most perfect confidence.

"I inclose a list of persons transmitted to me by the commissioners of Albany, to be offered in exchange, and against which I have no objections, provided that those that are marked as inhabitants make their application to me, for the purpose, in writing, agreeable to law, to be filed in the Secretary's office of the State.

"If the enemy should consent to an exchange, due attention must be paid to give preference to those of our friends who have been longest in captivity, as this is consonant with justice, and the contrary would occasion discontent.

"Agreeable to your request, I transmit your inclosed warrant of impress for forty wagons for ten days. You will please observe that you may, by the letter of the warrant, in the first instance, employ the whole number of wagons for ten days, to transmit provisions or stores, and the warrant will expire. But I conceive the public service would be advanced by employing a small number of them only at a time; and that in this way will be sufficient, with what the quartermaster may furnish, to transmit provisions for your troops during the season. It is justice to make the disaffected, who in other respects, bear least of the common burthen, the objects of the impress, which I am sure will not be disagreeable to you. I am with great respect and esteem, Your most obed't serv't, GEO CLINTON."[4]

Funding and provisions never materialized during Stark's tenure at the Northern Department. His frustration is evident in the following letter:

"To his Excellency, Governor Clinton.

Albany, 31st, August, 1781.

Dear Sir—My embarrassments in this department are almost intolerable. I have not a single grain of forage nor can I procure any. When I apply to the quartermaster, he says, 'what can I do?' and this is all I can get from him. It is all that he does, and almost all that he says. You must be sensible that it will be impossible to transact business without some magazine of forage is laid up or at least some for immediate consumption.

"It is a month since I have been on the ground, and I have received nothing from the quarter master except a little swamp hay, and none of that for ten days.

"I have almost daily calls from the frontier for provisions, but am not able to send them any assistance, as the quartermaster has no money to hire teams, and no authority to impress them; and as you promised me every assistance in your power, to facilitate my command and the public business, I must now claim the benefit of your promise, and beg your assistance at this critical period . . . I shall be very happy to be favored with your advice, and shall apprise you of all intelligence that shall appear to affect the State.

Your most obedient servant, JOHN STARK."[5]

Stark was requested to provide a company of troops to augment the community security forces at Albany. There was great unrest along the frontier, so he organized and detached several small bands of scouts to range through the forests, much as he did when he was one of Robert Rogers' Rangers. Their presence helped to discourage lawlessness. Negotiations with Canadian officials for the exchange of prisoners was successfully conducted on several occasions. The war was winding down, yet the scarcity of basic provisions remained intolerable. The following letter to Major Heath with vintage Stark sarcasm is another example of Stark's frustration with his position. It was written September 11, 1781 from Saratoga:

"Dear Sir—Yours of the 3d and 7th inst. Are now before me. . .By your not acknowledging the receipt of my former letters, I am led to believe you never received them, for certainly they must have reached you long before this. In them you will find the reason of my not sending you a return; and the same difficulty that then existed is not yet removed. Therefore, you must not expect a return until the materials are supplied to make it with. However, I can tell the number in this garrison, which consists of two majors, seven captains, eleven lieutenants, twenty-seven sergeants and three hundred and sixty rank and file. We have about ten rounds of cartridges per man, and no more ammunition in store. I wrote to General Knox for a supply some time ago, but have neither received the ammunition, or an answer; but hope for them every hour. I have no deputy adjutant general, nor have I one that I can appoint, capable of the business, who is willing to undertake it. Be assured sir, whenever you shall think proper to order a supply of paper, and appoint a deputy adjutant general . . .the business shall then be done with regularity, and I hope, to your satisfaction; till then, I can not tell how it will be transacted. You will perceive, by the number of men in this garrison, that it would be imprudent to detach any of them to Albany . . . I can not think of myself justifiable in sparing any men from this, or any frontiers, without your positive orders, until we are stronger than we are now.

". . . were I to send a company there [Albany], I should expect they would have one half of them in jail, and the other half to keep them there, in a month. . .they have had more than one continental soldier in jail, for debts, or pretended debts; now they are calling for more, for perhaps the same purpose . . .

". . . Albany is able to turn out five hundred men for its own defence; and a larger body than fifty can not well come against them; and, if ten virtuous citizens are not able to defend themselves against the assaults of one skulking rascal of a tory or an Indian, it is very remarkable, as they have got forts and walls to cover them, almost beyond the power of human force to shake. But, my dear, sir, if you have men to spare from the army, I expect they will soon be wanted at this place, as I have this day almost certain intelligence of there being a large detachment of the enemy at St. Johns, destined for this quarter. Perhaps they may come before you can possibly send me assistance; but I hope not.

"I am sorry that, among the rest of my calamities, it is not in my power to send an express forty miles, unless by detaching a soldier on foot, with provisions on his back; and in case the enemy shall approach, I shall be under the necessity of sending expresses to Hampshire and Berkshire counties, to Albany, and to the Grants. This, sir, requires good horses and horsemen. Neither of them are to be had here; and, were there any horses, there is no money to pay their expenses, nor forage to keep them on; nor any either can I get.

"I have applied to the governor for forage, but he says that Congress has never require it of the State, and, without that requisition, he can not give a warrant to impress it; and that he supposes Congress has lodged the money in the hands of the proper officers, to procure it.

I am, sir, your obedient Humble servant,

JOHN STARK."[6]

On September 11, General Philip Schuyler wrote to Stark about the retreat of the British fleet and of Benedict Arnold's burning of New London, Connecticut, and included a general update on the war effort. Stark had a much warmer and personal relationship with Schuyler than he did with Gates. Major Caleb Stark had lived with the Schuylers for an extended period of time, and they were favorably impressed with his manners and courteous demeanor. Their daughter and Caleb became good friends. She taught him how to play chess. The elderly General Schuyler always referred to the young major with affection and admiration. Stark replied in a letter dated September 13:

"Dear Sir—I am honored with yours of the 11th instant. The extra flood of good news it contains diffuses a joy through my senses little short of delirium, and makes me almost forget my declining years, and wish for health and vigor and an opportunity of distinguishing myself of our illustrious general, in aiding to humble the haughty, arrogant, and ostentatious Earl Cornwallis. I should be very happy to have a share in his defeat and capture—two events which either already have occurred or infallibly must take place in a few days.

"Poor Rivington [publisher of Rivington's *Gazette*, a notorious Tory] must be in a wretched dilemma. What excuse can he make? How [to] extricate the British from their present difficulties? If he, or any other power short of omnipotence can, they must be adepts indeed.

"I am so pleased with the good news you send me, as almost to forget to thank you for your generous offer to send me intelligence. Be assured, sir, that I feel exceedingly grateful for this and every other expression of your favor. I have no doubt of the willingness of that infamous traitor, Arnold, to do his country all possible injury, but hope he has not been able, in the case you mention, to give us fresh evidence of his hateful disposition.

With esteem, sir, your friend, and humble servant,

JOHN STARK."[7]

Early in October, a group of Tory thugs was operating within the American lines marauding, looting, and murdering innocents. Thomas Lovelace was caught with a copy of a British commission on his person and was given a trial by officers assembled by Stark at Saratoga. The board pronounced him a spy and sentenced him to death. General Stark wrote out the order:

"DEATH WARRANT OF THOMAS LOVELACE. By John stark, Esq., Brigadier General in the Army of the United States, and Commander of the Northern department, &c.

At a general court martial, held at Saratoga, October second, 1781, whereof Colonel Wiessenfels was president, Thomas Lovelace, of the Tory forces in the British army, was brought before the court, charged with being a spy; and the court, after hearing the examinations, and other testimony, have pronounced their opinion that he was a spy, and, by the usages of war, he be hanged by the neck until he be dead; which sentence being approved by me, you will remove him from the main guard tomorrow, the 8thy instant, at half past ten o'clock AM, and exactly at eleven o'clock cause him to be hanged by the neck until he be dead—for which this is your sufficient warrant." John Stark. [Signed by Major Caleb Stark, Brigade Major][8]

The day after Lovelace was hanged, Stark notified General Schuyler about the event. He also discussed the prospects of an attack by British and Tory forces from the Lake George area, and pleaded with Schuyler for more men and equipment.

Schuyler informed Stark that the French fleet was then in Chesapeake Bay transporting American and French soldiers after their long march from Connecticut through New York and New Jersey to the head of the bay, where French ships were carrying them to Yorktown. General Washington was beginning the siege of Yorktown by encircling Cornwallis's army and placing heavy artillery capable of bombarding the British fortifications. The British were dangerously low on supplies as the noose circling them was slowly tightened.

On October 17, 1781, Cornwallis sent a flag of truce to Washington to work out the terms of surrender. Two days later, on the nineteenth, the British and American forces turned out in formation to witness Cornwallis's surrender of his army. Actually he did not have the courage to carry out that official duty, so he had his deputy, General Charles O'Hara, officiate. Washington, always a stickler for protocol, had his second in command, General Benjamin Lincoln, receive the surrender from O'Hara. The British soldiers sullenly turned in their muskets, while their band was playing *The World Turned Upside Down*. British hopes for victory over the rebellious colonies were dashed, even though large detachments of soldiers were present in the south and in New York City.

The British Parliament shortly took steps to bring the costly war to a close. Parliament was forced to acknowledge that the United States of America was an independent nation. The Treaty of Paris was signed by Great Britain and the United States on September 13, 1783, with Congressional ratification coming on January 14, 1784.

When news of the British defeat at Yorktown reached General St. Leger, commander of British forces at Fort Ticonderoga, he and his men loaded up all of their supplies and sailed from Lake Champlain to Canada. One more threat on the frontier had just been eliminated.

After the surrender of Cornwallis, some anxiety on the northern frontier was relaxed and Stark was preparing to leave. General Heath had asked him to stay at his position for a while longer, until he could locate another general officer to replace him. A General Hazen was suggested and if he was not available, Colonel Reid would exercise command. Tensions on the New York—Vermont border were running high and Stark reported the situation to Meshesh Weare, Chairman of the New Hampshire Congress on December 14, 1781:

"Dear Sir—Not withstanding my letters to you seem to be treated with silent contempt, yet, when anything intervenes where I think my country or the State of New Hampshire in a particular manner deeply interested, I conceive it my duty, apart from common politeness, to inform you of it. Such I deem the late riotous conduct of the State of Vermont, in extending their pretended claim to the westward, and threatening to support it by a military force; and, indeed, those within the twenty-mile line are actually in arms, in open defiance and violation of the rules of Congress; and are actually opposing themselves to the troops raised by the State of New-York to put their constitution and laws into execution. Two detachments, one acting under the authority of Vermont, and the other under officers owing allegiance to the State of New-York, are assembled now at St. Coick, in opposition. For farther particulars I refer you to Captain Fogg who will have the honor of delivering this.

"I have been favored with perusal of the proceedings of the legislature of Vermont State, on the subject of their being received into the Union of the United States, and find that they have not only rejected the resolutions of Congress, but in reality have disavowed their authority; and I farther perceive that, in their great wisdom, they have thought proper to appoint a committee to determine whether New-Hampshire shall exercise jurisdiction to Connecticut river or not. This proceeding appears too weak and frivolous. For men of sense to suppose that New-Hampshire would ever consent to an indignity so flagrant, and an abuse so pointed as this seems to be, is what I own surprises me. However, I hope, and indeed have no doubt, that New-Hampshire will be more politic than to take notice, of this daring insolence. What I mean by notice, is to think of treating with them upon this or any other subject until Congress shall come to a final determination with respect with these people.

JOHN STARK." [9]

Stark's final report to Washington dated December 21, 1781 from Albany, before he and Caleb departed Saratoga, summarizes his activities in the Northern Department.

"My Dear Sir—Although I am not the first that has addressed a congratulatory letter to on account of your late glorious and unequalled success in Virginia, yet be assured that I am not behind the others in respect, or in the high opinion I entertain of the important and very essential service rendered my country by your capital acquisition. British standards will no more be the dread of neighboring nations, nor will her armies in future be deemed invincible. You have taught them the road to submission, and have manifested to the world that they are vulnerable; no doubt the warlike nations with whom they are at variance, stimulated by your noble example, will give them farther proofs of their inability to trample on the laws of equity, justice and liberty with impunity. I hope that this may be the case, and that they may shortly be brought to a sense of their duty and relinquish to us the invaluable blessings that the power of omnipotence has placed in our view, and leave our country once more to taste the sweets of tranquil peace.

"My exile has not been attended with any very interesting events. The enemy, to be sure, came as far as Ticonderoga; but when they learned the alacrity with which the militia turned out to defend their country, they returned, with shame and disgrace, without striking a blow at the northern frontiers. But the Mohawk river felt some of the effects of their inveterate malice. However, by the timely interposition of Colonel Willet, they were driven from that country with indignity. As the particulars must have come to your knowledge before now, I will not give you the trouble of reading them here.

"During the time the enemy were hovering about Ticonderoga, a sergeant and a scout of the Vermont militia were attacked by a scout of the enemy. They killed the sergeant and took the party prisoners. When the party was brought to Ticonderoga, the commanding officer showed great dissatisfaction at the accident, treated them with all imaginable tenderness, sent for the sergeant and had him buried with the honors of war; after which he released the prisoners, with what provisions they chose to take, and they returned home with a letter from Lt. Col. St. Leger to Gov. Chittendon (as it was said), apologizing for the accident.

"Upon this coming to my knowledge, I addressed a letter to the governor, of which I inclose a copy, as likewise a copy of his answer. You will perceive, by his letter, he gives his reason for not sending to me by affirming that he has sent the account to you. If so, I should be much obliged for a copy of the letter . . .

"The proceedings of the Vermonters have been very mysterious, until ten days ago, when they in a manner threw off the mask, and publicly avowed their determination to continue their claim of jurisdiction to the North river on the part of New-York, and to Mason's patent on the part of New-Hampshire, and did actually send an armed force, with a piece of artillery, to protect and defend their adherents on the west side of the twenty-mile line; and indeed have done little less than to wage war with the United States, who, I conceive, are bound by every tie of justice and policy, to defend all its members from insults of any enemy, internal or external.

"I believe, sir, that I may venture to predict that unless something decisive is done in the course of this winter, with respect to these people, we may have everything to fear from them . . .

"This may be considered as strange language from me, who have ever been considered a friend of Vermont; and, indeed, I ever was their friend, until their conduct convinced me that they were not friendly to the United States . . . During my command, I have been promised everything from their government and their leading men that I could wish for; but they have taken particular care to perform nothing, while, on the other hand, the militia of New-York, and those of Berkshire, attended to my requisitions with alacrity and uncommon spirit; and I believe the northern and western frontiers are in a great measure indebted to them for the protection of their houses, etc. I most sincerely wish that matters may turn out better than I expect, and am. With my best wishes for your health and happiness,

Your most obedient servant, JOHN STARK."[10]

Stark spent 1782 severely invalided with rheumatism. Fighting on the southern and western frontier continued as the Mohawk Indian chief, Joseph Brant continued his raids in Pennsylvania and Kentucky. The boundaries and independence of the United States of America were agreed to in a preliminary peace treaty. It also spelled out the terms of the withdrawal of all British forces in America.

Molly Stark gave birth on June 2, 1782, to the couple's last child—a girl they named Sophia.

Stark's last communication with General Washington was on September 23, 1782, a short letter that ended: "Most sincerely wishing you success . . . and that you may soon be able to restore to your country a safe, honorable and lasting tranquility, it is the ardent wish of your most obedient and humble servant, JOHN STARK."[11]

John Stark settled into domestic routines with the companionship of those he loved. He had marched to sound of the guns for the last time.

20

Fading Shadows (1783-1822)

Early in 1783, there was a general dissatisfaction among army officers at Congress's reluctance to provide pay and benefits, especially for the wounded. A mutinous atmosphere pervaded the army detachment stationed at Newburgh, New York. A letter written by an aide to General Horatio Gates had been circulated among the troops attacking Congress for its lack of attention to the plight of the soldiers. General Washington condemned the letter as soon as he had knowledge of its existence and forbade officers to meet secretly in opposition to the government. He scheduled an open meeting to discuss the situation at Newburgh.

General Stark and his son, Major Caleb Stark, attended the meeting and received the thanks of General Washington for his presence. Washington was able to appease the disaffection of the men by the time the conference was adjourned.

A patriotic order was founded at Fishkill, New York, by officers of the Revolutionary War to perpetuate remembrance of friendships formed during the conflict. Membership in the original order comprised only those officers who had served three years and was available to the eldest male descendant of any officer killed in action. Washington held the office of president of the Society of the Cincinnati until his death.

If it had remained a patriotic fraternal order, it would have had more widespread appeal, but it soon became an elitist society that perpetuated and honored the aristocratic system the country had sacrificed so much to defeat. Cincinnatus, for whom the society was named, was a Roman warrior who temporarily became dictator. He resigned his office and returned to his farm to plow his own land.

General Stark made several objections to the formation of the organization because its principles were not in line with those of the Roman officer. He wrote: "To imitate that great man, we should return to the occupations we have temporarily abandoned, without ostentation, holding ourselves ever in readiness to obey the call of our country."[1]

❧

The historian, Edward Everett, described Stark's objections: "Leading the life of a real Cincinnatus he[Stark] declined associating himself with the Society, formed by the officers of the newly disbanded army under that name. He shared the apprehensions which prevailed so widely of the dangerous tendency of that institution and he had something severe and primitive in his taste which disinclined him from the organization."[2]

❧

Life during that colonial period centered on family and home. Stark participated very little in civic matters, primarily because of rheumatism, which left him semi-mobile. He was not interested in the social goings-on that many politicians enjoyed. In Portsmouth, for example, the Langdons, Whipples, and others in public life entertained and dined in luxury. That lifestyle was simply not for Stark. He eked out a living from the land and became comfortable, but he was never wealthy, nor did he desire to be. He was too much a man of the forest and the soil to feel comfortable in the higher echelons of society. He did, however, retain an interest in national politics for the rest of his life. He accepted the position of town moderator from 1784 to 1794.

Having frequently felt unappreciated by Congress, and been passed over for promotion, Stark had to swallow his pride when he saw younger and inexperienced officers commissioned ahead of him. Perhaps, the following letter, made up for some of the disappointment:

"In pursuance of an act of Congress, of the thirtieth day of September, A.D. 1783,

JOHN STARK, Esquire, is to rank of Major General by Brevet, in the Army of the United States of America. Given under my hand, at New-York, the ninth day of June, 1786.

NATHANIEL GORHAM, President.

Entered in the war office—

HENRY KNOX, Secretary of War."[3]

Molly and John Stark lost their son Archibald, in September 1791. Archibald had served with his father as a lieutenant during his last tour of duty in the Northern Department. Archibald had accompanied General John Sullivan on his campaign against the Six Nations Indian confederacy. After the war, Archibald went into business with his cousin Stephen (son of William Stark), operating a small store in Goffstown.

Comfortable in his role as patriarch of the family, John Stark had the gift of appreciating what was really important in life: fulfilling his duty to his country and his responsibilities for his family.

Derryfield was beginning to grow and the Starks' home place and land were at the center of that growth. Their land covered much of what is now the main business section of Manchester. A wooden bridge was constructed across the Merrimack River just north of the Amoskeag Falls by Colonel Robert McGregor, one of Stark's aides at the battle of Bennington. The aged General was skeptical of the venture and good-naturedly kidded McGregor: "Well, Robert, you may succeed but when the first passenger crosses over, I shall be ready to die."[4]

❦

Within sixty-five days, the structure was completed and Stark used it occasionally. About that time, 1789, he was retiring from the lumber business, and sold off his sawmills. A year later a smallpox epidemic broke out and all of the Stark family were inoculated for the disease. None contracted it.

The canal in Derryfield was funded by soliciting subscriptions. Stark did not participate in the project. Its purpose was to harness the sixty-five foot drop of Amoskeag Falls. A canal would allow boats and barges to bypass the falls, and it was primarily responsible for the growth of the city of Manchester. The canal opened for business in 1807.

Even though Stark had only an elementary education, he was a prolific reader. His personal library contained most of the contemporary authors. Reading a good book was an enjoyable pastime and he especially enjoyed the Scottish poets of the period.

In 1805, Thomas Jefferson was elected president of the United States. He was a favorite of Stark, who saw in the man those qualities that he associated with the true values of the American people. The following letter written from Monticello and dated August 19, 1805 from the president had to have been most welcomed:

"Respected General—I have lately learned, through the channels of the newspapers, with pleasure that you are still in life, and enjoy health and spirits. The victories of Bennington—the first link in the chain of success which issued in the surrender of Saratoga—are still fresh in the memory of every American, and the name of him who achieved them dear to his heart.

"Permit me, therefore, as a stranger who knows you only by the services you have rendered, to express to you the sincere emotions of pleasure and attachments which he felt on learning that your days had been prolonged—his fervent prayer that they still may be continued in comfort, and the conviction that whenever they end, your memory will be cherished by those who come after you, as one who has not lived in vain for his country.

I salute you, venerable patriot and general,

With affection and reverence.

THOMAS JEFFERSON."[5]

Stark's humble reply:

"Derryfield. October, 1805.

Respected Sir—Your friendly letter of August 19th came to hand a few days since; but, owing to the imbecility enseparably connected with the wane of life, I have not been able to acknowledge it until now.

"I have been in my 77th year since the 28th of August last; and, since the close of the revolutionary war, have devoted my time entirely to domestic employments, and in the vale of obscurity and retirement, have tasted that tranquility which the hurry and bustle of a busy world can seldom afford. I thank you for the compliment you are pleased to make to me, nor will I conceal the satisfaction I feel in receiving it from a man who possesses so large a share of my confidence.

"I will confess to you, sir, that I once began to think that the labors of the revolution were in vain, and that I should live to see the system restored which I had assisted in destroying. But my fears are at an end; and I am now calmly preparing to meet the unerring fate of men, with, however, the satisfactory reflection that I leave a numerous progeny, in a country highly favored by nature, and under a government whose principles and views I believe to be correct and just.

"With the highest considerations of respect and esteem, I have the honor to be, sir, your obed't serv't.

JOHN STARK."[6]

Severe attacks of gout, a metabolic disease characterized by severe inflammation of the joints, often caused by excessive uric acid in the blood, were frequent during his retirement years. It may be that the general's condition was aggravated by his daily intake of rum, his favorite beverage. He was not an excessive drinker, but he had a portion of his grog, as he called it, every day.

During the first decade of the 1800s he was the recipient of numerous letters and notices from veterans groups and individuals who paid tribute to him on the anniversary of the Bennington battle. The Veterans of the Bennington Campaign had formed a fraternal order and kept in touch with their leader over the years, even though the membership shrank a little every year. In many ways, the memories of the men involved became more reflective and meaningful as time passed. The bond of brotherhood among soldiers in combat lasts a lifetime and the spirit that originally brought them together on the battlefield sustained that bond, and maybe even strengthened it, to the end of their days. For their 1809 celebration, the committee wrote the following invitation to General Stark. It was dated July 22, 1809:

"To General Stark.

Honored and Respected Sir—You can never forget that, on the memorable 16th of August, 1777, you commanded the American troops in the action called Bennington battle, and that, under divine providence, astonishing success attended our arms. Our enemy was defeated and captured, and this town and its vicinity saved from impending ruin. It has been usual to hold the day in grateful remembrance, by a public celebration.

"On Thursday last, a large and respectable number of leading characters in this and the neighboring towns, met to choose a committee of arrangements for a celebration on the 16th of August next. More than sixty of those who met were with you in the action. They recollect, sir, with peculiar pleasure, and have directed us to write and request you, if your health and age will permit, to honor them with your presence on that day. All your expenses shall be remunerated.

"No event could so animate the brave 'sons of liberty,' as to see their venerable leader and preserver once more in Bennington; that their young men may once have the pleasure of seeing the man who so gallantly fought to defend their sacred rights, their fathers and mothers, and protected them while lisping in infancy.

"Should this request be inconsistent with your health, we should be happy in receiving a letter from you, on that subject, that we may read it to them on that day. Sentiments from the aged, and from those who have hazarded their lives to rescue us from the shackles of tyranny, will be read by them with peculiar pleasure, and remembered long after their fathers have retired to the silent tomb.

"Accept, sir, our warmest wishes for your health and happiness, and permit us, to assure you that we are, with great esteem,

Your cordial and affectionate friends,

GIDEON OLIN
JONATHON ROBINSON
DAVID FAY."[7]

General Stark's answer dated July 31, 1809:

"At My Quarters, Derryfield,

My friends and Fellow Soldiers—I received yours, of the 22nd instant, containing your fervent expressions of friendship, and your very polite invitation to meet with you to celebrate the 16th of August in Bennington.

"As you say, I can never forget that I commanded American troops on that day in Bennington. They were men who had not learned the art of submission, nor had they been trained to the arts of war; our 'astonishing success' taught the enemies of liberty that undisciplined freemen are superior to veteran slaves.

"Nothing could afford me greater pleasure than to meet your brave 'sons of liberty' on the fortunate spot; but, as you justly anticipate, the infirmities of old age will not permit it, for I am now more than fourscore and one years old, and the lamp of life is almost spent. I have of late had many such invitations, but was not ready, for there was no oil in the lamp.

"You say you wish your young men to see me; but you who have seen me can tell them I never was worth much for a show, and certainly can not be worth seeing now.

"In case of my not being able to attend, you wish my sentiments. These you shall have, as free as the air we breathe. As I was then, I am now, the friend of the equal rights of men, of representative democracy, of republicanism, and the declaration of independence—the great charter of our national rights—and of course a friend to the indissoluble union of these states. I am the enemy of all foreign influence, for all foreign influence is the influence of tyranny. This is the only chosen spot of liberty—this the only republic on earth.

"You well know, gentlemen, that at the time of the event you celebrate, there was a powerful British faction in the country (called tories), a material part of the force we contended with. This faction was rankling in our councils, until it had laid a foundation of subversion of our liberties; but, by having good sentinels at our outposts, we were apprised of the danger. The sons of freedom beat the alarm, and, at Bennington, they came, they saw, they conquered.

"These are my orders now, and will be my last orders to all my volunteers, to look to their sentries; for there is a dangerous British party in the country, lurking in their hiding places, more dangerous than all our foreign enemies; and whenever they shall appear, let them render the same account of them as was given at Bennington, let them assume what name they will be.

"I shall remember, gentlemen, the respect you and the inhabitants of Bennington and its neighborhood have shown me, until I go to the 'country from whence no traveler returns.' I must soon receive marching orders."

[Accompanying this letter, General Stark penned a toast to be made at the reunion celebration:] "Live free or die; Death is not the worst of evils."[8]

In 1809 Stark wrote a note to an old friend of many years, Reverend William Bentley, an ordained minister from Massachusetts, discussing his thoughts on James Madison. Stark frequently referred to Dr. Bentley as "my Chaplain."

"Peace is undoubtedly," Stark wrote. "our greatest good as long as peace can be honorable. But I fear that if we tip the cup of conciliation any higher we shall have to drink the dregs . . . I think Madison will not wait for the Arnolds or Pickerings of our country. Although he has not recommended a declaration of war to Congress I think he will not suspend it long . . . But it is the greatest consolation that I have that I shall leave the general government of my country in so good hands."[9]

President Madison wrote to General Stark on December 26, 1809, expressing his admiration of and respect for him as a hero and patriot who contributed to the independence of the country. Stark's reply on January 21, 1810, showed that he had not lost the fire of independence in his later years:

"Sir—I had yesterday the pleasure of receiving an address from the first magistrate of the only republic on earth. The letter compliments me highly upon my services as a soldier, and praises my patriotism. It is true, I love the country of my birth, for it is not only the land which I would choose before all others, but it is the only spot where I could wear out the remnants of my days with any satisfaction.

"Twice has my country been invaded by foreign enemies, and twice I went out with her citizens to obtain a peace. When the object was attained, I returned to my farm and my original occupation. I have ever valued peace so highly that I would not sacrifice it for any thing but freedom; yet submission to insult I never thought the way to obtain or support either.

"I was pleased with your dismissal of the man [British Envoy]sent by England to insult us: because she will ascertain by the experiment, that we are the same nation we were in '76, grown stronger by age, and having gained wisdom by experience.

"If the enmity of the British is to be feared their alliance is still more dangerous. I have fought by their side, as well as against them, and have found them to be treacherous and ungenerous as friends, and dishonorable as enemies. I have also tried the French: first as enemies, and since as friends; and although all the strong prejudices of my youth were against them, still I have formed a more favorable opinion of them than of the English. Let us watch even them.

"But of all the dangers from which I apprehend the most serious to my country, and our republican institutions, none require a more watchful eye than our internal British faction.

"If the communication of the result of my experience can be of any service in the approaching storm, or if any benefit can arise from any example of mine, my strongest wish will be gratified.

"The few days or weeks of the remainder of my life will be in friendship with James Madison.

JOHN STARK."[10]

On June 29, 1814, John Stark's beloved wife passed away. Molly had contracted typhus fever and succumbed four days later. It must have been the hardest blow the intrepid warrior ever had to accept. He was very feeble and could not get around. The funeral was held at the family home. The preacher eulogized Molly, but when he began to do the same for the general, Stark loudly tapped his cane on the floor and said, "Tut, tut, enough o' that an it please you." He was unable to accompany Molly's body to the burial place, and was heard to say, "Good-bye, Molly, we sup no more together on earth."[11]

With that, the sad old general bid adieu to his wife, companion, best friend, and confidante of fifty-seven years. Molly is the "invisible" lady. Her famous husband diligently avoided the trappings of celebrity, yet left behind some residues of his existence; Molly on the other hand, left no letters or anecdotes that have been found by researchers. We learn about her only through the eyes of those who knew her.

She was a hardworking frontier mother and wife who was devoted to her family. She was known as a no-nonsense lady who ran an orderly and clean home. General Stark's frequent absences left the major burden of providing for the family on her shoulders. If she complained, we do not know of it. Reverend Bentley paid this tribute to the lady:

> "July 23, 1814. News has reached us of the death of Elizabeth, wife of General John Stark of Manchester, N.H., at, 77 years, many years younger than the general. She had all the prudence of a good wife and all the affection of a good mother. Her character was mild and suited to make a complete whole with the independence and bold virtues of her Cincinnatus."[12]

Molly deserves the many tributes made in her name today. She is the embodiment of the strong pioneering woman who brought civility and order to the rustic conditions on the border, with the strong moral fabric that defined our country.

After Molly's death, John Stark was confined to his room. He derived pleasure from the attendance of his family as his health steadily declined. Eighteen days before his death, Stark suffered a paralytic stroke, and he passed away on May 8, 1822.

The *New Hampshire Patriot* ran a death notice of his death in the May 18 edition:

"The immortal Stark is no more. The last of April he suffered a paralytic stroke, some 18 days before his death, with choking and inability to swallow while eating. After that he ate no more and during the remaining time he was speechless, although to his watchful friends and relations who stood around him he retained his senses to the last. Until the last attack he had been able to walk about the house and, in pleasant weather, out of doors."[13]

General John Stark, hero of Bunker Hill and the Battle of Bennington, was buried in his Continental army uniform. True to his modest ways, he requested that his funeral be "simple unostentatious." The funeral has been described by an old comrade, Colonel Samuel Herrick:

"In the front of the house, beyond the road, a line of infantry, leaning on reverse arms, under the fragrant budding of the orchard, waited the time of their escort service. The day was quite oppressive in its heat and many of the soldiers suffered in their warm and close uniforms. At the close of the religious services by the Rev. Mr. Dana of Londonderry and the Rev. Ephraim Bradford of New Boston, the procession was formed. The military moved in front and at the sides as escort. Mr. Ray, a much respected neighbor, led the horse Hessian, decked out in war trappings, and the long procession of mourners moved from the lawn and at the sad funeral pace, proceeded to the family burying ground in the field, about a quarter of a mile distant. The young people of the town unbeknown to their elders obtained a small cannon and stationed it some distance from the grave and fired minute guns as the procession approached. The body was deposited in its last resting place and the infantry, filing right and left of the spot, fired three volleys as their last mournful tribute of respect to the memory of the beloved patriot and soldier."[14]

Stark's grave is located on the east bank of the Merrimack River on what was once Stark land. When General Stark was buried in the cemetery, North and South Uncanoonuc Mountains were clearly visible across the river in Goffstown. The gravesite is now sheltered from the harsh prevailing northwesterly winds by a stand of large white pine trees. On a quiet day one can hear the soft murmur of wind brush through the pine needles. It is a place of peace and tranquility, a fitting resting place for a deceased warrior. An American flag proudly waves above the grave, a silent sentinel paying tribute to a life dedicated to the peace and liberty symbolized by the red, white and blue banner.

> *His toil is past, and his work is done;*
> *And he is fully blessed;*
> *He fought the fight, the victory won,*
> *And enters into rest.*[15]

21

In Tribute

For more than two centuries John Stark has been the forgotten general of the Revolutionary War and the French and Indian War. His contributions to the formation of this nation have gone relatively unheralded, and his accomplishments are worthy of wider recognition and appreciation.

His heroic performance at the Battle of Bunker Hill was primarily responsible for the heavy losses suffered by the British troops, completely demoralizing them. By placing his New Hampshire militia at a key strategic location near the water's edge on Prescott's left flank, Stark and his men absorbed the initial thrusts and decimated line after line of attacking redcoats. They were responsible for the largest number of enemy soldiers killed on the battlefield. They were also the last to leave Breed's Hill when the order was given for the Americans to retreat. Stark's heroic blocking defense saved the lives of hundreds of Americans who were allowed to retreat back over Charlestown Neck while New Hampshire frontiersmen held the British army at bay in a brilliant fighting withdrawal.

With unerring tactical savvy, Stark had located the most vulnerable position on the hill and placed his men there. They fought with uncommon valor, and when they ran out of bullets they used their muskets as clubs to enable their comrades to file past to safety in the rear. The skill and tenacity of all of the colonial forces surprised the arrogant British, who saw them as a bunch of ragtag rebels who needed to be taught a lesson at the point of a bayonet. Bunker Hill made them reassess their thinking and their tactics, and they correctly perceived that success, if possible, was going to be expensive. The colonials' display of courage and commitment was responsible for the British withdrawal from Boston.

Through the years, Stark has been known as the hero of Bennington, a title he earned with a stunningly gallant display of common sense, inspirational leadership, and an acute tactical ability to read the terrain and to select where and when he would fight. Armed with New Hampshire, Massachusetts, and Vermont volunteers and an independent New Hampshire command, Stark came to the aid of his Vermont neighbors, who feared they would be overrun by General Burgoyne's army attacking southward through Lake Champlain and the Hudson River corridor.

His success against two strong detachments from Burgoyne's army, which he decimated in a ferocious battle at the Walloomsac River in New York, a few miles from Bennington, is a testament to his superb leadership. The destruction of the two detachments badly weakened Burgoyne's force and set up a chain reaction that led to the British surrender at Saratoga. It was also a key factor in winning the alliance of the French. That, in turn, led to the conclusion of the American Revolution. Stark deserves an honored place on the list of fighting generals who helped lay the foundation of our country.

The fact that Stark remains less known than some of his contemporaries can probably be attributed to the fact that he was a modest man, a product of the frontier wilderness in which he grew to manhood. When the war ended, he returned to his home in Derryfield and worked his farm and sawmills. He did not seek public office and shunned publicity. At times he could be cantankerous, and opinionated, and was capable of making snap judgments, not all of them correct. His respect for plain talk and action was legendary, and he was notoriously intolerant of those who did not have their facts straight. He was a generous relatively unlettered man who did not leave a large body of writings.

He fought the Abenaki Indians in his youth when they made war against helpless settlers in isolated locations, yet he came to respect many of their customs and beliefs when he was captured and taken to Canada. At their camp, he was able to earn their respect by being the independent self-sufficient man that he was, and he refused to be treated like a woman by hoeing corn as a hapless captive.

Wherever John Stark went, he made a difference. During the French and Indian War, he served as an officer with the famed Rogers' Rangers and performed several important patrols of the vast wilderness around Lake Champlain. He was with General Abercromby during that officer's futile attack against Fort Ticonderoga, held then by Marquis de Montcalm. Abercromby had a larger army than Montcalm and Stark advised Abercromby to place his superior artillery firepower where he could obliterate the abatis the French had felled around their defenses. As it turned out, his advice was ignored and the British suffered one of the most disastrous defeats in their military history.

Again at Fort Ticonderoga, this time during the early years of the Revolution, Stark stubbornly refused to abandon the fortifications he and his command were building on Mount Independence. He claimed that the mountain could be better defended than the fort, but his opposition was overruled by General Schuyler, and they abandoned the facility. Later, his tactical insight was validated when General Burgoyne recognized the strategic importance of the elevation and placed artillery on the mountain.

The true measure of a man is how he reacts in a crisis. Stark's performance at Bunker Hill, Bennington, and Fort Ticonderoga and as commander of the Northern Department of the Continental army showcase his skill as a leader of men and his commitment to the cause of liberty. He was a true patriot and sacrificed much during the wars. Even during the Battle of Bennington, he was suffering from rheumatoid arthritis, which incapacitated him in his later years. His legacy of excellence and courage mark him as an active member of the group who made it possible for the political statesmen to build upon his success on the battlefield.

The American Revolution was essentially a civil war. It began on the eastern seaboard, which was the traditional land used by the Native Americans, the eastern woodland Indians of New England and Canada. The war not only set Englishmen against Americans, who had always considered themselves to be English, but it also generated division and confusion within the tribal councils of the native population. Various tribes allied themselves with one side or the other, frequently alternating their support. Neither side offered much promise for the future of the Indian way of life. Even their survival was at stake.

When Benedict Arnold began his epic invasion of Quebec, he had a contingent of Indians as scouts. The Abenaki were once again placed at the center of a conflict that was not of their making. On October 4, 1777, General Horatio Gates was getting ready for the battle at Saratoga and optimistically called for, ." . . all the Saint Francis Indians who have lately come to Co'hos, with all those who from Friendship . . . and affection to Our Noble Cause, are ready to Step forth at this important Crisis, to put a finishing stroke to this campaign."[1]

The Indian community at Adanak, on the Saint Lawrence River was divided in how it should respond. Twenty years after Robert Rogers had burned the village at Adanak, there were Abenaki scouts serving with New Hampshire rangers patrolling the upper Connecticut River Valley. In general, the tribe was biding its time trying to be as neutral as possible. Several members of their tribe were enrolled in the Charity School at Dartmouth College, in New Hampshire, on the east bank of the Connecticut River. This may explain why they leaned more towards the colonials than the British during the conflict.[2]

At the end of the Revolution, the United States took its place among the nations of the world as the only republic on the planet. At its inception, there was some fear that, as a new nation, it would repeat some of the mistakes responsible for the immigration of large populations to the new land. The distaste for a strong central government was basic within the electorate. The people visualized the republic essentially as a collection of individual states in which most of the power should be concentrated. Then, the adoption of the Articles of Confederation was viewed as a framework for a new government that had the promise of working for the benefit of the people and won support for the adoption of the United States Constitution. Stark had followed this process with great interest, even though he never participated in the debates then taking place. He was by choice an observer.

John Stark avoided publicity and guarded his private world. Explosive, rude, opinionated, and bull-headed are but a few of the human characteristics attributed to him. He never had a problem stating his case or being understood by his subordinates or superiors. He was uneducated, but he possessed a keen intellect. Physically and emotionally strong, he was able to carry out difficult orders without complaint. He approached problems with a healthy dose of Scotch-Irish common sense and an intelligence that could easily have been overlooked by those who saw only his gruff ways and mannerisms. He was a four-square character without a trace of pretense, and he defined himself by his deeds, not his words.

Perhaps Stark's most endearing virtue was his ability to inspire men to maximum effort when things looked bleak. His calm demeanor in combat was reassuring to the men. The main ingredient of his ability to command stems from his strong character. The troops sensed that about him, and his honest respect for the men came from the top down. Once the troops realized that, respect was returned.

He will always be remembered by the sentiment he sent as toast for the veterans of the Battle of Bennington when he proclaimed: "Live Free or Die—Death is not the worst of evils." He, of course, was thinking of the evil of tyranny, the natural enemy of liberty and freedom, and nobody fought more valiantly than John Stark for that principle.

There is a granite monument at a large American military battlefield in the rolling hills of northern France, established in tribute to the sacrifice of young Americans who went to war in defense of freedom in World War One. Etched in the granite marker are a few simple words that apply not only to the brave young men who died in battle, but also to General John Stark, a rugged, modest frontiersman who faced grave challenges and was proved worthy:

> *"Virtue and Courage*
> *Are Their Own*
> *Monument and Reward."*[3]

Appendices

Bennington Flags

There are two unique flags associated with the Battle of Bennington and General John Stark.

The first, known as the Bennington Flag, consists of thirteen stripes alternating white and red with white stripes at the top and bottom. The canton is composed of thirteen seven-pointed-stars (known as Masonic Stars) arranged in an inverted U configuration, with two stars placed at each upper corner of the canton, all on a blue field. The State of New Hampshire flies this flag at the Statehouse in Concord, New Hampshire beside General Stark's statue for six days every year. It is a fairly large flag measuring five and half feet by ten feet. An original Bennington Flag now resides at the Bennington Museum, Bennington, Vermont.

The second flag, known as the Green Mountain Boys Flag, is also associated with the Battle of Bennington. It has a green field with thirteen white stars painted on a blue canton arranged in an approximate perpendicular 3-2-3-2-3 pattern. According to most authorities, this is the flag that Stark carried onto the battlefield. It was also used by Colonel Seth Warner's Vermont Regiment. In English folklore, green was used as a symbol for freedom and liberty, that is why trees were so popular as symbols in early colonial America.

The Green Mountain Flag is also known as the Stark Flag. The General took the original flag home with him and placed it on a wall in his house. Over the years, before his death, he snipped off small pieces of the field and gave it to friends. All that is left of the original is the canton section, and that holds an honored place at the Bennington Museum.

There are conflicting claims about which of the two flags actually flew over the battlefield. I side with the majority, who believe it was the Green Mountain Boys Flag. Both flags are treasured symbols of a time when our independence was still in doubt. They give reference to a violent military engagement that prepared the road to ultimate victory. Therein lies their importance and noteworthiness.

The Bennington Cannons

The four fieldpieces that General Stark's militia captured from two British regiments at the Battle of Bennington have a rich historical legacy that spans more than two hundred and twenty-five years. Some controversy exists concerning the famous Molly Stark Cannon, named after General John Stark's wife Elizabeth, whom he affectionately called Molly.

A thorough search of the records indicates that in the spring of 1777, British General John Burgoyne landed at Quebec, where he collected his army and supplies for an invasion of Lake Champlain and the Hudson Valley to divide the colonies. After his capture of Fort Ticonderoga, Burgoyne was low on supplies and horses and sent out two foraging detachments to fill that deficiency. One, under Colonel Baum, left with a brigade of German and British troops with two, three-pounder cannons. These were captured by Stark's men in their first engagement on the Walloomsack River west of Bennington, Vermont on August 16, 1777. That same afternoon, Colonel Breymann's relief column of German dragoons arrived at the scene with two, six-pounders. The destruction of Breymann's regiment was one of the most vicious battles of the Revolutionary War.

Shortly after the battle, General Horatio Gates wrote to General Stark that he was sending two officers and twenty artillerists to manage the four cannons captured in the battle. They probably accompanied Stark's newly recruited militia force in the Battle of Saratoga when he captured Fort Edward and placed a battery on the west side of the Hudson River, thereby blocking Burgoyne's retreat northward to Fort Ticonderoga.

The New Hampshire historian George F. Willey wrote the following on page 303 of his *History of Manchester:* "Two small bronze guns mounted are at the capital in Montpelier, Vermont, and one of the larger guns is at New Boston. Some of our old military records mention the remaining cannon, the mate to the last named, and assert that it was assigned to a privateer in the War of 1812, and was lost at sea."

The two three-pounders, manufactured in London, were given to Vermont during the seventy-first anniversary of the Battle of Bennington, in 1848, at which time they were engraved: "Taken at Bennington, August

16, 1777." In 1928, one of the pieces was moved to the Bennington Museum, where it is now on display in a controlled atmosphere.

When Burgoyne surrendered at Saratoga, the Continental army captured one hundred and seventy-five fieldpieces, including the Bennington cannons, and incorporated them into the army's ordnance inventory. After Saratoga, the military campaigns shifted south to New Jersey, Pennsylvania, and the southern states. Many of the fieldpieces were taken with the troops that evacuated the Northern Department, and were dispersed throughout the country.

New Boston's Molly was cast in a Paris foundry in 1743. Part of her legend is that she was poured with pure brass for the king's use. Guns cast by royal warrant had an oval shield with three leaves, cast on the barrel, and were not sent to newly acquired territories. Molly appears to be what is known in the literature as a trade gun, sent to New France during the reign of King Louis XIV. Molly's royal lineage is questionable.

According to legend, Molly was used in the War of 1812 by the incompetent General William Hull, who was captured by the British at Detroit. A year later, when the Americans under the intrepid General Winfred Scott forced a surrender at Niagara River, the fieldpieces from Fort George were placed in storage at the Watervliet Arsenal, an ordnance supply center north of Albany.

The remaining six-pounder was personally given to the Ninth New Hampshire Militia Regiment, New Boston Artillery Company, by General John Stark some time between 1813 and 1822, the time of Stark's death. He had often referred to it as "my cannon."

By all historical accounts, including much of Molly's legend, she should be a six-pounder, but Molly is a four-pounder. The bore of a six pounder is 3.66 inches and the bore of a four pounder is 3.21 inches when new. Molly's bore is 3.35 inches, which is about right considering normal erosion of the barrel. The only accurate conclusion to be made is that Molly is not, and could never have been, one of the cannons General Stark captured at Bennington.

The collision of historical truth with legend should not detract from Molly's storied past. In fact, it has enhanced the allure surrounding the historical icon, giving rise to the question: What other secrets has the illusive Molly hidden from us?

The list below is taken verbatim from Caleb Stark's *Memoir.* He had copied it from one of General Stark's memorandum books.

Children of John and Elizabeth Stark

John Stark, [Senior], son of Archibald Stark, born August 28, 1728.

Elizabeth Stark, [Molly] Alias Elizabeth Page, Daughter of Caleb and Elizabeth Page, born February 16, 1737. Married August 20, 1758. Died June 29, 1814.

Caleb Stark, born December 3, 1759. Died August 26, 1838.

Archibald Stark, born May 28, 1761. Died September 11, 1791.

John Stark, born April 17, 1763. Deceased.

Eleanor Stark, born May 4, 1765.

Eleanor Stark, Jun'r, born June 30, 1767. Deceased.

Sarah Stark, born June 11, 1769. Died January 29, 1801.

Elizabeth Stark, born August 10, 1771. Died May 14, 1813.

Mary Stark, born September 19, 1773. Deceased.

Charles Stark, born December 2, 1775. (He sailed from Boston in the brig Sibsburgh, Benjamin Wright, Master, November, 1776, and was heard of no more.*

Benjamin Franklin Stark, born January 16, 1777. Died July 25, 1806.

Sophia Stark, born January 21, 1782.

The above and foregoing children were born of the above Elizabeth Stark.

**The vessel was owned by Major (Caleb) Stark. His brother–in–law, Thomas McKinstry and one of his clerks, Mr. Heath, were also lost in her.*

Bibliography

Alden, John R. *A History of The American Revolution 1775-1783.* New York: Knopf, 1969.

Ambrose, Stephen. New York: *To America.* Simon and Schuster, 2002.

Amory, Thomas C. *The Military Service and Public Life of Major General John Sullivan of the American Revolutionary Army.* Boston: Wiggin and Lunt, 1868.

Anderson, Leon. *Major General John Stark, Hero of Bunker Hill.* Concord: Evans Printing Co., 1972.

Asprey, Robert. *War In the Shadows.* vol. I. New York: Doubleday, 1975.

Axelrod, Alan and Charles Phillips. *The Macmillan Dictionary of Military Biography.* New York: Simon and Schuster, 1998.

Baker, Henry Moore. *New Hampshire at Bunker Hill.* Concord: Rumford Press, 1903.

Barney, Jesse A. *Rumney, Then and Now.* Town of Rumney, New Hampshire, 1967.

Bedford, Town of. *History of Bedford From 1737.* Concord: Rumsford Press, 1903.

Belknap, Jeremy. *History of New Hampshire.* New York: Johnson Reprint Co., 1970.

Bellico, Russell P.. *Sails and Steam in the Mountains.* New York, Fleischmanns, Purple Mountain Press, 1992.

Bobrick, Benson. *Angel in the Whirlwind.* New York: Penguin Books, 1997.

Bouton, Nathaniel. *History of Concord,* 1856.

Bouton, Nathaniel, editor. *Documents and Records, State of New Hampshire, 1776-1783,* volumes XIII. E. Jenks, State Printer, 1874.

Boyer, Paul s., editor. *The Oxford Companion to United States History.* New York: Oxford University Press, 2001.

Brewster, Charles W. *Brewster's Rambles About Portsmouth.* Somersworth Somersworth: NH Publishing, 1859.

Brumwell, Stephen. *White Devil: A True Story of War, Savagery and Vengeance in Colonial America.* New York: De Capo Press, 2005.

Calloway, Colin G. *The American Revolution in Indian Country.* New York: Cambridge University Press, 1995.

Calloway, Colin G., editor. *The World Turned Upside Down: Indian Voices from Early America.* Boston: Bedford/St. Martins, 1994.

Catlin, George. *North American Indians.* New York: Penguin Books, 1989.

Clarence, John. *Bunker Hill: Battle of 1775.* New York: Broadstreet Press, 1868.

Coburn, Frank. *A History of the Battle of Bennington.* Vermont Historical Society, 1912.

Coffin, Charles, Editor. *History of the Battle of Breed's Hill.* Selected Pamphlets, volume 117, New York: 1831.

Cogswell, Elliott C. *History of New Boston.* Boston: Rand co., 1864.

Commanger, Henry Steele. Editor in Chief, *The American Destiny, An Illustrated Bicentennial History of the United States.* New York: Danbury Press, 1975.

Commager, Henry Steele and Richard Morris, Editors. *The Spirit of Seventy-Six.* New York: Castle Books, 2002.

History of Concord. New York: City of Concord Historical Commission, 1903.

Cook, Frederick, editor. *Journals of the Military Expedition of Major General John Sullivan Against the Six Nations of Indians in 1779.* Auburn, New York: Peck and Thomson, 1887; reprint, Bowie, Md. Heritage Books, 2000.

Ellis, Joseph J. *Founding Fathers.* New York: Alfred A. Knopf, 2000.

Ellis, Joseph J. *His Excellency George Washington.* New York: Alfred A. Knopf, 2004.

Ellsberg, Commander Edward. *Captain Paul.* New York: Dodd, Mead and Co., 1941.

Elson, William Henry. *History of the United States of America,* Macmillan co., New York, NY, 1904.

Ferling, John. *A Leap in the Dark.* New York: Oxford University Press, 2003.

Fisher, David Hackett. *Liberty and Freedom A visual History of America's Founding Ideas.* New York: Oxford, 2005.

Fleming, Thomas J. *Now We Are Enemies.* New York: St. Martin's Press, 1960.

Foner, Eric, and John A. Garraty, editors. *The reader's Companion to American History.* Boston: Houghton Mifflin Company, 1991.

Foster, Herbert D. and Thomas W. Streeter. Stark's Independent Command at Bennington, With Appendices. New York State Historical Association, (1904).

Garratye, John A. and Mark C. Carnes, editors. *American National Biography,* Twenty-Four Volumes. New York, 1999.

Hadley, George Plummer. *History of the Town of Goffstown, 1733-1920.* Published by Town, 1922.

Hamilton, Duane. *History of Merrimack and Belknap Counties.* Philadelphia Lewis Co., 1885.

Hamilton, Edward P.. *Fort Ticonderoga, Key to a Continent.* Boston: Little, Brown Co. 1964.

Hatch, Robert M. *New Hampshire at Bunker Hill.* Historical New Hampshire, 1975, 30(4): 215-220.

Herr, John K. and Edward S. Wallace. *The Story of the U.S. Cavalry, 1775-1942. New York:* Crown Publishers, 1984.

Hibbert, Howard. *Redcoats and Rebels.* New York: W.W. Norton, 1990.

Holden, James Austin. "Influence of Death of Jane McCrea on Burgoyne Campaign." *Proceedings of the New York State Historical Association* 12 (1913).

Howarth, Stephen. *To Shining Sea, A History of the United States Navy, 1775-1991.* New York: Random House, 1991.

Hoyt, Edwin P. *America's Wars and Military Excursions.* New York: McGraw-Hill, 1987.

Keller, Allan. *Life Along the Hudson.* Burlington, Vermont: Lake Champlain Publishing Company, 1997.

Ketchum, Richard. Bennington, *MHQ: The Quarterly Journal of Military History,* 1997, 10(1): 98-111.

Ketchum, Richard. *Saratoga—Turning Point of America's Revolutionary War.* New York: Henry Holt, 1997.

Ketchum, Richard M. *The Winter Soldiers: The Battles for* Trenton *and Princeton.* New York: Anchor Books, 1991.

Kidder, Frederic. *History of the First New Hampshire Regiment in the War of the Revolution.* Hampton, New Hampshire Hampton, NH, Peter E. Randall, 1973.

Leckie, Robert. *The Wars of America,* Vol. I. New York: Harper and Row, 1968.

Leckie, Robert. *George Washington's War, The Saga of the American Revolution.* New York: Harper Collins, 1992.

Lengel, Edward G. *General George Washington: A military Life.* New York: Random House, 2005.

Little, William. *History of Weare.* Town of Weare, 1888.

Longguth, A. J. *Patriots, The Men Who Started the Revolution.* New York: Simon and Schuster, 1998.

Lord, Philip. *War Over Walloomsac.* New York State Bulletin Number 473, 1989.

Maine Writers Research Club. *Maine Past and Present. Boston:* DC Heath Co., 1929.

Manchester, City of. *Early Records of the Town of Derryfield.* Manchester Historical Society, 1905.

Mayo, Lawrence. *Stark at Winter Hill.* Concord, N.H., 1921.

McCullough, David. *1776.* New York: Simon and Schuster, 2005.

McClintock, *History of New Hampshire.* Boston: Algonquin Press 1888.

Merrill, William E. *History of* Derryfield, *New Hampshire.* 1897.

Miles, Lion. *The Battle of Bennington.* Graduate Seminar Paper, University of Massachusetts, Amherst, May, 1987.

Miller, Nathan. *Sea of Glory.* Annapolis, Maryland: Naval Institute Press, 1992.

Mintz, Max M. *The Generals of Saratoga, John Burgoyne and* Horatio *Gates.* New Haven: Yale University Press, 1990.

Monk, Linda R. *The Words We Love, Your Annotated Guide to The Constitution.* New York: Stonesong Press, 2003.

Moore, Howard Parker. *A life of General John Stark of New Hampshire.* Self-published, 1949.

Morison, Samuel Eliot. *John Paul Jones, A Sailor's Biography.* New York: Little, Brown Co., 1959.

National Park Service. U.S. Department of the Interior. *Saratoga.* GPO, 1997.

Naval Documents of the American Revolution, 10 Vol. Naval History Division, Washington, D.C. 1964.

Neumann, George C.. *Battle Weapons of the American Revolution.* Texarkana: Scurlock Publishing Co., 1998.

Newman, Joseph, directing editor, *200 Years, A Bicentennial History of the United States.* Washington, DC: Books by US News and World Report, 1973.

New York Office of Parks, *Bennington Battlefield, State Historic Site,* 1997.

New York Office of Parks, Crown *Point, State Historic Site,* 1998.

Palmer, Peter S. *History Of Lake Champlain, 1609-1814.* New York: Fleischman's, 1992.

Parker, Rev. Edward L.. *History of Londonderry.* Boston: Perkins and Whipple, 1851.

Parkman, Francis. *Montcalm and Wolfe.* New York: Da Capo Press, 1995.

Pike Robert E. *"Note on General Stark" in,* Vermont History, 1965, 33(2): 349-350.

Potter, Chandler E.. *History of Manchester.* Concord: NH Historical Society, 1856.

Potter, Chandler E.. *Military History of New Hampshire, 1623-1861.* Concord: NH Historical Society, 1972.

Purcell, Edward, and David F. Burg, editors, *The World Almanac of the American Revolution.* New York: Pharos Books, 1992.

Risch, Erna. *Supplying Washington's Army.* Washington, D.C.: U.S. Army Center of Military History, 1981.

Sanborn, Edwin P.. *History of New Hampshire From Its First Discovery to the Year 1830.* Clarke, Manchester, N.H. 1875.

Savas, Theodore P., and David Dameron. *A Guide to the Battles of the American Revolution.* New York: Savas Beatie LLC, 2006.

Scales, John. *Colonial Era History of Dover.* Bowie, Md.: *New Hampshire,* Heritage Books, 1977.

Scheer, George F. and Hugh F. Rankin. *Rebels and Redcoats.* Cleveland, Ohio, World, 1957.

Schwartz, Seymour I. *The French and Indian War 1754-1763, The Imperial Struggle for North America.* New York: Simon and Schuster, 1994.

Secomb, Daniel F.. *History of the Town of Amherst.* Somersworth: NH Publishing, 1883.

Squires, J. Duane. "*A Summary of Events of 1777 Which Led to General Stark's March to Victory at Bennington.*" *Historical New Hampshire,* 1977 32(4): 165-170.

Stark, Caleb. *History of Dunbarton. Concord*: Parker Lyons Co., 1869.

Stark, Caleb. *Memoir and Official Correspondence of General John Stark of New Hampshire also a Biography of Captain Phinehas Stevens and Robert Rogers.* Originally published by Edson C. Eastman, Concord, NH 1877, and a facsimile has been reprinted by Bowie, Md. Heritage Books, Inc. 1999.

Sweetman, Jack. *American Naval History.* Annapolis: Naval Institute Press, 1991.

Thwaites, Reuben G., and Louise P. Kellogg, editors. *Frontier Defense on the Upper Ohio, 1777-1778.* Madison: Wisconsin Historical Society, 1912.

United States Army, *Regulations for the Order and Discipline of the Troops of the United States.* Boston: Compiled by Frederick William Baron von Steuben, Boston, 1794.

United States Army, *Small Unit Actions,* Washington, DC, Center of Military History, 1982.

United States Military Academy, *West Point Museum.* New York: West Point, 2001.

Vermont Division for Historic Preservation: *Mount Independence, State Historic Site.* 1997.

Vermont Division for Historic Preservation: *Hubbarton Battlefield State Historic Site.* 1996.

Washington, George, *1732-1799, The of Writings of George Washington.* Electronic Text Center, University of Virginia Library, Charlotsville, Va.

Washington, Ida H. and Paul H. Washington. *Carleton's Raid.* Weybridge, Vermont: Cherry Tree Books, 1977.

Weintraub, Stanley. *General Washington's Christmas Farewell.* New York: Free Press, 2003.

Weir, William R., *Turning Points in Military History.* New York: Citadel Press, 2005.

Whisker, James B.. *Arms Makers of Colonial America.* Cranbury, N.J.: Associated University Presses, Inc., 1992.

Wickman, Donald H. *Built with Spirit, Deserted in Darkness; The American Occupation of Mount Independence, 1776-1777,* Master's thesis, University of Vermont, October, 1993.

Wiench, Henry. *An Imperfect God: George Washington, His Slaves and the creation of America.* New York: Farrar, Strauss and Giroux, 2003.

Wiley, George F. *Semi-Centennial Book of Manchester, 1846-1896.* Manchester, N. H.: Geo. F. Wiley,1896.

Wilkinson, James. *Memoirs of My Own.* Philadelphia: Vol. 1, Abraham Small, 1816.

Williams, Glenn. *Year of the Hangman: George Washington's Campaign Against the Iroquois.* Yardley, Penn.: Westholme Publishing, LLC, 2005.

Windrow, Martin and Francis K. Mason. *A concise History of Military Biography.* New York: John Wiley and Son, 1975.

Zaboly, Gary, *American Colonial Ranger; The Northern Colonies 1724-64.* Oxford, Osprey Publishing, 2004.

Comments on Sources and Notes

I have used material from a large number of sources included in the Bibliography. These have been helpful in providing background material and a fresh perspective on events surrounding General John Stark, and the period in which he lived. I have used quotations to allow General Stark to speak for himself about events where appropriate material is available. He was not a great man of letters, but he had a unique way of expressing himself and of portraying his feelings, thereby giving the reader a fresh insight into his thinking.

There are two sources devoted solely to General John Stark. The first was written by his Grandson Caleb Stark in 1831 and revised in 1860. Both documents contain much of the General's correspondence. The second is a biography written and self-published by Howard Parker Moore in 1949. His book reflects impeccable scholarship. However, he frequently masks the chronology and essence of major events with lengthy amounts of minutia, suppositions, and editorializing. Moore's authenticity has been verified, but his zeal to uncover conspiracies to mislead makes it difficult, at times, to determine the facts. His work richly deserved a more professional publishing effort, but it still stands as a monumental effort to tell General John Stark's story, and I pay tribute to his diligence in researching material.

Volume XIII, *Documents and Records, State of New Hampshire, 1776-1783,* edited by Nathaniel Bouton in 1874, has been invaluable. The *Clinton Papers* at Ann Arbor, Michigan were also extremely helpful.

I have also reviewed material from the following:

Newspapers and periodicals
American Heritage
American History
Army Time

Boston Globe
Concord Monitor
Military Heritage
Naval History
Time
Marine Corps Gazette
National Geographic
New Hampshire Union Leader
Newsweek
New York Times
Proceedings of the Naval Institute
Reader's Digest
The Quarterly Journal of Military History
US News and World Report

I have visited all of the locations where General John Stark served—Lake Champlain, Lake George, and the Hudson River Valley. I've toured Fort Ticonderoga, Fort William Henry, Fort Anne, Fort Edward, Saratoga National Historic Park and Monument, Crown Point, and the Bennington Battlefield Park and the surrounding landscape where the battles and patrols took place.

I worked one year in Warrensburg, near Lake George, and can testify that winters in the Adirondacks are severe and long. John Stark, Robert Rogers, and everyone else who served in the area, especially in wintertime, deserve our respect and admiration.

The people responsible for the reconstruction and administration of Fort Number Four at Charlestown, New Hampshire also merit praise and appreciation. The fort is an authentic icon of our historic legacy.

Notes

Chapter 1: The Formative Years (1728-1753)

1. Howard Parker Moore. *A Life Of General John Stark of New Hampshire,* (hereafter Moore). 43.
2. Caleb Stark. *Memoir and Official Correspondence of General John Star,* (hereafter Stark). I am using a facsimile reprint of the original manuscript, which also includes a short biography of Robert Rogers and Captain Phinehas Stevens, printed by Heritage Books, Bowie, Md. 1999. 14.
3. Stark, 15.
4. Moore, 44.
5. Stark, 374.
6. Ibid., 101.
7. Moore, 45.

Chapter 2: Frontier Warfare (1753-1755)

1. Blaine Taylor, "France and Britain Vie For a Continent," in *Military Heritage* (February 2000) 77-89.
2. Seymour I. Schwartz. *The French and Indian War 1754-1763,* 1-14.
3. Moore, 46.
4. Francis Parkman, *Montcalm and Wolfe,* 251.
5. Stark, 387.
6. Moore, 52-53.
7. Ibid., 55. See also Stephen Brumwell, *White Devil: A True story of War.*
8. Col. John P. Sinnott, AUS (Ret.), "Braddock's March on Fort Duquesne," in *Military Heritage* (October 2000); 44.
9. Don Wambold Jr. "Sailing through the Mountains," in *Naval History* (October 2001); 36.
10. Moore, 59; Brumwell, 71-72.
11. Moore, 66.
12. Stark, 408, also Moore, 67.

Chapter 3: War on the Hudson (1755-1758)

1. Parkman, 256-258. Brumwell was also helpful in this chapter.
2. Stark, 19.
3. Moore, 76.
4. Schwartz, 89.
5. Parkman, 296.
6. Moore, 88-89. Stark, 428.
7. Stephen L. Smith, "Timber's Protective Shield," in *Military History* (February 1988), 19.
8. Ibid., 20.
9. Ibid., 23.
10. Stark, 26.

Chapter 4: End of the Conflict (1758-1759)

1. Moore, 104. Taken from General Jeffrey Amherst's journal.
2. Ibid., 105.
3. Stark, 27, also Moore, 105. Evidently John Stark's men were to be equipped with arms from British regimental depots.
4. Parkman, 443.
5. Ibid., 445, written in General Orders of August 13, 1759.
6. Moore, 107. Taken from Amherst's journal.
7. Ibid., 108. Taken from Amherst's journal.
8. Parkman, 453. Also Robert Rogers journals in Caleb Stark's Memoir, 447. Also George Plummer Hadley, *History of the Town of Goffstown, 1733-1920,* 1922. 101.
9. Moore, 111.
10. This statement is confirmed by Caleb Stark, Howard Moore, and the historian Francis Parkman.

Chapter 5: A Time of Discontent (1759-1775)

The New Hampshire Bicentennial Committes', *New Hampshire: Years of Revolution,* This volume was referred to extensively. Also, several town histories, too, were helpful.

1. Stark, 345.
2. Parkman, 547. Also, Eric Foner and John A. Garraty, Editors, *The Reader's Companion to American History,* 985.
3. Foner and Garraty, 1008.
4. Moore, 125.
5. Henry Steele Commager and Richard B. Morris, editors, *The Spirit of Seventy-Six,* 10. This is a most useful volume of source material of the

Revolutionary War period. Hereafter it will be noted as Commager and Morris.

6. The Division of Parks and Recreation, *History of Fort Constitution,* May, 1997. This small pamphlet is a treasure of pertinent Portsmouth area history.
7. Commager and Morris, 36."
8. Moore, 126.
9. Ibid., 127.

Chapter 6: The Line is Drawn(1775)

1. John Ferling. *A Leap in the Dark,* Oxford University Press, New York, 2003, 108.
2. Robert Leckie. *George Washington's War, The Saga of the American Revolution,* 110. Hereafter Leckie.
3. Ibid., 112.
4. Ferling, 135.
5. Moore, 130-131. According to a pamphlet created by the Baltimore and Ohio Railroad for its dining car Molly Stark, Molly discovered that her husband had forgotten his wallet. She rode to Medford and stayed overnight with her husband before returning to Derryfield. (Taken from the Stark folders at the Manchester Historical Association.)
6. Stark, 29, also, Moore, 131. *History of the First New Hampshire Regiment,* by Frederick Kidder, 1868, was most helpful for this section.
7. Moore, 135-136.
8. Ibid., 137.
9. Commager and Morris etc., pp. 104-105.
10. Ibid., 118-119.
11. Moore, 142-143.
12. Ibid., 143.

Chapter 7: Bunker Hill (June 17, 1775)

1. Thomas J. Fleming. *Now We Are Enemies,* 64. Hereafter Fleming.
2. Stark, 346.
3. Ibid., 346.
4. Commager and Morris, 121-122.
5. The John Stark Page, WWW/Stark. Html, 2 of 5.
6. Moore, 154.
7. Hibbert, 51-52, *Redcoats and Rebels.* Hereafter Hibbert.
8. Moore, 156.
9. Ibid., 157.
10. Ibid., 158.

11. Fleming, 220.
12. Moore, 161-162.
13. Stark, 31.
14. Brumwell, 313. The "continuous fire" concept was also used successfully by a British garrison stationed at Rourke's Drift, Africa, against the Zulus in 1879, and was a standard tactic of the famous British "Square."
15. Fleming, 256.
16. Stark, 30.
17. Commager and Morris, pp. 131-132.
18. Stark, 30.
19. Ibid., 112.
20. Anne and Charles Eastman, originally published in *New Hampshire: Years of Revolution,* Profiles Publications and the NH Bicentennial Commission, 1976.
21. Longguth, A.J. *Patriots,* Hereafter Longguth, 285.
22. Henry Moore Baker. *New Hampshire at Bunker Hill,* 23.

Chapter 8: British Evacuate Boston (1775-1776)

1. Stark, 346.
2. Moore, 216-217.
3. Leckie, 116-117.
4. Henry Steele Commager, editor in Chief. *The American Destiny,* 26. Hereafter called, Commager.
5. Leckie, 125.
6. Longuuth, 307-309.
7. Margaret Stoler. Benjamin Church, Son of Liberty, Tory Spy, *American History Illustrated,* November/December 1989, 28-35.
8. George C. Neumann. "American Made Muskets," *American Rifleman,* October 2003, 70-75 and 84-89. Also, *American Rifleman,* March 2006, 54-44.
9. Ibid., 70-75 and 54-44.
10. Commager and Morris, 172.
11. Ibid., 172-173.
12. Ibid., 173.
13. Ferling, 183.
14. Leckie, 241.
15. Moore, 223.
16. Stark, 114.

Chapter 9: Canada to Trenton (1776)

1. Leckie, *Washington's War,* 203-215. Also in Hibbert, 88-100.

2. Stark, 115-116.
3. Moore, 235.
4. Stark, 116-117.
5. Ibid., 118.
6. Moore, 237-238.
7. Russell Bellico, Battle of Lake Champlain, *American History Illustrated,* March, 1985, 10-21. Also in Commager and Morris, 220-221.
8. Moore, 243. Taken from Stark.

Chapter 10: Trenton and Princeton (1777)

1. William Press Miller. Victory By Precise Plan, *Military History, February,* 1992, 45. This is a well-researched description of the battle for Trenton by a noted military historian.
2. Ibid., 42-49. Moore contains some description for Trenton but nothing on Princeton. Caleb Stark has almost nothing on the two battles.
3. James Wilkinson. *Memoirs of My Own Times,* 1816. Caleb Stark quotes Wilkinson, 40.
4. Edward G. Lengel. *General George Washington, A military Life,* Random House, NY. 2005, 191-210.
5. Edited by Otis G. Hammond. *Letters and Papers of Major-General John Sullivan. Continental Army,* Three Volumes, New Hampshire Historical Society, Concord, NH,1930-1939, Vol. I, 319-320.
6. Moore, 249. Originally in Caleb Stark.
7. Stark, 42.
8. Anderson, 13-14.
9. Stark, 43.
10. Moore, 253.

Chapter 11: Loss of Fort Ticonderoga (July 1777)

Several works were used to prepare this chapter. Of course, Moore and Caleb Stark served as a guide, but for a different perspective I utilized several exceptional works as follows: William Seymour's "Turning Point at Saratoga," in *Military History,* December 1999; and Richard M. Ketchum's excellent volume, *Saratoga: Turning Point of America's Revolutionary War.*

1. The story of the Beaumarchais muskets is taken from Caleb Stark 356-357. It is interesting to note that fifty-eight years after the fact, the heirs of Mr. Beaumarchais were still requesting payment for the muskets and powder. Evidently the family had been reduced to poverty during the French Revolution.
2. Moore, 256-257.

3. From an Associated Press newspaper article titled, "*Remnants of Revolutionary War Engineering,*" by Wilson Press, 2005. The 26 foot beam that washed ashore at Lake Champlain weights 1,500-1,800 pounds. Steps are being taken to stabilize the beam. Once that has been accomplished by the Lake Champlain Maritime Museum, it will be returned to Fort Ticonderoga for display at a new visitor center.
4. Mike Phifer. Campaign to Saratoga, *Military Heritage* August, 2000. 42,
5. Ibid., 43.

Chapter 12: Vermont Requests Assistance (July 1777)

1. Stark, 119.
2. Commager and Morris. 547-548.
3. Stark, 119-121.
4. Ibid., 122-123.
5. Moore, 262.
6. Ibid., 265.
7. Stark, 124.
8. Ibid., 46-47.
9. Ibid., 121-122.
10. Ibid., 124-125.
11. Moore, 271-272.
12. Moore, 279.
13. Foster and Streeter, "Stark's independent Command at Bennington," 56-57.

Chapter 13: Fear on the Frontier (Summer 1777)

Throughout the chapters pertaining to the Battle of Bennington, I have used several authoritative sources including Ketchum's fine book on Saratoga, and Foster's and Streeter's excellent study of the battle. Lion Miles' study of the battle has been most informative; also Scheer and Rankin's volume.

1. Lawrence Cortesi. "The Tragic Romance of Jane McCrea," *American History Illustrated,* April, 1985, 10.
2. Ibid., 10.
3. Ibid., 13.
4. Ibid., 14. Also in Commager and Morris, 558-559; Leckie, 396 and John Koster, Jane McCrea, *Military History,* June, 2000, 12-16. It is interesting to note that after the incident, Jane's body was exhumed. The examiners found bullet holes in her body. It is most likely that she was the victim of friendly fire from those who sought to rescue her.
5. Commager and Morris, 551.
6. Moore, 278-279. Taken from the NH Historical Society.

7. Moore, 279. Taken from Foster and Streeter.
8. Ibid., 285. Taken from NH Historical Society, Stark Papers.
9. Moore, 285-286. Taken from the NH Historical society.
10. Excerpts taken from Stark to Schuyler on August 13, 1777 in Moore, 287. Taken from NH Historical Society.

Chapter 14: The Battle of Bennington (August 16, 1777)

1. Stark, 57.
2. Ibid., 58
3. Ketchum,(Saratoga), 307.
4. Stark, 62. Caleb Stark attributes the story of the exploding ammunition wagon from a lecture by a Colonel Butler to the Vermont legislature. Throughout this chapter I have used several sources listed in the bibliography. To use footnotes for every source would be cumbersome. Foster and Streeter, Ketchum, Leckie, Commager and Morris, and Hoyt were my primary sources.
5. Stark, 65-69.

Chapter 15: The Aftermath (August—September 1777)

Ketchum's book on Bennington, Foster and Streeter's volume on Bennington, and Wiley's *History of Manchester* have been helpful. Caleb Stark and Moore have been valuable guides in developing a chronology of events. Caleb Stark's priceless volume of General Stark's correspondence continues to be used wherever appropriate.

1. Stark, 351.
2. Stark, 71.
3. Moore, 331-333.
4. Stark, 129.
5. Ibid., 136.
6. Ibid., 135.
7. Commager and Morris, 577-579.
8. Commager and Morris, 572-573.
9. Stark, 137.
10. Ketchum, (Saratoga), 327-328.
11. Foster and Streeter, 45.

Chapter 16: Saratoga (September-October 1777)

I have studied several versions of the Battle of Saratoga. Some taken from works cited in the Bibliography. A few articles that were beneficial are as follows: William Seymour. "Turning Point at Saratoga," in *Military History,* December, 1999, 46-52: Eric Etheir. "The Making of a Traitor," *American History,* August, 2001, 24-

30; and Mike Phifer. "Campaign to Saratoga," in *Military Heritage,* August, 2000, 40-51, 94.

1. Stark, 138-139.
2. Ibid., 140.
3. Ketchum, 411.
4. Ibid., 417.
5. From the John Stark folder at the Manchester Historical Association.

Chapter 17: Post Saratoga (1777-1778)

1. Morison, 106-117.
2. Ketchum, 431.
3. Moore, 386.
4. Stark, 140.
5. Moore, 387. From Gates Papers at New York Historical Society, 8.137.
6. Moore, 405.
7. Stark, 79.
8. Ibid., 142.
9. Moore, 410.
10. Leckie, 451.
11. Stark, 144.
12. Ibid., 160.
13. Ibid., 172-173.
14. Ibid., 182.
15. Ibid., 190.
16. Ibid., 194.
17. Glenn F. Williams, 159.
18. From *George Washington's Writings*, vol. 13, Electronic Text Center, University of Virginia Library.

Chapter 18: Rhode Island to the Northern Department (1779-1780)

1. Russell Bellico, The Great Penobscot Blunder, *American History Illustrated,* December, 1978, 5-9, 44-48. Also, John Henry Fay. Disaster on the Penobscot, *Naval History,* December 2000, 31-33. Also, Maine writer's Research Club, 107-111.
2. Moore, 439. Taken from *Writings of George Washington,* Vol. XVII.244.7
3. Stark, 81-82. Also Commager and Morris 728-730.
4. Willard Stein Randall. Why Benedict Arnold Did It, *American Heritage,* September-October, 1990, 60-73.
5. Commager and Morris, p. 753.
6. Stark, 82-83. Also, Commager and Morris, 761-762.
7. Commager and Morris. 762-763.

8. Ibid., 765-767.
9. Moore, 452.
10. Ibid., 454.
11. Ibid., pp. 455-456. Taken from Stark Paper Collection at the New Hampshire Historical Society.
12. Ibid., 459.

Chapter 19: Last Post (1781-1783)

1. Moore, 460-461.
2. Stark, 215-216.
3. Ibid., 225.
4. Ibid., 228-229.
5. Ibid., 231.
6. Ibid., 247-249.
7. Ibid., 251.
8. Ibid., 85.
9. Ibid., 301-302.
10. Ibid., 303-305.
11. Moore, 480.

Chapter 20: Fading Shadows (1783-1822)

In this chapter I relied heavily on the original source material found in Caleb Stark's *Memoir,* and Moore's *STARK*, and I am in their debt.

1. Stark, 87.
2. Moore, 482.
3. Stark, 91.
4. Moore, 491. Molly had experience in dealing with smallpox. During the war she cared for twenty sick soldiers at the family's home in Derryfield.
5. Ibid., 496.
6. Stark, 309-310.
7. Ibid., 311-312.
8. Ibid., 312-313. The wording of Stark's toast was acknowledged the next year by the anniversary committee (the original is in the Stark Paper Collection at the New Hampshire Historical Society, in Concord).
9. Moore, 501. Rev. Dr. William Bentley was a Harvard graduate and a pastor of a church in Boston. He and Stark maintained a long and friendly correspondence before Bentley's death, four years before Stark's.
10. Stark, 316-317.
11. Moore, 507.
12. Moore, 507.
13. Ibid., 512.

14. Ibid., 513.
15. From a Currier and Ives lithograph that was used by the Union army in the Civil War to notify my great-grandparents of the death of their son Pvt. Eli Stilson, of the Thirty-first Maine Regiment, Company G, on 30 July 1864 at Petersburg, Virginia, during the Battle of the Crater.

Chapter 21: In Tribute

1. Colin G. Calloway. *The American Revolution in Indian Country,* Cambridge University Press, 1995, is an invaluable source about the native population during the conflict. Pages 65-75 are especially relevant to this treatise.
2. Ibid., 65-75.
3. General John J. Pershing. "Our National War Memorials in Europe" in *National Geographic,* Volume LXV, No. 1, 1-35, January, 1934.

Index

Abenaki Indians, xi, 4–7, 8–9, 39, 40, 97, 198, 222, 223
Abercrombie, James, 32
Abercromby, James, xv, 18, 19–20, 23, 29, 30, 31, 32, 33, 34, 37, 72, 113, 222
Acland, John, 173, 174,178
Acland, Harriet, 174
Adams, John, 48
Adams, Samuel, 52–53, 62, 82
Adanak, 223–224
Albany, New York, 181–185, 202, 203
Allen, Ethan, xvi, 58, 80, 81
Allen, Ira, 95, 122, 124
Allen, Thomas, 144
Allen family, 133
American Revenue Act (1764), 50
American Revolution, 221
  Canada and, 90–92, 114, 158, 179–180
  causes of, 43, 44–45, 47–48, 52
  France and, xiii, 111, 177, 199–200
  Hessians in, 102, 103, 116, 118, 134–135, 146–149, 151-156, 167–168, 172–174
  in Maine, 186–187
  in Massachusetts, xii, xvi, 51, 52–55, 57–58, 62–77, 65*m*, 79–84, 86–88, 187
  Native Americans and, 97, 129, 133, 140, 147–148, 154, 182, 183, 184, 209, 223–224
  in New Hampshire, 48–51, 206, 208
  in New Jersey, 99–108, 105*m,* 188, 189
  in New York, xii, 88–89, 99, 111-118, 157–158, 166, 169*m,* 170–175, 181–185, 189–191, 194, 197–209, 222
  in Rhode Island, 186–188
  Treaty of Paris (1783), 206
  in Vermont, 58, 119–129, 154–155, 162–164, 166, 198, 206, 208
  Washington in, xvi, 81–82, 85–86, 88, 98, 99–100, 103–107, 162, 166
  weapons in, 148–149
Amherst, Jeffrey, 34, 35–39, 40, 46
Amoskeag Falls, xv, 3, 42, 212
André, John, xvii, 190–194
Archelaus, Henri, 168
Arlington, Massachusetts, 54
arms. *See* weapons
Arnold, Benedict, xvii, 58–59, 80–81
  at Crown Point, 95
  at Fort Schuyler, 160
  at Fort Stanwix, 166

at Fort Ticonderoga, xvi
Gates and, 171, 172, 174–175
in Northern Department, 157
in Quebec, 90–92, 95, 98, 223
at Saratoga, 171, 172, 174–175
treason of, 189–190, 204
in Vermont, 128, 130
Arnold, Peggy Shippen, 190, 191
Arnold's Bay, New York, 98
Articles of Confederation, 224
Augusta, Maine, 187

Badger Island, 50–51, 176
Bald Mountain, 29
Baldwin, Captain, 76
Barrett, Colonel, 53–54
Batten Kill, 173
Baum, Fredrich, 103, 134–136, 139–147, 148–150, 153, 160, 163, 227
Bayley, General, 182
Bear's Tavern, 102
Beaumarchais, Monsieur, 111
Bedell, Timothy, 123
Bellows, Colonel, 127
Bemis, Jotham, 157
Bemis Heights, 157, 171
Bennington, Battle of, xiii, xvii, 142–153, 154–155, 161–162
cannons of, 227–228
flags of, 226–227
"Live Free or Die," 224–225
prisoners from, 155–156, 164
Stark and, 142, 143, 144, 145-153,158–160, 162–164, 166-167, 221–222
Bennington, Vermont, 129
Bennington Flag, 226-227
Bentley, William, 216, 218
Blanchard, Colonel, 15, 16, 17
Blood, Captain, 51
Boston, ix
in American Revolution, 79–84, 86–88
siege of, 54, 79–84, 86–88
Boston Tea Party, 48, 52
Bourlamaque, Commander, 37
Braddock, Edward, xv, 15, 16, 18
Bradford, Ephraim, 219
Brant, Joseph, 198, 209
Brant, William, 183, 184
Breed's Hill, 35, 63, 66, 67, 68, 73, 74, 79, 87, 221. *See also* Bunker Hill, Battle of
Breymann, Heinrich, 227
Battle of Bennington and, 143–144, 146, 149–150, 153
at Saratoga, 174
Brown, Arthur, 46
Brown Bess, 83, 111
Brudenell, Edward, 174
Brush, Colonel, 163
Bunker Hill, Battle of, xii, xvi, 62–77, 65*m,* 80, 87, 221. *See also* Breed's Hill
Bunker Hill Monument, 75
Burgoyne, John, xii–xiii, 63
Battle of Bennington and, 143–144, 154–155, 166–167
at Fort Edward, 132–133
at Fort Ticonderoga, xvii, 113–115, 117, 118, 119, 155, 178, 227
letter to Germain, 161–162
in New York, 97–98, 157–158, 170-178, 228
in Quebec, 91, 92
at Saratoga, 170–178, 228
Stark and, xii-xiii, 178
in Vermont, 119–120, 125, 129–130, 134
Butler, J.D., 151

Butler, John, 129, 183, 184, 198
Butler, Walter, 129, 183, 184
Butler, William, 184, 185

Cabot, John, x
Cadwalader, John, 105, 181
Caldwell, James, 189
Campbell, Daniel, 51
Canada
 in American Revolution, 90–92, 114, 158, 179–180
 England and, 90
 in French and Indian War, 10, 18, 34, 35, 36, 40–42
Canceaux (sloop), 49
Cane, Major, 82
cannons, 150, 227–228
Cape Breton Island, 34
Carleton, Guy, 97, 114
Carr, Captain, 117
Castine, Maine, 186. *See also* Fort George
Catamount Tavern, 143, 156
Charlestown, New Hampshire. *See* Fort Number Four
Chimney Point, 92, 93
Chittendon, Governor, 208
Christo (Abenaki Indian), 5
Church, Benjamin, 66, 82
Cilley, Joseph, 109, 112, 170
Cincinnatus, 210–211
Clark, Peter, 128, 151
Clerk, Colonel, 32–33
Cleveland, Colonel, 60
Clinton, George, 199, 200–202
Clinton, Henry, 63, 71, 155, 161, 173, 190, 199, 200
Clinton, James, 192
Cogan, Mr., 112, 127
Committee of Correspondence, 50
Conceau (man-of-war), 84
Connecticut Farms, 189
Constitution, U.S., 224
Continental Congress (First), 50
Continental Congress (Second), 52, 81, 85
Conway, General, 180, 181
Cooper, James Fenimore, 28
Coos Intervale, 40
Coos Meadow, 8–9, 16
Copp's Hill, 71
Cornwallis, Charles, 200, 204
 at Battle of Trenton, 104, 105
 at Battle of Yorktown, 205, 206
Coville, New York, 170
Crown Point, New York
 in American Revolution, 59, 80, 92, 93, 95, 98, 184
 in French and Indian War, 15, 18, 19, 38
Currency Act (1764), 44

Dana, Reverend Mr., 219
Daughters of the American Revolution, 47
Dawes, William, 53
Deane, Silas, 111
Dearborn, Henry, 61, 68–69, 172, 173, 174
Declaration of Independence, xvi, 94
De Grasse, Count, 200
Delaware River, 101, 103, 104, 105*m*
Derryfield, New Hampshire, 42, 44, 46, 51, 185, 211-212, 222
Dieskau, Ludwig, 17
Dinwiddie. Robert, 11, 12, 14
Dorchester Heights, 79, 86
Dovegate. *See* Coville, New York
dragoons, 147, 148, 166
Duane, James, 179–180

Duluth, Chief, 133
Duquesne, Marquis, 12

East India Company, 47–48, 52
Eastman, Amos, 5, 6, 7
Eastman, Jonathon, 55
Eastman, Phinehas, 125
Emerson, Colonel, 152
England, 79–84, 86–88
  Battle of Bunker Hill, xii, xvi, 62–77, 65*m*, 80, 87, 221
  Boston Tea Party, 48, 52
  Canada and, 90
  colonies of, 11, 43, 44–45, 47–50, 51, 177
  Fort Ticonderoga and, 111–118
  in French and Indian War, x, xv, 10, 15-20, 22–24, 42–43
  Native Americans and, x–xi
  New Hampshire and, x
  taxation policies, 43, 44–45, 47–48
  Treaty of Paris (1783), 206
Evangeline (Longfellow), 18
Evans, Edward, 128
Everett, Edward, 211
Ewing, James, 101, 103

Falmouth, Maine, 84–85
Fay, David, 215
Fellows, General, 199
firearms, 82–84
fires, xiv, 3, 26
First New Hampshire Regiment, 60–61, 67, 79–80, 82–84, 105, 109, 112, 170
Fishery Act, 52
Fitch, Captain, 125
flags, 226–227
  American, xvii, 176
  Green Mountain Boys Flag, 226
  Stark Flag, 226
Fleming, Thomas J., 67
Fogg, Captain, 206
Folsom, Nathaniel, 17, 60, 61, 179
Folsom, Samuel, 126
Forbes, General, 30
Fort Anne, 118, 166
Fort Beausejour, 15, 18
Fort Carillon, 22, 26-30, 32, 34-37. *See also* Fort Ticonderoga
Fort Champly, 97
Fort Clinton, 155, 173
Fort Constitution, 48
Fort Duquesne, xv, 14, 15, 30
Fort Edward, xvii, 16, 18-20, 26-28, 35, 116, 118, 130, 132–133, 175, 198, 227
Fort Frederick, 15, 17, 19, 38
Fort George, 14, 36, 130, 186, 187, 228
Fort Lake Erie, 11
Fort Le Boeuf, 11, 12
Fort Louisbourg, 4, 26, 34
Fort Lyman, 16
Fort Montgomery, 173
Fort Necessity, xv, 15
Fort Niagara, 15, 36
Fort Number Four, xiv, 4, 7–8, 38, 40
  in American Revolution, 126–128, 130, 153, 182
  in French and Indian War, 16, 18
Fort Oswego, 16, 20
Fort Pitt, 36
Fort St. John, 81, 119
Fort Schuyler, 158, 160, 198
Fort Stanwix, 155, 158, 166
Fort Ticonderoga, xv, xvi, xvii, 38
  in American Revolution, 58, 80, 81, 86, 92, 93, 98, 111–119, 155, 178, 227
  England and, 111–118

Stark at, 94, 222–223
See also Fort Carillon
Fort Vaudreil, 30
Fort Western, 187
Fort William and Mary, 49, 77
Fort William Henry, xv, 18, 19, 20, 23–28, 30, 32, 36, 48
France
in American Revolution, xiii, 111, 177, 199–200
in French and Indian War, x, xv, 10, 15–20, 22–24, 177
Native Americans and, 8–9, 15–20, 22–24
Spain and, 177
See also New France
Francis, Colonel, 117, 118
Franklin, Benjamin, xiv, xvii, 12, 16, 176
Fraser, Simon, 115, 117, 133, 154–155, 172, 173
Fraternal Order of Freemasons, 50
Freeman's farm, 172, 173
French and Indian War, x, xv
in Canada, 10, 18, 34, 35, 36, 40–42
causes of, 10
on Hudson River, 21–33
Native Americans in, 12, 15–20, 22–24, 38–40
Rogers' Rangers in, 21–24
Stark in, 13–14, 17–19, 21-24, 30-31, 33, 35-36, 38, 40-41, 97, 221–223
Treaty of Paris (1763), 42
in Vermont, 38
Washington in, xv, 11–12, 14–15
Frye, Joshua, 14–15
fur trade, 11

Gage, Thomas, xvi, 32, 35, 52–53, 59–60, 62, 63, 66, 71–72, 82
Gansevoort, Peter, 130
Gates, Horatio, 31, 48, 81, 88, 155-157, 160–164, 210, 223, 227
Arnold and, 171, 172, 174–175
at Crown Point, 95
in New Jersey, 188, 189
at Saratoga, 171–175
Stark and, 167, 178–181
Gentleman Johnny. *See* Burgoyne, John
George III, King of England, 46, 74
Germain, George, 114, 161–162
Gibraltar of the North. *See* Fort Ticonderoga
Gilman, Lieutenant Colonel, 69
Gist, Christopher, 11
Goffe, Captain, 5
Gorham, Nathaniel, 211
Gove, Jonathan, 51
Grant, Mr., 126
Greene, Nathanael, 99, 101, 102, 105, 106, 108, 189, 192, 200
Green Mountain Boys, 58, 80, 81, 153
Green Mountain Boys Flag, 226
Gregg, William, 140, 158, 163
Gridley, Richard, 66–67, 77
gunpowder, 74, 77, 111

Half-King (Indian chief), 15
Hamilton, Alexander, 134, 141
Hamilton, Brigadier General, 172
Hamilton, Captain, 39
Hancock, John, 52–53, 62, 82, 160, 168–170
Hand, Edward, 185, 188, 192
Harper, William, 188
Harrytown, New Hampshire, 3
Hazen, General, 206
Heath, William, 54, 88, 202–203, 206

Herrick, Samuel, 145, 147, 150, 159, 163, 178, 219
Hessians, 102, 103, 116, 118, 134–135, 146–149, 151–156, 167–168, 172–174
History of Manchester (Potter), 71
Hobart, David, 145, 159
Hobbs, Captain, 20
Hog Island, 57–58
Holland, Colonel, 76
Howe, Augustus Vincent Lord George, 28-31, 33, 41, 63, 72
Howe, Richard, 99, 114, 192
Howe, William, 63, 70, 72, 74–75, 86, 88, 99, 114, 118, 134, 162, 183, 200
Hubbard, Colonel, 164
Hubbardston, Battle at, 117–118, 160
Hudson River, 21–33, 156, 158, 170
Hull, William, 228
Humphrey, Colonel, 194
Hunt, Colonel, 126
Huntington, J., 188, 192
Huron Indians, 133
Hutchins, Gordon, 124–125

Isle-aux-Noix, 92

Jay, John, 134
Jefferson, Thomas, 212–213
Johnson, Noah, 13
Johnson, William, xv, 16–17, 46, 183
Johnston, William, 184
Joliet, Louis, x
Jones, David, 132–133
Jones, John Paul, xvii, 176–177

Kennedy, Captain, 39
Kennedy, Lieutenant, 22
Kimpton, B., 120
Knowles, Charles, 8
Knowlton, Captain, 70–71, 73
Knox, Henry, 83, 86, 102–103, 108, 190, 192, 202, 211
Knyphausen, Wilhelm, 189
Kosciuszko, Tadeusz, 171

Lafayette, Marquis de, 107, 180, 192, 200
Lake Champlain
  American Revolution on, 58, 59, 89, 90, 92, 98, 114, 118
  French and Indian War on, 16, 17, 18, 19, 22, 37
Lake George, 16, 24, 30, 36, 37
Lake George, Battle of, xv, 17
Lake Memphremagog, 40
Langdon, John, xvii, 45, 48, 49, 50–51, 123–124, 176
La Salle, Rene-Robert Cavalier, x
The Last of the Mohicans (Cooper), 28
Laurens, Henry, 200
Lawrence, John, 192
Learned, Ebenezer, 172, 173, 174
Lee, Charles, 55, 81
LeLoup, Chief, 133
Lexington and Concord, Battle of, xvi, 51, 52–54
Lincoln, Benjamin, 128–130, 136–139, 160, 163, 205
Little Ox-Bow, 9
"Live Free or Die," xviii, 216, 224–225
Livingston, Henry B., 121
Logstown encampment, 12
Londonderry, New Hampshire, xii, xiv, 2, 3
Longfellow, Henry Wadsworth, 18
Loudoun, Lord, 20
Louis XIV, King of France, 10
Lovelace, Thomas, 204–205

Lovewell, Colonel, 8, 51
Lovewell, Solomon, 187
Lyman, Phineas, 17

Madison, James, 216–217
Maine, 186–187
Majabagaduce. *See* Castine, Maine; Fort George
Marquette, Jacques, x
Martin, Jonathon, 51
Massachusetts
  American Revolution in, 51, 52–55, 57–58, 62-77, 65*m*, 79–84, 86–88, 187
  Battle of Bunker Hill, xii, xvi, 62–77, 65*m*, 80, 87, 221
  commendation to Stark from, 179
  Vermont and, 122
Massachusetts Committee of Safety, 55, 57, 62, 66
Massachusetts Provincial Congress, 52
Mast Road, 45
Maxwell, Colonel, 189
McClane, John, 188
McClary, Major, 60, 68, 70, 76
McClean, Francis, 186
McCoy, Mrs., 5
McCrea, Jane, 132–133, 154
McGinnis, Captain, 17
McGregor, Robert, 212
McKinstry, Thomas, 198, 199, 229
McKonkey's Ferry, 101, 103
McNeil, Sara, 133
Mellon, Thomas, 151–152
Menotomy. *See* Arlington, Massachusetts
Mercer, Hugh, 105
Mifflin, Thomas, 88
Miltimore, Lieutenant, 152
Minute Men, 53
Mohawk Indians, 140, 184, 209
Mohawk River, 156
Molly Stark Cannon, 227–228
Monroe, James, 103
Montcalm, Marquis de, xv, 27–28, 31, 37, 40, 222
Montgomery, Richard, 90–91
Monument Hill, 117
Moore, John, 13, 71
Morgan, Daniel, 157, 172
Mount Defiance, 32, 115, 116
Mount Hope, 115
Mount Independence, 94, 95, 98, 113, 114–115, 116, 178, 223
Mowatt, Henry, 186
Munro, George, 27
muskets, 83, 111

National War Board, 179
Native Americans, ix, x–xi, 1, 2
  American Revolution and, 97, 129, 133, 140, 147–148, 154, 182, 183, 184, 209, 223–224
  captivity by, 4–7
  France and, 8–9, 15–20, 22-24
  in French and Indian War, 12, 15–20, 22–24, 38–40
  Pontiac's Conspiracy, 43
  Rogers and, 39–40
  Six Nation Indian Confederacy, xvii, 12, 212
  Stark and, xiv, 4-7, 40, 222
  See also Abenaki Indians; Huron Indians; Mohawk Indians; Saint Francis Indians; Wyandot Indians
Nautilus Island, 187
Navy, U.S., 92, 98
Neilson's house, 171
Newburgh, New York, 210

New France, 10–11
New Hampshire
  in American Revolution, 48–51, 79, 206, 208
  as English colony, 45–46, 48–50, 51
  in French and Indian War, x
  military units from, xvi, 60-61, 67, 79-80, 82-84, 105, 107, 109, 112, 116-117, 170
  Vermont and, 122, 123–129, 136–141, 153, 166
New Hampshire Committee of Safety, xvi, 47, 52, 95, 136, 161
New Hampshire Congress, 60, 182-183
New Hampshire Grants, xii–xiii, 5, 9, 119, 162, 200, 203
New Hampshire Militia, xvi
New Ireland, 186
New Jersey, 99–108, 105*m,* 188, 189
New York
  American Revolution in, xii, 88–89, 99, 157-158, 166, 169*m,* 170–175, 181–185, 189–191, 194, 197–209, 222
  French and Indian War in, 21–33
Nichols, James, xii, 2, 159, 163, 164
Nichols, Moses, 145, 147
Nixon, Colonel, 58, 93
Noodle Island, 57
North, Lord, 59
Northern Department, 160–161, 194
  Schuyler and, 156–157
  Stark's command of, xviii, 170, 181, 197–209
Northwest Passage (Roberts), 40
Nova Scotia, 34
Number Four. *See* Fort Number Four
Nutfield, New Hampshire. *See* Londonderry, New Hampshire

O'Hara, Charles, 205
Olin, Gideon, 215
Orr, Samuel, 14
Otis, James, 45

Page, Caleb, 8, 19, 35, 42, 64, 229
Page, Captain, 8
Page, Elizabeth, 229
Paine, Thomas, 132
Parker, Captain, 53
Parkman, Francis, 43
Parsons, Samuel H., 192
Patriot's Day, 86–87
Patterson, John, 192
Peabody, Stephen, 128
Penet (brigantine), 177
Penobscot Bay, 186, 187
Perry, Abraham, 13
Philips, Lieutenant, 29
Phillips, William, 115, 172
Pigot, Robert, 72
Pitcairn, Major, 53, 73
Pitt, William, 26, 30, 31, 34
Plains of Abraham, x
Plan of Union, xiv, 12
Plattsburgh, New York, 98
Point Judith, 186, 188
Pontiac's Conspiracy, 43
Poor, Enoch, xvii, 61, 79, 107, 109, 119, 172, 173
Portsmouth, N.H., ix
Potter, C.E., 71
Powers, Captain, 9
Prescott, William, 66, 67, 70, 72, 73, 77
Princeton, Battle of, xvi, 103–107
prisoners, 155–156, 164, 167–168
privateers, 44, 45, 84, 186

Putnam, Israel, 30–31, 66, 67, 69, 77, 81, 162

Quebec, 90-91, 223
Quebec, Battle of, 40–41

Raleigh (ship), 51
Rand, John, 150–151
Ranger, USS (sloop), xvii, 176–177
Rattlesnake Mountain, 32, 96
Ray, Mr., 219
Reed, James, 55, 61, 65, 66, 69, 76, 79, 87, 93, 112, 206
Revere, Paul, 48, 53, 66, 82, 187–188
Revolutionary War. *See* American Revolution
Rhode Island, 185, 186–188
Riedesel, Frederick Adolph von, 114, 117, 134, 149
 Battle of Bennington and, 143–144
 at Saratoga, 172, 173, 174
Rising Castle Island, 50–51, 176
Roberts, Kenneth, 40
Robinson, Jonathon, 215
Rochambreau, Jean-Baptiste, 199–200
Rogers, Elizabeth Brown, 46
Rogers, Richard, 13, 17, 18–19, 20
Rogers, Robert, 12-14, 17, 18, 20, 21, 22, 223–224
 in American Revolution, 64, 72–73, 78–79
 Amherst and, 35–36, 39–41
 in French and Indian War, 23, 24, 28–30, 35–36, 39–41
 journals of, 46–47
 Native Americans and, 39–40
 Pontiac's Conspiracy and, 43
 treason charges, 46, 78–79
Rogers' Rangers, xii–xiii, xv, 185
 in American Revolution, 64, 72-73, 78-79
 in French and Indian War, 21–24, 28-30, 35-36, 39-41
 Pontiac's Conspiracy and, 43
 Stark in, xii-xiii, 13–14, 17–19, 21-24, 29-31, 33, 185, 222–223
Rogers' Rangers (movie), 40
Rogers' Rock, 29
Royal Navy, 84, 186
Rumney Camp, 5

Saffords, Samuel, 150
St. Clair, Arthur, 115–118, 176, 192
St. Francis Indians, 4–7, 38–39, 223
St. Lawrence River, 90
St. Leger, Barry, 114, 130, 134, 155, 158, 166, 208
St. Patrick's Day, 86–87
Saltonstall, Dudley, 187
Saratoga, Battle of, xiii, 169*m,* 170–175, 227
 Stark at, 166, 175, 177–178, 197-209
 surrender of Burgoyne at, 175, 176–178
Saratoga, New York, 197–209
Sargent, Paul Dudley, 51, 55
Sargent Hill, 117
sawmills, xvi, 44, 46, 212
Scammel, Colonel, 194
Scarborough (frigate), 49
Schuyler, Philip, 81, 92–96
 at Crown Point, 95
 at Fort Ticonderoga, 112, 115
 in Northern Department, 156–157, 160–161
 Stark and, 127, 138–139, 160–161, 198, 199, 204, 205, 223

in Vermont, 120–121, 127–130, 136, 137
scorched earth policy, 120–121
Scott, Charles, 104
Scott, Winfred, 76, 228
scurvy, 37
Second New Hampshire Regiment, 60, 61, 79, 116–117
Seven Years War. *See* French and Indian War
Sheepscot, Maine. *See* Wiscasset, Maine
Shirley, William, 16, 18
Short Hills Battle, 189
Sibsburgh (brig), 229
Simmons, Colonel, 163
Six Nation Indian Confederacy, xvii, 12, 212. *See also* Native Americans
Skene, Philip, 120, 140, 143, 144, 149–150, 152, 158
smallpox, 1, 24, 26, 28, 91, 92, 93, 212
Smith, Stephen, 32
Society of the Cincinnati, 210–211
Sons of Liberty, 45, 48
Spain, 177
Spikeman, Captain, 20, 22, 24
spruce beer, 37
Stamp Act (1765), 44–45, 50
Stark, Ana, 2
Stark, Archibald, Jr., 2, 5, 29, 42, 55, 181, 194, 196, 212, 229
Stark, Archibald, Sr., xi–xii, xiv, xv, 1, 14, 33, 35
Stark, Benjamin Franklin, 229
Stark, Caleb, xv, 205, 207, 229
in American Revolution, 64–65, 74, 75, 156, 170, 177–178, 181, 183, 185, 196
André and, 194
appointment as adjutant, 109, 112
Native Americans and, 26
Rogers and, 78
Schuyler and, 204
Washington and, 210
writings of, 23-24, 33, 46, 55, 99, 125
Stark, Charles, 229
Stark, Eleanor, Jr., 56, 229
Stark, Eleanor, Sr., xi–xii, xiv, 1
Stark, Elizabeth, Jr., 56, 229
Stark, Elizabeth Page (Molly), 19, 98–99, 110, 146, 185, 209, 212, 227
children of, 42, 229
death of, xviii, 218
home of, 47
marriage of, xv, 35
Stark, Isobel, 2, 13
Stark, Jean, 2
Stark, John, Jr., 229
Stark, John, Sr., xiv, 79–80, 82–84, 88, 176, 221
at Albany, 181–185
Amherst and, 35–36, 38, 40–41
André and, 191–192
attitude toward British, 41
at Battle of Bennington, 142, 143, 144, 145–153, 158–160, 162–164, 166–167, 221–222
at Battle of Bunker Hill, xvi, 62–77, 221
at Battle of Trenton, 101–103, 105*m*, 106
birth and childhood of, xii, 2
in Boston, 79–80, 82–84
Burgoyne and, xii–xiii, 178
children of, 42, 55–56, 229
command of First New Hampshire Regiment, 60–61, 67, 79–80, 82–84, 105, 109, 112, 170

command of Northern Department, xviii, 170, 181, 197–209
in Committee of Safety, xvi, 47
in Continental Army, xvii, xviii
death of, xviii, 218–220
in Derryfield, 42, 44, 46, 51, 185, 211–212, 222
family life of, 98–99, 112–113, 211–212
father's death, 33, 35
financial situation of, 195–196
at Fort Number Four, 18
at Fort Ticonderoga, 94, 222–223
at Fort William Henry, 24–26
in French and Indian War, 13–14, 17–19, 21–24, 30–31, 33, 35–36, 38, 40–41, 97, 221–223
Gates and, 162-164, 167, 178–181
as a guide, 8, 9
Hancock and, 168–170
health of, 194, 196, 209, 211, 214, 218–220
home of, 47, 109–110
horse of, 164, 165
independent command of, 123–131, 136–137
injury to, 26
letter to New Hampshire Congress, 182–183
"Live Free or Die," xviii, 216, 224–225
Lovelace and, 204–205
Madison and, 216–217
marriage of, xv, 35
in Massachusetts militia, 54–58
at Mount Independence, 95, 98, 115, 223
Native Americans and, xiv, 4–7, 40, 222
in New Hampshire Militia, xvi
in New Jersey, 101-103, 105*m*, 106, 188, 189
in New York, 88, 94, 166, 175, 177-178, 181-185, 189–191, 197-209, 222-223
parents of, xiv, 1–3, 33, 35
pep talk of, 146
pincer movement of, 145–151
promotions and, 96–97, 107, 168–170, 211–212
reenlistment episode, 107
resignation of, xvi, 108–109
in Rhode Island, 185, 186–188
Robert Rogers and, 78
in Rogers' Rangers, xii–xiii, xv, 13–14, 17–19, 21–24, 29–31, 33, 185, 222–223
at Saratoga, 166, 175, 177–178, 197–209
Schuyler and, 127, 138–139, 160–161, 198, 199, 204, 205, 223
at Short Hills Battle, 189
siblings of, 1, 2, 4, 87–88
Society of the Cincinnati and, 210
Sullivan and, 50
as Town Grand Juror, xvi
as town moderator, 211
treatment of prisoners by, 155–156, 164, 167–168
tributes to, 179, 221–225
at Trois-Rivieres, 91–92
in Vermont, 123–131, 136–153, 158-160, 162–164, 166-167, 221-222
Veterans of the Bennington Campaign and, 214–215
Washington and, xiii, 14, 101–107, 105*m*, 108, 158, 183, 184, 194–195, 197–199, 207–210

Stark, Mary, 229
Stark, Mary Stinson, 35
Stark, Samuel, 2
Stark, Sarah, 56, 229
Stark, Sophia, 209, 229
Stark, Stephen, 212
Stark, William, 2, 5, 6, 14, 35, 44, 87–88, 212
Stark Flag, 226
Stark's Pond, 44
Staten Island, New York, 194
Stevens, Phineas, 4, 7-8, 126
Stickney, Benjamin, 109, 128
Stickney, Thomas, 145, 151, 159
Stinson, David, 5, 6
Stirling, Hugh, 13
Stockbridge Indians, 19
Sugar Act, 44
Sullivan, John, 212
  in American Revolution, 79, 87, 88, 91–92, 95, 99, 101, 102, 105, 162, 181, 183, 195, 196
  in French and Indian War, 49-50
Sunshine Patriots, 132
Surprise (frigate), 91
Symonds, Colonel, 144

Talford, Major, 8
Tarbox, Increase N., 77
tea tax, 47–48
Thacher, James, 192–193
Third New Hampshire Regiment, 61, 79, 107
Thomas, John, 66, 91
Thompson, Charles, 168
Thompson, Samuel, 125
Thompson, William, 91–92
Thornton, Matthew, 76
trade gun. *See* cannons
treason, 46, 78-79, 189-190, 204
Treaty of Alliance (1778), 177
Treaty of Amity and Commerce (1778), 177
Treaty of Convention, 176
Treaty of Paris (1763), 42
Treaty of Paris (1783), 206
Trenton, Battle of, xvi, 99–100, 101–103, 105*m*, 106
Trois-Rivieres, 91–92
Trumbull, General, 88
turpentine, 3
Tyler, Major, 125

Valley Forge, xvii, 178
Vermont
  American Revolution in, 58, 119–129, 154–155, 162–164, 166, 198, 206, 208
  Battle of Bennington, xiii, xvii, 142–155, 161–162, 226–228
  Burgoyne in, 119–120, 125, 129–130
  French and Indian War in, 38
  Green Mountain Boys, 58, 80, 81, 153
  Massachusetts and, 122
  New Hampshire and, 122, 123–129, 136–141, 153, 166
  Schuyler in, 120-121, 127-130, 136, 137
  Stark in, 123–131, 136–153, 158-160, 162-164, 166-167, 221-222
Vermont Council of Safety, 165
Veterans of the Bennington Campaign, 214–215
Villiers, Joseph Coulon de, 15
Vulture (sloop), 190

Waite, Colonel, 95

Walker, Reverend, 125
Walloomasac River, 222
Ward, Artemus, 57–58, 64, 66, 67, 76, 81
War for Independence. *See* American Revolution
Warner, Seth, 178, 226
 in New York, 80, 116–118, 181
 in Vermont, 123, 125–127, 129, 134, 136, 139-140, 149-151, 153, 156, 159, 163, 164
Warren, Joseph, 52, 62–63, 73
Washington, George, xiv, 52, 132
 in American Revolution, xvi, 81–82, 85–86, 88, 98, 99–100, 103–107, 162, 166
 André and, 191–192
 Arnold and, 190
 at Battle of Princeton, 103–107
 at Battle of Trenton, 99–100, 101–103, 105*m,* 106
 in Boston, 81–82
 Burgoyne and, 154
 criticism of, 180
 in French and Indian War, xv, 11–12, 14–15
 letter to Second Continental Congress, 85
 Robert Rogers and, 78
 smallpox and, 28
 Society of the Cincinnati, 210–211
 Stark and, xiii, 14, 101–107, 105*m,* 108, 158, 183, 184, 194–195, 197–199, 207–210
 use of privateers, 44
 at Valley Forge, xvii, 178
 at Yorktown, 205, 206
Wasmus, Julius Fredrich, 148, 149, 156
weapons, 82–84, 86, 102, 111, 148–149. *See also* cannons; muskets
Weare, Meshech, 124, 126, 161, 206
Weare, New Hampshire, 45–46
Webb, Daniel, 27, 93
Wentworth, John, 8, 9, 13, 17, 49, 50
West Point, New York, 189–191
Wheelwright, Mr., 7
White, Benjamin, 66
Whitney, Colonel, 164
Wiessenfels, Colonel, 205
Wilkinson, James, 87-88, 103
Willett, Colonel, 197, 207
Williams, Colonel, 127, 163
Winter Hill, 84
Wiscasset, Maine, xii, 1
Wolfe, James, 34, 35, 38, 40
Wooster, David, 91
Wright, Benjamin, 182, 229
Wyandot Indians, 133
Wyman, Lieutenant Colonel, 60, 68

Yorktown, Battle of, 205, 206
Young Chief. *See* Stark, John, Sr.

Clifton La Bree is a forestry graduate of the University of New Hampshire and is a long-time resident of the state. He worked two years as a county forester for the University Extension Service, two years as a supervisor for the New York State College of Forestry at Syracuse, and many years as a private consulting forester. Long a student of military history, he is the author of *The Gentle Warrior, General Oliver Prince Smith, USMC, Ret.*, and now works as a freelance writer.